W9-BFN-217

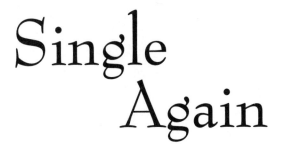

Single
Again

a guide for women starting over

Victoria Jaycox

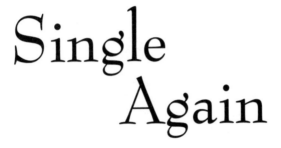

W. W. Norton & Company
New York ⌗ London

Excerpts from *The Change* by Germaine Greer. Copyright © 1992 by Germaine Greer. Reprinted by permission of Alfred A. Knopf, Inc. Excerpts from *Full Catastrophe Living* by Jon Kabat-Zinn. Copyright ©1990 by Kabat-Zinn. Used by permission of Dell Books, a division of Bantam Doubleday Dell Publishing Group, Inc. Excerpts from *New Passages: Mapping Your Life Across Time* by Gail Sheehy. Copyright © 1995 by G. Merritt Corporation. Reprinted by permission of Random House, Inc. Excerpts from *One's Company: Reflections on Living Alone* by Barbara Holland (Ballantine Books, 1992). Copyright © 1992 by Barbara Holland. Reprinted by permission of the Fox Chase Agency. Excerpts from "Rolling Stones Tune Helps Woman Turn Life's Corner" by Donna Damico Mayer (*All Things Considered*, National Public Radio). Copyright © 1996 by Donna Damico Mayer. Used by permission of the author. Excerpts from *Women of a Certain Age* by Lillian Rubin Copyright © 1979 by Lillian Rubin. Reprinted by permission of HarperCollins Publishers. "Lament" is reprinted from *Solo Flight* (Small Poetry Press) by Jean Kalmanoff by permission of the author. Copyright © 1991 by Jean Kalmanoff. "In Praise of Solitude" by Jean Kalmanoff is reprinted by permission of the author. Copyright © 1995 by Jean Kalmanoff.

For information about permission to reproduce selections from this book, write to Permissions, W. W. Norton & Company, Inc., 500 Fifth Avenue, New York, NY 10110

The text of this book is composed in Sabon
with the display set in Bernhard Modern
Composition by Platinum Manuscript Services
Manufacturing by The Haddon Craftsmen, Inc.
Book design by Lane Kimball Trubey

Library of Congress Cataloging-in Publication Data

Jaycox, Victoria.
Single again : a guide for women starting over / Victoria Jaycox.
p.   cm.
Includes bibliographical references.
ISBN 0-393-04699-0
1. Divorced women—Life skills guides. 2. Widows—Life skills guides
3. Divorce—United States—Case studies.
4. Widowhood—United States—Case studies. I. Title.
HQ814.J39   1999
646.7'0086'52—dc21
98-41561
CIP

W. W. Norton & Company, Inc., 500 Fifth Avenue, New York, NY 10110
http://www.wwnorton.com
W. W. Norton & Company Ltd., 10 Coptic Street, London WC1A 1PU

Contents

Contents

Contents

Contents

Contents

Preface

XXXXXXXXXXXXXXXXXXXXXXXXXXXXXXXX

This Book and Why I Wrote It

This book is about women becoming single after many years of marriage. Written for women who have recently become "single-again," the overall theme is that self-transformation after the death or divorce of a husband isn't an extraordinary event that happens only to special women. There are simple, practical ways to make it happen. Along with the sadness, anger, and confusion from the loss come new opportunities for personal growth. Women who capitalize on these opportunities often develop in ways they describe as truer to the selves they always hoped, deep down, they would be.

In a nutshell, that is the good news that I unearthed from interviews with scores of women who were either divorced or widowed after marriages of long duration. Their experiences are the core of *Single Again*. But the book also provides the wisdom of professionals in mental health and experts on topics like bereavement, finance, and employment, culled either directly through interviews or indirectly through their published reports.

Millions of women every year face the ominous transition to life on their own after many years of marriage, but I am not one of them. I am still married to a man I met when I was sweet sixteen, fell in love with in college, and wed in 1960, the week before I graduated. We've been through rough patches together, but are more in harmony now than ever, with a strong mutual commitment to our life together.

So why, almost everyone asks, am I writing a book on this topic? It seems a strange choice for someone who hasn't been through the process. What is the source of my fascination with a topic that isn't really relevant to my life?

After more than twenty years of marriage, my husband and I separated. Although I had already started to build a more independent life for myself by going back to work part-time (after ten years at home with our two daughters), I found the idea of starting a new life on my own overwhelming. Thanks to a huge dose of marriage and individual counseling while we both hung in there, my husband and I later reconciled. But the emotions I faced and the difficulty I had finding my way then are still fresh.

They remain so because I know that, realistically, I can expect to outlive my husband and will once again face the predicament of being unmarried. A woman who was 65 in 1990 could expect to live 4 years longer than a male of the same age (18.6 years versus 14.2 years for the man). If the trend continues, a woman in 2020 can expect to live 12 more years than her male counterpart.[1] That fact, combined with the high divorce rate and low remarriage rate of mature single women, means that while 85 percent of men die married, an equal percentage of women die unmarried.[2] Some 19 million women over the age of 35 in this country (over 30 percent) are widowed or divorced.[3]

I also know that it's *not* a given that when and if I find myself single, I'll live happily ever after. I learned that from my professional life, which I've devoted for some twenty years to issues that affect mature women. I have worked in many capacities—as an advocate, a grassroots organizer, a program manager, and now as a writer. For several years, I was even director of a national advocacy organization, the Older Women's League (OWL). I've been deeply involved in issues that affect women, like pensions, criminal victimization, abuse, health care, and death with dignity.

In the course of working closely with mature women, I began to recognize that women who have spent a good part of their lives as wives and mothers adapt very differently to the loss of a husband. Some make the transition to exciting, involved lives as singles, while others seem to fall by the wayside.

Why some succeed—and how *I* can hope to—became the fixation that fueled the research for this book.

⁂⁂⁂⁂⁂

Finding Out What I Needed to Know

My method in doing the research for this book was to gather the stories of many women who had built independent lives after years of marriage. Although I wanted as much diversity as possible in my sample, I remained true to two criteria: I chose women who had been married at least ten years, followed by at least two years of being single-again. I chose both numbers arbitrarily—the ten years of marriage to ensure that a woman had become accustomed to her identity as a married person, and the two years alone to make it likely that she had already passed through the initial stages of disorientation following her separation or her husband's death.

A third criterion was meant specifically to stack the deck in favor of my objective for this book. (Whoever said authors were unbiased?) I wanted to interview women who felt proud of what they had done in making new lives for themselves. Ideally, these would be women who had taken advantage of the opportunities that being single provides by choosing lives substantially different from their earlier, married ones. Their stories illustrate the possibilities for growth and change as individuals, as friends and family members, and as volunteers and paid workers.

Who Are These Women?

In the end, I found eighty-eight divorced and widowed women willing to discuss with me what they had been through.[4] The ages of my interviewees ranged from forty to eighty-nine—with almost one-half between forty and sixty, the other half between sixty and eighty. (Two were over eighty.)[5] About three-fourths of them were working for pay, while the rest were either retired or working as volunteers. About 80 percent were white, 10 percent African American, the remaining 10 percent either Asian American or Hispanic. All except one said she was heterosexual.

Nine of the eighty-eight women had remarried or were in permanent relationships when I talked to them. Of the rest, more than one-half had been without a permanent partner for under ten (but more than two) years, another third had been single between ten and twenty years, and eleven (14 percent) had been unmarried for over twenty years (one for more than forty years).[6]

The length of their former marriages was equally diverse. Twenty-six women (30 percent) had been married for between ten and twenty years when they became single. The other sixty-two women (70 percent) had been married for more than twenty years: thirty-three (44 percent) between twenty and thirty years; twenty (22 percent) between thirty and forty years; and nine (10 percent) over forty years.[7]

Exceptional Women. Unexceptional Women

When I began my interviews in 1993, I was struck by the compelling stories the women told me about the devastation they faced and their successful comebacks. I wondered then whether these first few women were exceptions. Perhaps their successful recoveries were due to extraordinary intelligence, or competence, or good luck. Now, almost ninety interviews later, I know they were not all that exceptional. I found scores of women who exhibited the same resilience and success. Faced with the loss of a husband who was the locus of their adult emotional life, they turned that loss into an opportunity. They looked at themselves with fresh eyes, added up their strengths and weaknesses, got back in touch with their early dreams, and headed in a new direction. They transformed themselves.

This book tells the stories of dozens of fairly ordinary widows and divorcées who, despite hardships and disadvantages, succeeded in giving up firmly held notions of themselves as married. Many did not have the advantages of a good education, a happy childhood, or adequate money. But they moved ahead, most with a great amount of satisfaction, to new experiences and lives—at least for a while—as singles.

Sometimes the changes they made were mainly internal—new ways of viewing themselves and the world around them, a new valuing of their separateness and integrity. But often the alterations were visible as the women took on entirely new lives—new work, new home, new friends. Either way, these women all saw themselves as dramatically different, and usually improved, as a result of becoming single.

✕✕✕✕✕

Why Both Widows and Divorcées?

Although the experiences leading widows and divorcées to become single are radically different, once these women are on their own, they face many of the same problems. Both widows and divorcées must adjust to fundamental changes in their lives and consolidate new identities.

Some of the obstacles they face do differ, however. A divorcée can find, for example that while society is usually supportive of a widow's predicament, *her* friends and family are more critical than supportive. Negative attitudes about divorce can also cause her to harbor a sense of shame about the failure of her marriage, to feel that because she didn't stay married, she is somehow defective.[8] What is more, the need to continue interacting with her ex provides new opportunities for anger, confusion, and misery, making it difficult for her to put the relationship behind her.

A widow, on the other hand, can find that the "support" she receives is a double-edged sword. Friends' fixed notions about how she should feel, and about how quickly she should move on, can make it difficult for her to experience what she is really feeling, including perhaps a lot of anger at her former husband. Suppressing these feelings, studies show, makes for a poor recovery from grief.[9] And while the finality of a husband's death should make it easier to put closure on the relationship, a widow's knowledge that any unfinished business with her spouse must remain so forever can make that closure difficult to achieve.

So while the obstacles they face differ, clearly neither widows nor divorcées, as a *group,* have it any easier or harder. Some women, both widowed and divorced, have an easier time of it because they understand right away that they're better off single. (That's obvious with women who choose a divorce. But it also applies to widows who had an unsatisfactory marriage. Psychologist Margaret Huyck refers to these women, when their husbands are still alive, as "widows in waiting.")[10] Others, both widowed and divorced, have a hard time, depending on factors like age, the traumatic quality of the death or divorce, the level of self-esteem, the availability of support, the happiness of the marriage, feelings of control or victimization, and other types of stress.[11]

Every loss of a longtime husband, whether through divorce or death, is unique, and its impact will vary depending on the circumstances. Those particulars will make it relatively more easy or more difficult for a woman to recover and will influence the length of her recovery. But even the worst set of circumstances will never make recovery impossible. That holds true for *both* widows and divorcées.

✕✕✕✕✕✕

How This Book Can Help

Calling on all their skills and resources—some they never even knew they had—the average women in this book have carved out new and exciting paths in their transition from married life to singlehood. They have come to grips with what happened, with their new identities as single women, and with the frustrations and joys of life without a partner. They are not "exceptional," but most have, with very little guidance, found their way to good lives on their own. I firmly believe there could be a lot more of them. Making it possible for *you* to be among them is what this book is about.

Single Again will give you insight into how other widows and divorcées go about creating order and sense out of turmoil and nonsense. By telling, in their own words, about the paths they took and the obstacles they met, these women will share their experiences and the insights they ultimately achieved. In addition to offering you many hard-won tips, their stories may also inspire you to muster the courage to meet your new challenges.

These women's stories provide hope because they show that starting over, as difficult as it is, can bring its own rewards. They demonstrate that it can take a while, and it can be painful. But with a lot of willpower and persistence, you can accept your loss and move on to a new, stronger sense of who you are and what you want from the rest of your life.

Their experiences reveal that adapting to your loss isn't impossible and that the changes that will occur aren't all that threatening. You can alter yourself and your self-image gradually, one step at a time, trying out new ways of being and acting that would not have been possible if you were still married. And in the course of finding your new identity, you can carve out a satisfying new life for yourself, either on your own or in a new kind of union.

Acknowledgments

The essence of this book is derived from the stories of an amazing assortment of widowed and divorced women. Without exception, these women were willing to tell me precisely what had happened to them, warts and all, in the aftermath of becoming single-again. I've taken their confidences seriously. Even though I've changed their names to protect their privacy, my overriding goal in writing this book has been to give them full credit for their struggles and accomplishments. To the extent that I succeeded, I hope that this book will repay, in part, the debt I owe them for their candor, warmth, and unfailing cooperation.

Finding these women was not all that onerous, thanks to what I call my "old girls' network." Until I began this book, I never fully appreciated that network. Without hesitation, friends eagerly introduced me to their single-again friends. And former colleagues from my days at the Older Women's League, as well as OWL's allies in the Women Work! Network, contacted people all over the country, distributing screening questionnaires for me. For responding with enthusiasm and great suggestions, I'm especially grateful to Jane Adams, Harriet Baldwin, Dory Stacks Bentos, Essie Burnworth, Sally Cleaver, Judy Falk, Sandra Gillis, Merna Guttentag, Carleen Joyce, Joan Kurianski, Evelyn Lim, Jill Miller, Nancy Mitchell, Jan Piercy, Kathy Rose, Aurea Irene Singh, Kathy Soady, Kathy Sullivan, Mara Thorpe, and Jean van der Tak.

The dynamic executive director of OWL's Metro Atlanta chapter, Jeanne Scher, gave me access to some phenomenal interviews in that part of the country. And a special entry to the Chicago area resulted from the zeal of former colleagues Junia Hedberg of OWL's Illinois chapter and Jill Miller, co-director of Women Work! I owe them a great deal.

But the network functioned well beyond this initial set of contacts. My friends' friends and colleagues—women I was meeting for the first time—were equally energetic and productive. Among them, thanks go in particular to Teresa Gallo, Lettie Geiger, Augusta Gross, Lee Horsey, Jean Kalmanoff, Susan Kendall, Anne Mesmer, Carol Randolph, Judy Ruffatti, and Peggy Treadwell.

I'm also deeply in debt to the professionals who helped me penetrate to the heart of the issues single-again women face. Special thanks go to Elsie Bliss, Sarah Ellis, Margaret Hellie Huyck, Edie Irons, Joan Kurianski, Jacquelyn Mattfeld, Mary Lou Randour, Martha Farnsworth Riche, Elizabeth Smith, and Alice Umbach. Chicagoans Jean Ellzey, Lucille Lopez-Wark, Sheila Rogers, and Deborah Walker-Johnson not only shared their expertise but also put me in touch with more successful single-agains.

Two professionals I consulted, Rand Corporation psychologists Lisa Jaycox and Andrew Morral, are more than just experts. They are my daughter and son-in-law. They gave me sensible advice as I was doing my research and were willing to read and comment on the whole manuscript, in several different versions. And they say motherhood doesn't pay! Two other special friends helped me with essential editorial comments: political scientist Richard Hofrichter (a former colleague from eons ago); and my brilliant, perennially supportive husband (of even more eons), Kim Jaycox. I also treasure the contributions of my other daughter and son-in-law, Tamara and Lewis Kessler. Their unflagging moral support kept me going.

The miracle of getting the book published by Norton was also accomplished through friends—three Wellesley College class-mates. Linda Gottlieb, Marilyn Nissenson, and Susan Jonas have all written and published successful books. Apparently intrigued by a bleary-eyed description of the book I gave them at a thirty-fifth-reunion breakfast, they succeeded in linking me to their indomitable agent, Pam Bernstein.

With amazing efficiency, Pam was able to find the book just the right editor, Jill Bialosky, at W. W. Norton & Company. Jill's dedication to the book never wavered, even when she was ini-tially confronted with *many* too many stories of women's suc-cesses at various aspects of becoming unmarried. I am grateful to her for paring the book down to a more palatable size.

Finally, for helping me to transform myself into a profession-al writer, I want to credit the devoted pros who lead such great workshops at the Writer's Center in Bethesda, Maryland. I'm especially grateful to the center's Tim Wells for his pragmatic, no-nonsense advice about crafting the basic concept for this book.

Single
Again

Introduction

The Challenge of Being Unmarried

American women are spending their adulthood in an increasing number of life stages, each one with a different set of resources and responsibilities, each one with a different balance between public and private worlds. . . .

In particular, women are spending a smaller share of their adult lives raising children. They are spending a smaller share of their adult lives married. They are even spending a smaller share of their adult lives in families. They are spending more of their adult lives making decisions as individuals, investing in their skills and caring for themselves.

—Population Reference Bureau[1]

✕✕✕✕✕✕

"The Bravest Thing You've Ever Done"

When she reached her fifties, Felicia could look back with pride at her accomplishments. She and her husband of thirty years had successfully raised four children—two boys and two girls. To make sure that she was available when her family needed her, she had never worked for pay, sticking to volunteer work in order to accommodate their schedules. Her husband's fast-paced career in the federal government required her to spend a lot of time and energy traveling with him and helping him entertain, a role she found fascinating.

But it all ended in a flash when she reached fifty-three—on the day her husband told her he wanted a divorce. Felicia went into a full-blown panic. How on earth was she going to manage a life on her own? And how, she wondered, could she persuade anyone in the working world to hire her, at her age?

Felicia is just one among millions of women who face the predicament of being single-again after spending much of their adult lives married. Often they marry quite young, before they have a firm idea of who they are. And like Felicia, they spend most of their adult years putting the concerns of their family members ahead of their own. This sacrifice all too often eats away at their self-confidence, leaving them uncertain about their ability to do without the support of a husband.

When a woman does lose that support, it can be a crisis of major proportions, somewhere near the top on measures of stressful life events. And while every woman's crisis is unique, they are all similar in one important respect. Whether her husband dies or divorces her, whether the marriage is happy or unhappy, and whether or not she initiates the divorce, in all cases a woman finds herself on her own, perhaps for the first time. She must make a sudden transition from seeing herself as part of a couple to viewing herself as single.

In addition to coping with the sometimes overwhelming emotions of her loss, a newly single woman faces an identity crisis. Not only is she without the marital relationship that was fundamental to her self-image, but also she has lost most of the friends and interests that came with the territory of "wife."

That threat to her identity can be quite traumatic. For a woman to move to a fundamentally different lifestyle, one without the familiar props and oriented mainly toward herself, can lead to feelings, as one psychotherapist put it, "that [her] very self is disintegrating."[2] Not being married means that she must revamp her image of herself and how she relates to the world. She must face both a steady stream of discouraging stereotypes about single women and the realization that she may no longer be considered part of mainstream society. And in addition, many women feel that the older they become, the more society renders them invisible. [3]

In the face of this assault on her psyche, it would be easy enough for a woman emerging from a long marriage to fall into the trap of identifying herself as one of life's victims. To do otherwise—to meet the new challenges and master them—requires great courage. It can be, as one mature divorced woman put it, "the bravest thing you've ever done."

⊠⊠⊠⊠⊠

Recoiling from the Blow

A PANOPLY OF REACTIONS

The situation you face when you first become single after many years of marriage can be summed up in one word: chaotic. Your life has been turned upside down. "I was blitzed. I didn't know what had happened. I felt like I had been run over by a truck," one divorcée said. "I didn't know who 'me' was," said a widow.

Whether the chaos extends to both your exterior world *and* your interior world, or just exists in one of those realms, it is invariably there. What varies is the response divorcées and widows have to that disarray. Just as there is no one typical woman, and no one typical way of being divorced or widowed, so there is no one way that women who face this dilemma react.

Although they are certainly not the norm, some women, both widows and divorcées, walk away from the loss of a husband with minimal emotional turmoil. Louella, for example, calmly explained that she didn't grieve the death of her husband of forty-four years because "my family is not a grieving family. We are very accepting of the will of God." Darleen explained that she was able to accept the departure of her alcoholic husband of forty-two years because "he had already left emotionally. There was no presence of him in the house." And some women who endure unhappiness or long illnesses with their husbands often feel more relief than grief once they're through the initial shock.

Still others fall apart completely—either immediately or after a number of months—and have to slowly reconstruct their identities. Judith, for example, was disconsolate when her husband and soulmate left her completely unexpectedly, the unsuspected outcome of a serious affair she was certain he had abandoned ten years earlier. She described how she "hit bottom and bellied up" after his ex-mistress "came to claim him."

But most women fall somewhere in the middle, terribly upset but still able to function day-to-day. Psychotherapist Edie Irons has run a grief group for women in Charlotte, North Carolina, who, like herself, have been widowed. She says she has come to believe "that each grief is as unique as each love affair and each marriage."[4]

The dissimilar reactions of women to their losses are not so strange once you consider the circumstances and total context. Factoring all that in makes it easier to explain, for example, why a woman who takes the initiative in a divorce often has an easier time of it. Mercy took her three children and slipped away from her abusive husband with the help of some neighborly Catholic nuns. "It's easier to be the 'leaver' than the 'leavee,'" she said. Mercy, who was the "leaver," recently summed up her feelings to a divorcing woman she found sobbing outside her home in her snowbound car. "You're looking at it the wrong way," Mercy told her. "You need congratulations. You haven't been abandoned. You've been liberated."

Because the contexts of these losses can differ so radically, psychiatrist Jon Kabat-Zinn believes that arbitrarily assigning stress points for the loss of a spouse, either through divorce or through death, does not make much sense. Doing that, he writes, "does not take into account the *meaning* of the experience for the surviving spouse and the degree of adjustment or adaption that he or she will have to make as a result."[5]

Is There a Typical Comeback?

If you are just beginning your pilgrimage to a new unmarried life, understand that you will have to count on some trial and error as you meet challenges along the way. Just as there is no such thing as a typical reaction to being widowed or divorced after a long-term marriage, so there is no typical way to recover and build a new life. The paths women take to new lives cover a wide spectrum. No one solution is appropriate for every new widow or divorcée. Nor does any one set of rules apply in every situation.

But although the paths that women take vary widely, they are often parallel. Once a woman has stumbled through the worst of the pain and anger from her loss, she usually realizes that her unmarried status presents an opportunity to claim a new identity. She seems to figure out intuitively what will work best for her under her circumstances. And perhaps most important, she reacts with great courage, forging ahead to make an interesting new life for herself, providing a model for those who come after.

In writing this book, I found all sorts of these women—even

ones who didn't much believe in themselves or had rarely taken risks before—who were able to build satisfying, independent lives for themselves. By telling you their stories, I will show you how you can too.

⊠⊠⊠⊠⊠

Rewriting Your Narrative

DISMANTLING THE PAST

In her book *Writing a Woman's Life*, Carolyn Heilbrun contends that in order for women to change their lives, they must first realize what "narratives," or societal expectations, have been controlling them so far. By recognizing and articulating those narratives, women can then move on to dismantle them and to reimagine their futures.[6] Heilbrun writes:

> Acting to confront society's expectations for oneself requires either the mad daring of youth, or the colder determination of middle age. Men tend to move on a fairly predictable path to achievement; women transform themselves only after an awakening. And that awakening is identifiable only in hindsight.[7]

Divorce or widowhood often awakens women to one particular narrative in their pasts: having turned the direction of their lives over to others. A number of women described the moment when it dawned on them that although they had never been in charge of their lives, now they could be. This is divorcée Lucille's moment:

> I finally got sick and tired of spending my money on a fifty-minute hour telling the same stuff over and over with no intervention, no change. . . . And I realized if I was going to have a life, I had to do something. No one was going to do it for me. We are all looking for someone out there to take care of us. Let me tell you some-

thing. There isn't anyone. Nobody wants to hear that. It makes them furious. But the day you find that out and believe it and start to do something for yourself, good things will come into your life.

Fifty-eight-year-old Joanne, a widow for only two years when I interviewed her, had already made that discovery: "For the first time in my life, I'm not answerable to anyone. . . . If I wanted to live in the south of France for six months, I could go live in the south of France for six months." And Corinne says that her discovery that she wanted her freedom more than she wanted her marriage also came after two years of being separated from her husband. "At that point, I was so delighted to be an 'I'—all of 'I'—that I realized I didn't want to go back."

These women and others we meet later in the book go on not only to imagine new futures for themselves but to live them. They make significant changes in where and how they live, in their work, and in how they relate to others. But even more fundamental, they change their images of who they are and who they want to be.

CHOOSING TO REINVENT YOURSELF

Psychologist Joan Borysenko explains that many of us return to familiar ground once a crisis is over. That happens because, she explains, "It's simply human to seek the path of least resistance."[8] So although you may toy with the idea of starting over, making the necessary changes is *not* the path of least resistance. It's tough and requires you to face guilt if you slack off and disappointment if you fail.

If change is all that difficult, then how was I able with such ease to find so many women who had succeeded in transforming major aspects of their lives? One answer may lie in what psychologists are uncovering about how normal women change as they mature. Illinois Institute of Technology professor Margaret

Huyck is one of these psychologists. Huyck explains that even across cultures, women take on increasing self-direction and power as they grow older. And while some of these changes may appear rather drastic, they may just be aspects of a woman that had lain dormant since her youth.

"Sometimes what looks like more dramatic outward change is really variations on an internal theme," Huyck explains. "The internal theme may have been there and been quite well-masked. It's not that you're inventing powers you never had or becoming something you never were."[9] Huyck says that psychologist David Gutmann refers to this midlife metamorphosis as "reclaimed powers."[10] It's a kind of maturation that both men and women undergo, but which Huyck believes is particularly conspicuous among women.

While men often reclaim their right to be vulnerable, what women reclaim, more often than not, are traits that as young adults they had projected onto men—like power and creativity. As girls grow up, they often have conflicting feelings about being gifted or creative and so abandon these talents to take on safer, more "feminine" roles. But as they grow older and find more support for (and less opposition to) reclaiming these talents and interests, they begin to rethink the rules.[11]

Huyck says that this self-empowerment can just happen of its own accord, but it may be especially likely to happen after some kind of wake-up call like children leaving home or divorce or widowhood. That accords with one conclusion that Gail Sheehy makes in her book *New Passages*. Sheehy states that a loss can propel you toward a stage of maturity she calls "second adulthood":

> Involuntary losses can become the catalyst for voluntary changes in the practice of our lives, altering the efforts we make to connect with others, the values we choose to make congruent with our actions, the habits we change to support better health, the responsibilities we accept for mentoring the next generation and civilizing our communities, country, and planet.[12]

WHAT MATTERS MOST

When I began these interviews, I had a number of ideas about what characteristics would make it easier or harder for a woman to move ahead to a new life. Many of my ideas proved untrue. I never found in my interviews that money (or the lack of it) is an important determinant of whether a woman can manage in the maelstrom of being single-again. A number of the widows and divorcées I talked to had been left with little or nothing and yet were thriving.

Nor did I find, as I expected I might, that whether a woman had a happy childhood is key. Some women were children of alcoholics or abusive parents and yet had not let that handicap keep them from moving on. Nor did a common perception prove to be true—that the age at which a woman becomes single has a lot to do with her ability to adapt. Sixty- and seventy-year-olds set off on new ventures about as often as forty- and fifty-year-olds—often with different goals but full of risk nonetheless.

What *does* matter is a woman's determination to use everything at her command to put the event behind her and her willingness to take the risks needed to make a new life. "To me it was a question of 'Will I live or will I die?' That's the question I put to myself," says Olivia, a sixty-two-year-old African American woman, in the throes of pulling herself out of a slump after the breakup of her third marriage. "I had been raised to depend on a man, and my identity lay in what a man felt about me," Olivia laments. It took her years to understand that she had been sold a bill of goods.

Pulling yourself free of the myth that you can only have a *real* life if you're part of a couple—an idea we all absorbed from nursery rhymes and popular songs, from movies and TV—is a Herculean task. Whether you can purge yourself of that fiction and risk writing a new narrative—where it's okay to be a woman on your own—has less to do with your past and present circumstances than it does with the kind of grit and bravery you bring to the task.

Part One

making order out of chaos

1

Facing
the Chasm

Just as with physical pain, you can be mindful of emotional pain and can use its energy to grow and heal. The key is to be willing to inquire into your suffering, to observe it, to open up to it consciously, in the present, and work with it just as you would with a symptom, with physical pain, or with a thought that surfaces repeatedly.

—Jon Kabat-Zinn
Full Catastrophe Living[1]

Mastering the Tightrope

PICTURE THE CHALLENGE

One way to imagine the challenge of being single-again is to picture yourself at the top of a mountain that overlooks a huge two-sided abyss. You need to walk a tightrope stretched across that chasm to reach the mountaintop of recovery on the other side. Below you, on one side of the tightrope, is all your pain, anger, and confusion about what happened. On the other side are distractions and diversions from your plight. On the tightrope, you must take care not to lean with your balance pole too far in either direction—dipping it so far into your grief work that you fall into isolation and depression or so far into distractions that you never really face up to what happened. Too far in either direction, and you won't make it across.

This chapter describes what lies on each side of the ravine. It provides a sampling of reactions from women immediately after losing a husband, an exploration of some of the different ways in which women do their grief work, and a discussion of some healthy escapes and diversions.

HOW IT FEELS TO FACE THE ABYSS

If you have recently become single after years of marriage, you may be feeling overwhelmed by emotions right now. Maybe you believe that your reaction is excessive, beyond what would be considered normal for someone who is newly single. Compare your reaction, then, with those of some widows and divorcées in this book:

- Sally believes that it would have been easier to have terminal cancer, even be raped, than go through what she did after her husband of thirty years left. "I felt like I'd been hit by a Mack truck, devastated, not knowing from minute to minute whether I'd be okay or in tears. I can't imagine anything worse to go through other than the death of a child." She became dehydrated from crying and stopped reading because she couldn't comprehend what was on the page. Constant exercising to rid herself of tension took its toll in excessive weight loss. "I couldn't sit still. Even in the middle of the night, I was up, walking around, because I couldn't sleep and it was an alternative to lying there and being overwhelmed."

- After her husband died, Dora "sat and wailed like an animal" for a whole year. Married at nineteen, she was dumbfounded by her loss and by being on her own for the first time in her life. She took a job she was entirely unsuited for and went off each lunch hour to cry. Missing terribly the intimacy and tenderness she had with her husband, she began a series of affairs with men. None of them turned out to be right for her.

- When Harriet and her husband decided to divorce, she became panicky about whether she could support herself. Unable to write checks because her arms went limp, she took to carrying a lot of cash with her. "I went to the grocery store and I felt like a bag lady. I'd pick up stuff and I'd put it down." She even had an "out of body experience" in which "I was walking but I felt blank and I had another person who was me walking right beside me." She was petrified that she was losing her mind.

- When Susan's husband of twenty-one years died in an airplane crash, she was so shattered that she had to stop working for a while. "I didn't think I'd survive," Susan recalls. She found it hard to concentrate, couldn't eat, and couldn't sleep. "I felt demobilized, totally dysfunctional. The pain was totally excruciating. I felt as if I had a big cinder block settled on my chest." She even developed a persistent cough, trying in vain to dislodge that weight.

- Anna was so distraught when her husband of twenty-two years left her just as she was recovering from leukemia that she considered suicide, even checking herself into a psychiatric hospital for a few days. For two years after that, she became a compulsive shopper. Her initial dreams that her husband was attacking her with a knife were soon replaced by an obsession that he would knock on her front door with flowers and ask her to take him back. "I was so panic-stricken I wanted to marry anyone who came along," Anna recalls.

The emotions these women describe—despondency, rage, longing, anxiety, disorientation, disillusionment, despair—are often all lumped together and referred to as "grief." Although their grief was profound, it was not abnormal. Studies of normal grieving point to an amazing number of symptoms that can come from the loss of a loved one: agitation, fatigue, crying, self-reproach, low self-esteem, helplessness, hopelessness, a sense of unreality, suspiciousness, interpersonal problems, preoccupation with the loved one, depression, exaggerated worry, guilt, anger, hostility, loss of feelings of pleasure, loneliness, retarded thought and concentration, loss of appetite (or the opposite), sleep disturbances, energy loss, bodily complaints, and susceptibility to illness and disease.[2]

Fortunately, say psychologists Margaret and Wolfgang Stroebe in their review of the consequences of partner loss, "not all of these symptoms appear in every bereaved person, nor at any one time in the duration of bereavement."[3] For most of us, grief runs "a normal, if harrowing, course,"[4] with a few symptoms at a time, replaced later by others. Even so, they conclude, "the notion of a broken heart seems to be more than a metaphor."[5]

Given the enormous range of what is considered normal grief, it's difficult to decide when a woman's grief has gone wrong and she should seek professional help in dealing with it. Here are some danger signals that the problem has gotten beyond what you can handle on your own:

- Your anxiety, depression, or anger dominates your life.

- Your anxiety is so extreme that it is out of proportion to any dangers you face.

- Instead of working toward solving your problems, you are paralyzed.

- You recognize recurring destructive patterns that you are unable to change on your own.[6]

The subject of when you should consult a mental health professional is covered in more detail in chapter 8, "Discharge Your Emotional Overload."

⋈⋈⋈⋈⋈⋈

Grief Work: Your New Assignment

WHY YOU MUST GRIEVE

Mending a broken heart is a tough order. There's no surgery for the kind of broken heart caused by the severing or disintegration of a strong bond between husband and wife. While that kind of break can cause as much turmoil and pain as the physical kind, there are no quick fixes. Healing can take years. And while on the mend, you may be vaguely demented—racked by conflicting emotions in the midst of radical life changes.

Mental health researchers and practitioners agree that curing your grief entails more than lying back and waiting for the feelings to subside. You must be an active participant. If you ignore the aftermath of a distressing life event, you may fall prey to a low-level, chronic depression. **Only by confronting both your**

**emotions and the difficulties you face being single can you expect
to resolve the trauma.**[7]

Someone who has suffered a loss normally goes through a
series of stages, according to grief therapists. The first stage is
characterized by shock, numbness, and disbelief. That frequently gives way to a period of intense yearning, anger, and protest.
That stage in turn often yields to feelings of despair.

Once through those excruciating early stages of grief, you will
presumably move on to periods when you feel better and begin to
make a new life.[8] But going through these stages is not necessarily orderly, nor is there steady progress from feeling bad toward
feeling better. The initial stages can take months, if not years, and
the stages can overlap, be reversed, or not occur at all.[9]

Getting through these stages means doing what therapists
describe as "grief work." Psychoanalyst Eric Lindemann, one of
the first to study the aftermath of loss, describes grief work as "a
natural and necessary process in the recovery from loss."[10] Even
if the loss was not traumatic, you still have to come to terms
with your new status—making order out of disarray, sense out
of confusion, calm out of bedlam, and amity out of discord. You
need to feel that you have regained control of your life.

Therapists point to three goals for the grief work of a woman
who has lost a long-time husband. The first two are mainly
internal, the third external:[11]

- *Understand what happened, and perhaps why.* Becoming
  unmarried was not anything you hoped or planned for when
  you married. Part of recovering from your loss is making
  sense of the events or, where that isn't possible, making
  peace with them.

- *Come to grips with your new identity as a single woman.* In
  "a world set up by the Noah's Ark principle," as one woman
  described it, it's hard to comprehend right away what it
  means to be really on your own. Understanding and accept-

ing both the positives and negatives of your new status is an essential step in your recovery.

- *Figure out how to master a life without a partner.* Being on your own means being responsible for everything, from finances to repairs to creating new intimate relationships. And it usually means facing a radical downsizing in almost every area of your life. Working toward self-sufficiency is an important goal of grief work.

TOOLS FOR YOUR GRIEF WORK

The women in this book handled their grief in many different ways. I've arranged their approaches into different kinds of tools for carrying out your grief work: (1) making room for your emotional demons; (2) putting your feelings into words; and (3) devising healing rituals.

Making Room for Your Emotional Demons

This tool for grief work is simply to allow yourself to feel the emotional impact of your loss. Although doing so sounds simple enough, it's probably instinctive to try to avoid pain. When Rose was divorcing, for example, she sought respite from her turmoil by driving across country by herself for six or seven days. She describes driving on deserted highways across Nevada and southern Utah, the desert covered with purple and yellow blossoms, her cruise control set at seventy-five, "just one little car bombing across vast spaces. I could just turn off the engine in my brain. . . . It was soothing, restful, and healing."

But this escape just put off for a while the inevitable day of reckoning—when she had to face up to the divorce and decide what to do about it. When she got to California, she says she spent three months mostly in tears. Her advice for others facing divorce or death of a spouse: "You might as well get on with it, because you don't have any choice."

As Rose learned, the shock and pain can and do intrude anywhere you run, creeping in unannounced. Writer Barbara Holland compares it to a "patient tiger" which "comes in on padded feet, through the locked windows and barred doors, and squats in all the corners, waiting while you try to sleep."[12] She writes:

> It's more comfortable in the long run to be on terms with the tiger. He won't go away, but if you've been looking into his eyes, at least he can't catch you off guard. . . . Sweat it out. Pace back and forth in the apartment, relearning such long-neglected talents as crying and biting your fingernails. Wrestle the demons hand-to-hand, like Jacob with the angel. After you've spent the evening with them, it's less of a shock to find them waiting for you in bed.[13]

Wrestling the demons accomplishes more than just becoming familiar with them, however. As Dr. Jon Kabat-Zinn of the University of Massachusetts Stress Reduction Clinic writes, "Facing our problems is usually the only way to get past them."[14]

> Feelings have to be acknowledged, at least to ourselves. They have to be encountered and felt in all their force. There is no other way through to the other side of them. If we ignore them or repress them or suppress them or sublimate them, they fester and yield no resolution, no peace. . . . Strange as it may sound, the intentional *knowing* of your feelings in terms of emotional suffering contains in itself the seeds of healing.[15]

Most of the women in this book sweated it out—either alone or with help, on their own turf or distant from it—as they faced down their emotional demons. Their pain and anger were aroused by hundreds of everyday events—doing the dishes, an unexpected strain of music, or, for many, a trip to the grocery store. They dealt with their emotional turmoil by acknowledging it, robbing it of its power to totally disrupt their lives. They dis-

covered what author James Miller prescribes: "The best \
handle your feelings is not to 'handle' them but to feel the

Putting Your Feelings into Words

Another essential tool for grief work is to verbalize your feelings. There are all kinds of creative ways you can talk through or write about your feelings:

- *Seek out a range of people you can talk openly with, including friends, family, support groups, and therapists.* (Ways to do that are discussed in chapters 6 and 8.) You have to let others know you need their support, something women told me was indispensable when they were first single. May, who had always prided herself on her self-reliance, says that "the one thing I learned after Joe died is that it's okay to ask for help. . . . I say 'I need you' more than I ever could have before because I recognize that I do need help. . . . I think it's kept me from feeling bitter or not socializing."

- *To clarify your thoughts and feelings, write in a journal.* Although writing down something shouldn't be all that different from thinking it or speaking it, if you've ever kept a diary or a journal, you know it is. Seeing your thoughts on the written page gives them a kind of intensity, precision, and reality they don't have when you just "know" them. For many women, writing in a diary or journal was so therapeutic that they made a daily ritual of it.

- *Write letters to him (that he'll never see).* Widows find that they can address unfinished business in letters to their late husbands, business that might otherwise preoccupy them. And divorcing women who write letters they never send can let off a lot of steam. Sue Ellen found writing her ex and tearing it up to be a big help: "I would just vent my rage. I would type all night sometimes. You have to write it, talk it. Now I don't even think about him."

- *Find some "computer pals," the newest version of pen pals.*
  A tool that combines aspects of journal writing and a support group is something I'll call "cyberventing." By signing up with one or more of the thousands of online "newsgroups," you can both read what others in the group have posted on an electronic bulletin board and leave your own messages for others to read. One such newsgroup is a forum for widows and widowers over age fifty-five, accessible to members of SeniorNet or subscribers to America Online. On this bulletin board, members can post notes about their feelings and experiences. And regular "posters" get to know other regulars' stories and feelings, offering each other advice and comfort.[17]

Devising Healing Rituals

Other than funerals, our society has few rituals to help us deal with change or loss. Rituals have come a long way since anthropologists first pointed to them as important figurative dramas in people's lives. Now psychotherapists such as Evan Imber-Black are turning to them as a way "to facilitate, mark and celebrate idiosyncratic life cycle transitions."[18]

Rituals can be as simple as setting the table for one before each meal with attractive linens and china, symbolizing that you are going to take good care of yourself. Or they can celebrate whatever good is surfacing in your life.

Or rituals can be aimed at letting go of the past. Dr. Imber-Black tells of a woman who felt trapped in her old home after her divorce, unable to invite people in because of all the house's associations with the past. She came up with the idea of a "house-cooling party," inviting people to "bring gifts appropriate for the lovely home of a single woman—I need to replace the 'his and her' stuff!"[19]

When her husband remarried, Margie decided to hold a funeral for her marriage. She got together the trappings of a funeral, a hymnal, candles, and drew a hot bath. Then she played sad music and sat in the tub and sobbed her heart out. ("Hot water has always helped me cry," she muses.) She had planned to go next to the cemetery to bury some symbols of their marriage. But once out of the tub, she felt so much better that she just cleaned up and went about her business.

Several widows described rituals they created to continue to feel linked to their husbands. Melinda keeps her husband's cremated remains on a shelf in the living room in a simple square box made of dark wood. On top of the box is a favorite statue of his that she gave him shortly after they were married. "I go in there every day and I put my hands on the box and thank him for the lovely life that I have now. Because if he hadn't worked for thirty-three years, I wouldn't be living like this."

Jocelyn takes a vacation once a year to tend a nature trail near the seashore that she created in memory of her husband. She also compiled a book of remembrances of him written by close friends. And Faye describes a ritual that gave her comfort early on: "I wore his clothes. I know it may sound silly, but sometimes when I went on walks outdoors, I'd wear his favorite jacket. Somehow I felt a little of his protection. And at nighttime I would wear the tops to his pajamas. It was very comforting."[20]

Healthy Escapes and Diversions

CHOOSE *NOT* TO WORK AT IT

I once read about a widow who spent the first two years after her husband's death in bed, not willing even to fake cheerfulness. Then one morning she woke up, got out of bed, sold her house and most of her possessions, and moved to Arizona— where she became a respected painter.

Surrendering herself to her grief worked for her, apparently.

But it's unrealistic, perhaps even unhealthy, to expect someone to focus totally on that struggle. Besides, as Germaine Greer puts it, we are all expected to "buck up":

> The middle-aged woman will not find it easy to get her mourning done. Our culture demands a smiling face; it is bad enough to know oneself an old trout, without having to add the epithet 'miserable'. We have no tolerance for female images that are solemn, thoughtful, or severe. . . . If she wants to sit and think and cry a little or a lot, she is made to feel that these are bad wishes, and may not be indulged. Such behavior makes other people feel bad.[21]

Even if it were possible to indulge yourself, a number of studies have shown that *total* immersion in mourning and introspection may not be all that good for you.[22] Constant rumination even led to increased illness among one group of surviving spouses.[23] Some theorize that one reason women become depressed more often than men is that they tend to dwell on their bad feelings while men tend to distract themselves.[24]

A certain amount of denial may actually be a good form of emotional first aid,[25] **then, if done in moderation and along with appropriate amounts of grief work.** Lindemann describes this process as "the effort of reliving and working through in small quantities your relationship with someone you loved."[26] Widows and divorcées told me how important it is to let loose occasionally and take time to play, laugh, or just to be entertained. It may sound like a contradiction, but even people who are sad, or lonely, or frightened can, at times, relax and have fun. Smart single-again women can gain a lot from giving in to their urges for pleasure. You have to give yourself permission to do so.

LEARN TO SEE THE GLASS HALF-FULL

Many women avoid becoming preoccupied by their loss by adopting a positive attitude. When optimism does not come naturally, however, they achieve it with a lot of willpower. Such women began their portrayals of how they achieved a positive outlook by talking about what attitudes they had *decided* to adopt or to avoid. Edith, a widow with cancer, heart disease, and diabetes, explains, "I've tried to make myself very positive and accept the things I can't do anything about. Because I've been so blessed by the other things that have come my way. And because, you know, you have to. You just make up your mind and do it." Fanny, widowed twice before she was fifty-six, told me, "I don't allow myself to get angry anymore."

But what kind of magic has enabled them to make this choice? Certainly not just willpower alone, even though it played an important role. And not their understanding that other people expected them to put on a happy face and get over their loss quickly. And most emphatically not the maintenance of a cheerful outlook at all costs. These women all walked the tightrope between experiencing their unhappiness and finding some relief from it.

For each woman, the process of finding her way to a generally optimistic outlook was different. But it always began with techniques she relied on when she was alone, routines and rituals that helped her to resolve her strong and conflicting emotions and come out on the other side. When Tilly's husband died, followed a few years later by her new love, she decided to work out her emotions on her own "because I don't think anyone wants to hear it." Tilly does "a lot of loud talking" to herself. "You'd be shocked. I say all kinds of things about what I'm angry about." Or sometimes she writes it all out on the typewriter and then tears it up. "You suddenly find that maybe you weren't as right as you thought you were. You start to see another point of view."

Joy describes her technique:

If I feel myself getting into a funky mood or something, I'll say, "Okay, tell me what's going on." I'll talk to myself like there's another person there. Then the "other person" will respond: "We're going to do this," or

"You've had enough of this. It's time to get over it, get on with it."

Joy laughs and says that it has saved her untold amounts in therapy over the years.

Melinda describes a process that she goes through, one she has relied on over the years after an unhappy childhood. "Essentially, if I get in a funk, I will sit down and think about it and get myself out of it just in my head. . . . I think of all the good things and I can very quickly rattle off twenty or thirty wonderful things in my life." She actually takes her fingers and ticks off the positives, like her health, not allowing herself to dwell on the "if only's." "I just sit down and I can turn it around in a matter of minutes."

Whether they know it or not, Tilly, Joy, and Melinda are doing their own versions of what cognitive therapists call "disputation." **Using disputation, you deal with pessimistic thoughts and negative feelings by attacking them, challenging them with the facts.** Psychologist Martin Seligman believes that disputation is effective

> because successfully disputed beliefs are less likely to recur when the same situation presents itself again. . . . By effectively disputing the beliefs that follow adversity, you can change your customary reaction from dejection and giving up to activity and good cheer.[27]

Disputation, Seligman says, is "the prime technique" you need to use to attain "learned optimism" in your daily life. He urges:

> Practice disputing your automatic [negative] interpretations all the time from now on. Anytime you find yourself down or anxious or angry, ask what you are saying to yourself. Sometimes the beliefs will turn out to be accurate; when this is so, concentrate on the ways you can alter the situation and prevent adversity from becoming disaster. But usually your negative beliefs are distortions. Challenge them. Don't let them run your

emotional life. Unlike dieting, learned optimism is easy to maintain once you start. Once you get into the habit of disputing negative beliefs, your daily life will run much better, and you will feel much happier.[28]

As essential as it might be to "feel your pain" and explore the causes of your problems, spending too much time doing so on your own is probably a bad idea. Alone, feeling bruised and battered, there's really nothing to serve as a reality check on your feelings.

FIND A FRIENDLY BURROW

Some people feel an impulse to run away after a major upheaval. Whether acting on that impulse is healthy or unhealthy depends on the circumstances. The healthy kind was recommended in 1902 by physician Emma Drake in her book titled *What Every Woman of Forty-five Ought to Know*. Drake writes:

> Run away from yourself and your surroundings for a while and forget for a little the every-day cares. Hunt up some old friend, the more closely associated with far-away times the better, and get away to her where you can talk over unmolested all the girlhood days.[29]

A healthy escape, then, is when you travel somewhere where you feel safe and can view the whole event from a distance— where you are accepted as a whole person. (Barbara Holland calls this spot a "friendly burrow.")[30] Often women find that shelter among family members or old friends. Forty-six-year-old Karen Blixen (who is the author of *Out of Africa* and who used the pen name Isak Dinesen), shattered by divorce and ill health, found it at her family home on the coast of Denmark. Abandoning her unhappy life on an East African coffee plantation, she was able to heal herself in Denmark and go on to become a best-selling author and celebrity.[31]

For Nadine, that friendly burrow was a three-year stint in the

Peace Corps. Divorced at the age of fifty-two and supporting herself as a seamstress, she was left behind in a circle of friends "where everyone had money but poor Nadine." But once she was settled in a Peace Corps assignment in Paraguay, Nadine reports that her work helping women to improve their self-esteem was "gorgeous. It was the best thing I did in my life. I could be myself there because they didn't know anything about me. I had no past—being married, and then losing a husband. I was right there." Nadine believes that her Peace Corps experience was essential because it let her "accept the change. I even changed my values."

How Long Does It Take?

How long the initial stages of disorientation, anxiety, and sadness take, or should take, is a matter of much debate. On one side are proponents of the "it takes as long as it takes" school of thought. On the other are those who believe that when someone takes more than a few years, she is stuck and needs professional help. Rather than being stuck in their grief, however, many women describe a process in which they take three steps forward and two steps back. One woman said that just as she felt that she had turned a corner, there was another corner up ahead. Many said that the hardest part was after the initial flurry of activities and emotions had subsided and they had to face the reality of making it on their own.

The debate about how long it takes emerged in full force among four widows in an online discussion group on SeniorNet Online[32]—Jane, Ann, and JanB on one side, Beatrice on the other. Jane set off the firestorm by confessing that she had been grieving for her dead husband for ten years. Beatrice advised Jane that she should stop wallowing in her grief: "You must let go of that wonderful life that you led before. . . . Life can still be fun, but you have to help it along."

Offended, Ann wrote in response: "I don't know how to judge the 'rightness' of another person's loss or grieving. So glad to find someone who does. Please tell me what is 'allowable'?? Is a month for each year together about right??" And JanB chimed in that "[Beatrice's] idea of 'letting go' is unrealistic. NO ONE CHOOSES TO SUFFER! . . . What I have treasured here is the total and complete acceptance of my feelings, and therefore of me, a total stranger." This in turn led the ten-years-in-grief Jane to respond that "We need to be here for each other, not give advice or preach lessons."

Beatrice was not about to be silenced, however. She wrote: "There is a time to grieve and a time to get on with your life. . . . [D]on't you and others feel that ten years is a bit much?" She relates that after she "carried the load" by herself as widow for a few years, she "decided that was enough—got to do for myself and stop worrying about what was. The children agreed and off I went into the wild blue world. . . . I love my life now."[33]

Nothing about an appropriate time frame was settled there, and it probably won't be soon. The psychologist Stroebes point out that many people who lose a partner find life tolerable, even enjoyable, after a year or two. But even then, symptoms of grief often recur on anniversaries.[34] The woman in my sample who had been married the longest—fifty-two years before her husband and the father of their eight children died six years ago—weighed in on Beatrice's side, however. Penny from Kansas wrote this advice: "Allow a short time to grieve or get rid of anger (if any), then get on with living."

* * *

Women who make it successfully across the tightrope are experts at making order out of chaos, learning or upgrading many skills in the process. In addition to learning to manage their grief, they take charge of other aspects of their lives, like their stress, their legal situation, and their finances. Finding a job or work is another important way to keep a balance, as are resources like wise friends, religious beliefs, and a support group or professional therapist. Stories of how women use some or all of these ways are told in the chapters that follow.

2

Coping with the Stress That Accompanies Change

XXXXXXXXXXXXXXXXXXXXXXXXXXXXXXXXXXXXX

Fear is a rabbit on the road, paralyzed in the glare of the head-lights. Courage is being the driver.

—Barbara Holland
One's Company[1]

Becoming single after years of marriage inevitably produces a lot of anxiety. Most newly single women report how fearful they are initially. Not only are their current lives turned upside down, but they have trouble believing they will ever settle down again.

Sometimes a woman's apprehension is so overwhelming that she decides to seek out a doctor or mental health professional. That's probably a good idea if your overall level of tension is so high that you're unable to take even small steps toward a new life or if you are troubled by insomnia or an inability to relax. You should certainly check with a doctor if exaggerated worries have plagued you for longer then six months.[2] (See chapter 8.)

With or without the help of a therapist, however, you need to begin to take control of your new life. As divorced writer Barbara Holland points out, it's much less stressful to be in charge sitting in the driver's seat than to be the rabbit waiting to see what might run you down.[3] This chapter shows you how to use simple techniques to reduce the impact that stress has on your psyche and body.

⬚⬚⬚⬚⬚⬚

Learn How to Relax

Although anxiety often feels as if it has a life of its own, unconnected to your body, it is really nothing more than a physical reaction triggered by the perception that your survival is threatened. The feelings you identify as anxiety are simply physical symptoms that come from the release of adrenal-gland hormones intended to let you take quick action to defend yourself or run away.[4]

Psychologist Eric Widmaier points out that this physical mechanism worked great for our cavewomen ancestors, but not today when most threats don't require a physical response. He writes, "A person in the midst of a divorce does not require the hormonal, neuronal, and metabolic responses of someone who falls through thin ice on a wintry pond—yet in both cases the same internal changes are occurring."[5] When there is no relief for these feelings, and you feel constantly bombarded by them, you can become hypersensitive to any new stresses.[6] In addition, reactions like chronic hyperarousal, headaches, and sleep disorders happen automatically with each new stressor, according to Dr. Jon Kabat-Zinn of the University of Massachusetts Stress Reduction Clinic.

When hyperarousal becomes automatic, Kabat-Zinn writes, "Each time we react, we stress our intrinsic balance even more. . . . Unfortunately hyperarousal can become a permanent way of life."[7] In addition to making it difficult to cope, this type of hyperarousal in response to stress can weaken your immune function. Neuroscientists at Rockefeller University have concluded that a continual oversupply of stress hormones, such as norepinephrine and cortisol, can increase your chances of infection or disease.[8]

To cut into the negative effects of too much stress on your body, learn as many antistress techniques as possible. That way, according to psychologist Robert Epstein, you will have ready "a bag of tricks that you can deploy proactively. If you turn to them during the day, that changes your stress tolerance."[9]

You already have some simple ways of calming yourself that you've used all your life; turn to these with more frequency now. Or come up with new ways. Several women told me about how they had soothed themselves during their early anxious months. For example, when Sugar was in the throes of her divorce, although she had never been a Catholic, she found that repeating the "Hail Mary" and "Our Father" prayers and whole pieces of the Latin mass over and over were "a very comforting thing." Debra describes taking long walks each week after Sunday mass to deal with her fear after her husband's death. While she walked, she spent the time "thinking it over, sorting it out in my head, getting a rhythm going, repeating, 'Yes, I can.'" Just getting outside and communing with nature is soothing for a lot of women.

The ability to relax is like a muscle that has to be exercised regularly, even when you don't need it. That way, it's ready and powerful when you do need it. And just as in muscle-building, the technique becomes cumulatively more effective as time goes on. In developing a bag of relaxation tricks, you'll need to practice them at least once a day for a minimum of twenty minutes.[10] When one technique doesn't work, either because your anxiety is too intense or because you've had so much stress in your life that you are overly sensitive to it, try another. You should eventually find one that suits you and helps you through rough periods.[11]

Here are some techniques that have been demonstrated to make anxiety more manageable:[12]

- *Progressive relaxation* is a way of releasing the tension in your body. You tighten and then let go of every muscle group, beginning with your toes, all the way up to the muscles in your forehead and scalp.

- *The Relaxation Response*, which has you focus on breathing deeply, repeating the word "one" as you exhale, is described in the book by that name by Dr. Herbert Benson.[13]

- A favorite of Dr. Epstein's is *the cleansing breath,* where you take a deep breath, hold it, then let it out very slowly, letting go of your tension at the same time.[14]

- *Biofeedback* trains you to lower your tension level by responding to signals from electrodes that measure your skin's electrical response and temperature, as well as muscle tension and heartbeat.[15]

- *Meditation* teaches you to calm down by becoming aware of when you "hyperrespond" to stress.[16]

Dr. Saki Santorelli, also of the University of Massachusetts Stress Reduction Clinic, says that meditation works because "when you start feeling stressed during the day you are able to retrieve the feelings of relaxation you get during deep meditation."[17] One analysis of a number of different studies showed that various relaxation techniques and types of meditation all reduced anxiety, but Transcendental Meditation (TM) worked the best of all.[18] TM, in which you close your eyes and repeat a mantra, is the most popular and widely available version of meditation.

Dr. Kabat-Zinn is a proponent of a form of meditation he calls "mindfulness," which he says comes directly from the Buddhist tradition. In his book *Full Catastrophe Living*, Kabat-Zinn writes, "Our thoughts are so overpowering, particularly in times of crisis or emotional upheaval, that they easily cloud our awareness of the present."[19] The goal of mindfulness meditation is to make you aware of that present, including your stress reactions, discomfort, and bad feelings:

It is the process of observing body and mind intentionally, of letting your experiences unfold from moment to moment and accepting them as they are. It does not involve rejecting your thoughts nor trying to clamp down on them or suppress them, nor trying to control anything at all other than the focus and direction of your attention.[20]

Just being fully aware of your emotions and sticking with them, Kabat-Zinn says, "is a powerful response, one that changes everything and opens up new options for growth and for doing."[21] More important than the technique you use, he believes, is whether you practice it regularly:

Over time, the practice tends to teach you what you need to know next. If you sit with your questions and your doubts, they tend to dissolve in subsequent weeks. What seemed impenetrable becomes penetrable. What seemed murky becomes clear. It is as if you are really just letting your mind settle. . . . You just sit . . . the mind settles itself. It *is* like that.[22]

Meditation can also work in dealing with anger, an emotion so distracting that it can take over your life. Barbara Lazear Ascher writes about how Sister Chan Khong, a Vietnamese Buddhist nun whose family and friends were murdered during the war, used meditation to deal with her anger while she was in prison. For six years, Chan relates, she did a walking meditation:

> I would start by breathing in and out, watching my breath, being aware of each step I took. Then I would say, "I'm angry, I'm angry, I'm angry." Then "Breathe in, breathe out, breathe in, breathe out." I would repeat this for twenty minutes, several times a day. In six years I forgave my captors.[23]

How this sort of meditation works with anger, according to psychologist Andrew Morral, is that it disrupts the otherwise automatic relationship between angry thoughts and a full-blown anger response. Morral explains:

> With meditation, the experience of anger becomes one among many different sensations or thoughts you might be having at any moment. This can be very liberating. Instead of always "seeing-red," or becoming a hostage of your anger, in meditation, many people learn to tolerate anger: "I'm furious, true, but I'm so much more in addition to that. I'm pleased by some news I heard this morning from a friend. I have some errands to run this morning. My joints ache, as usual. And the sun feels lovely on my arm."

Morral says that used in this way, meditation can help put anger in its proper context, so that it doesn't become the context for everything else.[24]

Visualization is another method people can use when overwhelmed by life events. Gail Sheehy writes about one image that psychiatrist Patrizia Levi uses with her patients who are facing life crises:

> Imagine yourself in the ocean. Sometimes the current of life is fairly calm, and you can move along with it. Even if it's choppy, you can take the waves, perhaps readjust your course, and push forward. But at other times, when a storm blows up, the waves swell so high they threaten to overwhelm you. At that point, you don't fight the waves; you go with them. And you try to retain a sense about yourself that you will eventually find your sea legs in spite of the storm. The chances are that if you remain calm and alert, you will land safely.[25]

Ascher also describes a visualization technique she uses in sibling-bereavement groups she leads to help deal with anger:

> [We] hold our hands in front of ourselves, palms up and slightly cupped. We close our eyes and imagine our hands filling with all our anger. Once our hands have grown heavy and are completely full, with our eyes still closed, we turn our hands upside down, emptying all that was "held." We then return to the former cupped position and imagine healing light and energy flowing into our hands.

Ascher thinks that techniques like this one are essential to release the energy you need to move forward. "The distraction of wrongs done to us merely increases the power of the wrong," she writes.[26]

⋈⋈⋈⋈⋈⋈

Physical Outlets

Many women who did not exercise regularly when they were married began to make a habit of some type of regular physical activity to release tension and generally make themselves feel better. A word they often used to describe what they did was "nonthreatening," meaning that for many, to be relaxing the activity needed to be noncompetitive. Mentioned most often as providing release and pleasure was taking long walks. Others ran or swam laps or attended aerobics classes. Melinda, for example, jogs four miles three times a week.

Activities like these can melt away anxiety and physical tension, while stimulating the endorphins that provide a sense of wellbeing.[27] Kabat-Zinn explains that physical activity helps because it allows a physical release (just like fighting or running away would) after which your muscles relax and your blood flow readjusts itself.[28] The exercise doesn't have to be all that strenuous either. A recent study showed that people who bicycled moderately experienced more improvement in their moods than those who cycled intensely and those who pushed themselves to their limits.[29]

Neuroscientists at Rockefeller University are among those who endorse regular, moderate exercise to counteract the negative effects of stress. Their research shows that such physical activity can bring stress hormone levels back to normal, lower blood pressure and the heart's resting rate, and make it easier to give up negative behaviors that people use to calm themselves—like overeating or excessive alcohol consumption.[30]

Studies also show that strength training may be beneficial in changing your mood.[31] When forty-two-year-old Evelyn and her husband divorced so that he could pursue a homosexual lifestyle, Evelyn began to work out with weights. Not only did it make her feel stronger, but it also alleviated some of the stress-related problems she was having with her stomach. She also took up roller blading (she had bruises on her elbows to prove it), ridding herself of excess nervous energy while delivering her graphics design work to nearby customers.

For some women, physical activity is what pulls them through the initial stage of being on their own. Nina, for example, had always used activities like dancing and swimming to help her cope. When she separated from her husband of twenty-two years, she says she "hit bottom" and just wanted to stay in bed all day. But she forced herself to work out hard daily,

> for strength to get me through. . . . I realized that my own resources were the best friend I had. When I'm running, I feel strong and hopeful and capable. I feel energy and strength running through me. Then I know I can make myself feel good.

Nina obviously loves her workouts and uses them to divert her attention away from her painful feelings. Perhaps that's why physical activity seems to work to alleviate depression and anxiety—by providing a true distraction, not just another setting where you can mull over your problems. At any rate, evidence is accumulating that even modest amounts of exercise, done regularly, can improve both your mood and your self-esteem.[32]

⬚⬚⬚⬚⬚⬚

Change Your Lifestyle

Many experts recommend that people under a lot of stress change some of their habits. **Examine your eating habits.** You may need to decrease caffeine intake, which can dehydrate you and jangle your nerves unnecessarily. Eat regular, well-balanced meals and take *much* more time at those meals, paying attention to and savoring what you are eating. Make sure you're getting enough protein and foods considered essential to your brain cells and mood-regulating chemicals—like fish, bananas, milk, eggs, and cereals, as well as vitamins B6 and E.[33] Cut back on alcohol or tranquilizers or cut them out entirely if you find that you are relying on them too much or if they worsen your mood immediately or later on.

Turn down the noise and velocity in your life generally,

whether at home or at work. Stress is physically tiring, so you need to get more sleep, taking catnaps during the day if you don't get enough at night. (Be aware, though, that a disturbance in your sleep pattern—either sleeping too much or experiencing early-morning insomnia—is one warning sign that you may be seriously depressed and should consult a mental health professional.)[34]

Finally, begin to take better care of yourself by saying the following two phrases over and over when you're alone—so that you can begin to use them regularly with others: "No, I can't do that" and "I need some help." Women have a strong tendency to tie their self-worth to how good they are at *giving* care. As a result, they often find that saying no to others' demands or asking *others* for help is disconcerting, if not downright impossible.[35] Becoming comfortable with these phrases should make it easier to use them in real-life situations, helping you to preserve the limited energy reserves you have during this difficult period.

Evelyn Vuko, recovering from cancer, counsels that vigilance against "energy leeches" is essential. She suggests a visualization where you close your eyes and think about all of your obligations, "all the places where you usually say, 'Yes, of course. Here let me . . .'" Vuko writes:

> Keep envisioning these things until your brain is packed and you sweat with nausea. Now you're ready. Place your hands on your hips, throw your head back, take another deep breath and bark "NO! NO! NO! NO! NO!" Usually by the fifth time, your tense shoulders dislodge themselves from their usual place by your ears and your breathing becomes longer and deeper. As this powerful little word resonates in your mind, its magical powers declaw the sense of responsibility that manacles you to the patterns of your life. The tension and anxiety of constantly doing is replaced by a joyous burst of purely being.[36]

Take Risks

A lmost everyone I talked to found that she was able to begin to feel in control again just by putting one foot in front of the other. Take each step one at a time. You'll eventually find the courage to take the next and the next. **As you begin to take small risks and to succeed, you'll gain the confidence that comes from feeling in charge.**

Divorced writer Barbara Holland recommends ridding yourself of anxiety by meeting head-on whatever it is that frightens you. In her book *One's Company: Reflections on Living Alone*, she writes:

> Working slowly, with small risks taken and survived, we can build up the sense of competence that fends off fright.
>
> Take money out of the savings account and put it in the stock market. Make eye contact in the streets. Criticize taxi drivers. Turn down boring invitations. Complain to the boss. Buy a motorcycle. Join a rock-climbing club. Take advanced riding lessons. Join a protest group and get arrested. Run for city council. Sue the landlord. Fall in love. Quit the job. Jaywalk. Exceed the speed limit. Make a speech. Try out for the drama group. Find something that makes your palms sweat at the very thought and go and do it.[37]

Many women talked about how much trepidation they had to overcome in order to attend their first singles' group. But familiarity breeds relaxation, and most of the women became regular members, some eventually taking a leadership role. Those who felt they didn't fit in usually found another group or even started one that better suited their needs. In every case, the initial small risks they took by attending led them into social contacts that eased their anxieties about being alone.

Melinda addressed her fear of becoming lonely after her husband died by signing up for ever more adventurous classes. She advises others who are newly single: **"To become stronger, you have to walk through your fears."** Debra's anxieties centered on her work future. She took a number of small steps, each involving some risk, to figure out what kind of career she was suited for and then to pursue it. As her plans came to fruition, her bag-lady fears began to disappear.

Seek Reinforcements

In the end, of course, self-help—in the limited sense of relying on *just yourself* to get a handle on your grief and anxiety—is not enough. As sturdy as your bootstraps and boots may be, if they're all you've got, you're bound to wear them out before you can get yourself back on your feet and moving forward. So when solitary pursuits like reading, exercising, meditating, or journal writing aren't really enough, you are going to need some outer resources to bolster your inner ones.

Happily, you will find that those resources exist. They can come in the form of good legal and financial advice. Or they might be in the form of a job that provides both psychic and financial rewards. Or they might be family members, old or new friends, a group of people you have something in common with, or a therapist. Or they may present themselves through a new or renewed sense of spirituality. If you're willing to seek out and cultivate these resources, they can make the job of moving from couplehood to a single life a great deal easier.

3

A Tiger by the Tail:
Dealing with Lawyers

Well-meaning family members and friends may offer legal or financial advice. Keep in mind they don't know the specifics of your situation, and as successful as they might be at managing their own affairs, their strategies may not be appropriate for you. So listen to them, but wait until you meet with your professional advisors before taking action. . . . The lawyer is usually the first advisor you see.

—Alexandra Armstrong and Mary Donahue
*On Your Own: A Widow's Passage
to Emotional and Financial Well-Being*[1]

Regardless of how much or how little contact you've had with lawyers in the past, it's a pretty sure bet you'll have to turn to one now. Lawyers play an essential role in a woman's transition to being single-again. That role, however, is quite different for widows than for divorcées.

Widows need lawyers because of their knowledge of the special laws on wills, probate, and property transferals. For divorcées, a lawyer's legal knowledge is vital, but perhaps more important is his or her advocacy skills. Those skills are the key to a woman's getting out of her marriage a fair share of the investment she put into it. Because finding and managing a good lawyer is generally much harder for divorcées than for widows, most of this chapter will be devoted to the topic of divorce lawyers.

⋈⋈⋈⋈⋈

Finding the Legal Help You Need

LAWYERS FOR SOUND ADVICE

There is one important characteristic that both widows and divorcées should seek in a lawyer. **A lawyer should be able to provide a much-needed stabilizing influence during your turmoil.** Jocelyn's lawyer friend, for example, walked her through the legal steps needed when her husband died, giving Jocelyn the sense that she was well taken care of while everything was crumbling around her. And when Sugar's husband began acting crazy, she thought the advice she got from a family lawyer was "the greatest thing in the world." He confirmed her instincts to try to save the marriage, rather than to follow the conflicting directions she was getting from friends and family.

When she was divorcing, Jan also got more than legal help from a very good woman lawyer she describes as a "bulldog."

Even though the lawyer was hard to reach, Jan says, she was "there for me during a few crises when I became totally unglued." She calmed Jan down, told her what they were going to do, and was very upbeat and determined. And, in addition, she got Jan a good settlement.

The kind of help that Sally got from her lawyer was even more important than legal assistance, she says. Sally hired a top-notch lawyer "who had a lot of psychodynamic insight. . . . She felt her job was helping me to get my life together in the best way she could." After talking to Sally and assessing the situation, the lawyer decided that it would be a good idea for Sally to negotiate directly with her lawyer husband at first, without any third parties. Sally discovered she could bargain skillfully with him, despite her lack of experience, which helped her regain a sense of control. She thinks that her lawyer is one of a new breed of women lawyers who can be extremely helpful simply because they see their jobs as including more than just the law. Such lawyers are worth searching out.

Keep in mind, however, that law schools don't offer courses in therapeutic techniques. If a lawyer has a good bedside manner, that's a nice bonus. But it's a lot less important than her competence and eloquence. So if you find yourself talking to your lawyer more about personal problems than about legal ones, you should consider consulting a professional therapist or a support group, where you might get more for your money.

Hiring Your Lawyer

Finding and hiring a good lawyer entails the same kind of trial and error you go through to find any good professional. You ask friends, and call women's groups, your local bar association, and lawyers' referral services. Women getting divorced should ask others whose divorces are final, and new widows should ask widows whose estates are settled.

Once you identify a few candidates, you should interview each one (which some lawyers charge for) and ask about his or her fee and track record. Try to find out as much as you can about the person's credentials before you see her. Check your library or the Internet for the *Martindale-Hubbell* directory of lawyers to see how much experience she has in family and matrimonial law (for divorcées) or estate and trusts (for widows). Try to find out whether she is well known in legal circles.

Michelle used that advice (which, ironically, she had learned from her husband) and hired as her lawyer a woman who was head of the county bar association. That lawyer's clout earned her custody of the children, alimony for six years, and child support. One well-known divorce lawyer, Glenn C. Lewis, who won an amazing award for the divorcing wife of professional football quarterback Joe Theismann, would approve. Lewis is quoted as saying:

> Alimony is, unlike child support or property division, much more of a mysterious process. There are no formulas; there are no guidelines. All there is, is what seems fair to the judge or the lawyer settling the case. . . . There's no question that lawyers on the top of the food chain tend to get better results.[2]

It's impossible to judge the competence of a lawyer in just one interview, but you need to have a good feeling about the person to whom you're entrusting so much. These are the questions you need lawyers you interview to answer:

- How many clients do you have?

- Will you be handling my case personally?

- How much experience do you have in dealing with marriages of long duration?

- (If you are widowed) How much experience do you have working with estates and trusts?

- What kind of background do you have in issues that may be particularly difficult in my case, like a family business?

- What kind of information do you need from me in order to do your job?

- What is your fee schedule and what might the total fee come to?

In addition, ask yourself the following few questions after the interview:

- Did she understand my specific needs for legal help?

- Did he explain the process he'll follow in a way I easily understood and without patronizing me?

- Was she sensitive to me?

Payment for a lawyer settling an estate can come from the estate's assets. Paying for a divorce attorney, however, is not that simple. Most want a retainer up front, and it's usual for them to want another payment "midstream." If you can't afford that, many states have laws that allow a court to order the divorcing spouse who earns more to pay part of the attorney's fees for the spouse who earns less. That is one avenue to pursue if the inequities between you and your husband are clear. But these court orders happen infrequently, so don't count on one.[3]

Once you feel comfortable about hiring an attorney, you need to formalize your agreement in a letter of engagement. Such a letter should state the fee arrangements you have agreed to and specify the written and other communications you expect from her. For example, if you don't ask for an accounting by hour of how she spent her time, you'll have no way of knowing how your money is being used. (One divorcée said her attorney spent her retainer of ten thousand dollars in seven weeks with no report or accounting.)

⚔⚔⚔⚔⚔⚔

For Divorcing Women Only: Lawyers as Hired Guns

WHY YOU NEED A POWERFUL ADVOCATE

Sue Ellen treated her divorce as a problem to be solved by calling in the experts: "I learned that somewhere along the way. **You cannot do things by yourself. So go to the experts. And pay for it. Shop around and pick out the best.**" The experts in Sue Ellen's case were a family therapist who "helped me believe in myself," an aggressive female lawyer who "didn't give a goddamn" what happened to Sue Ellen's husband, and a female financial consultant who taught her about managing and investing her money. These three people helped her through the worst of the mess in record time—six months, as she recalls.

Sue Ellen relates how she found the lawyer she finally hired. "I went through six lawyers before I found [one to suit me]. If anyone said to me, 'But what's your husband going to live on?' I'd say, 'Forget it,' and walk out. You're supposed to have a lawyer that only thinks about you and to hell with your husband," she insists.

Realizing that her husband didn't have much money, Sue Ellen and her lawyer decided to get the house instead. "That's number one. Get the house. Forget anything else. Find a job in the dime store [for income]. Get the house." Sue Ellen describes with delight the way her lawyer "negotiated" with her husband in the pursuit of their goal—drinking wine during the sessions and blowing smoke from a cigarette in a long holder in his face. "Psychological warfare. She was marvelous. She didn't care if he ever had anything to eat."

Obnoxious? Unnecessarily provocative? If you think so, that's because you may not fully grasp how adversarial the whole process of divorce is, under our legal system. Attorney Frances

Leonard explains that divorces *need* to be full of conflict in order for the American system of resolving disputes to work:

> The theory [in the U.S. system] is that "truth and justice" will be revealed when each party puts his or her own case forward in the best possible light, before a neutral fact-finder and judge. For this system to work the adversaries should *not* be neutral, objective or conciliatory. . . . The system is at its best when the parties are irrevocably opposed.[4]

That works well in criminal cases, Leonard says,

> But this system, when applied to divorcing parties, approaches its worst. . . . Unfortunately, the nature of the adversary system tends to increase the tensions, divisions and pain at the worst possible time, even though 90% of [divorce] dissolutions are settled without need of a trial.[5]

Terrible or not, a woman in a long-term marriage is stuck with the system. If you hire a cheaper, less competent lawyer, or a more accommodating one, you put yourself in a precarious position. Leonard warns that when women, especially older women, try to economize, they are likely to lose out. Employing a good independent counsel, she believes, "may represent the most important 'purchase' of the midlife or older woman's lifetime."[6]

To get what is fair, you need a lawyer who is aggressive and who knows all the ins and outs of the arguments that can gain you an equal division of marital property—often including a portion of a husband's pension. You need someone who is able to get you adequate support by arguing, for example, that because you have sacrificed your own earning power to care for your family, you should be compensated now.

Sue Ellen's "pit bull" lawyer got her the house, which, with the help of a realtor friend, she sold for a nice sum. She then invested part of her proceeds in a townhouse and the rest in the stock market. That's what Anna did too, when she won the house in her divorce settlement. Her husband had initially locked Anna out of their home. When she was finally able to force him out instead, he told her that he would hire a cutthroat lawyer and show her. Accepting the challenge, Anna hired the best woman divorce lawyer in town. She won alimony, health insurance coverage, and their house, which she then sold to a wealthy friend. "Finally," Anna says, "I felt free."

Sue Ellen and Anna got good settlements because they sought out (and were able to pay) the best lawyers. But women who have fewer resources than their husbands often don't fare that well. That was illustrated in the immensely popular (among women) movie *First Wives' Club*. Women recognized that the movie's horror stories of women going up against husbands with more assets were true-to-life. Which they were. The author of the book on which the movie is based, Olivia Goldsmith,[7] says all the outrages in the movie happened to her or to one of her divorcing friends. The only part that is fiction, she notes, is the ability of the divorcing women in the movie to get revenge.

Once you've received an unfair settlement, unless you have very deep pockets, there's little you can do. The anguish and rage of several women I talked to who had an inadequate lawyer were palpable. One woman, A J Brand, turned her outrage into advocacy for changes in the legal system. But others were left to cope with drastically reduced lifestyles (one woman called it "downsizing in a big way") and fantasies of revenge. Those women who were able to feel all right about what they considered to be less than fair settlements rationalized it as a trade-off for staying on good terms with their ex-husband.

MANAGING YOUR LAWYER

In his book *Divorce War! Fifty Strategies Every Woman Needs to Know to Win,* lawyer Bradley Pistotnik advises that, even if you hire "the toughest, best-liked, and most highly connected lawyer money can buy," you should not just rely on her or him to get the kind of settlement you deserve.[8] As soon as you decide to divorce, he urges you to prepare a "master battle plan" that you keep absolutely secret.

That plan should include gathering the evidence you will need, such as whatever you can uncover about your husband's activities, plans, and assets. You can find this out by copying any evidence you can find, questioning his financial advisors, stockbrokers, attorneys, and secretaries, even tape recording conversations and hiring a detective.[9] Pistotnik admits that some of his fifty strategies "may seem aggressive and even deceitful." But, he goes on, "Keep in mind that they may be the only way to rectify the injustices that have been committed against you."[10]

Although his advice may be somewhat extreme, Pistotnik's book includes vital information if you're facing divorce. For example, he explains how in some states an abused or neglected spouse can use a "marital tort" lawsuit to get a monetary settlement. Under a marital tort, you can bring a civil suit against your spouse to get compensation for any personal injuries he caused you, including harm from emotional stress in your marriage.[11]

Using this and other techniques, Pistotnik makes it absolutely clear that *you* need to be the one in charge, making the important decisions, and keeping a tight hold on your lawyer's tail. **Remember that, although it may not always feel like it, the attorney you hire works for you, not the other way around. So while you can't tell him or her how to manage the case, you should always expect a full explanation of what your lawyer's up to and why.**

If you don't approve, you can always fire him or her. But before you do that, you should put your complaint in writing. If things don't change to your satisfaction, you should then send your complaint to the state bar association. If you're still unhappy, then find another attorney.[12]

TAKING THE ROAD LESS TRAVELED: MEDIATION AND SELF-HELP LAWYERING

Some divorcing women decide on a much less adversarial process—mediation. In mediation, husband and wife work out an agreement with an impartial third party (usually an attorney), without resorting to demands and counterdemands. **Where mediation works well, it is because both husband and wife are intent on making the divorce as equitable as possible, from the outset.**

If you and your husband qualify in this respect, count yourself as lucky. As linguist Deborah Tannen points out, our culture's increasing reliance on adversarial processes to settle disputes has long-term ramifications: "Requiring people to behave like enemies can stir up mutual enmity that remains long after a case has been settled or tried, and the lawyers have moved on."[13]

But mediation that produces a fair settlement for both parties may be rare, perhaps because couples are not equally matched going into it. A paper on "Divorce and Older Women" prepared for the Older Women's League states that

> after a few years of experience, the reports on mediation for the longtime homemaker or underemployed wife are not favorable. The short-term emotional gain, if any, is obviated by later economic distress, as the former wife realizes she traded away spousal support or property in the process.[14]

Becoming an amateur lawyer yourself in order to avoid or cut back on the atrocious hourly rate you have to pay for a good lawyer is often not useful either. Like every other area of the law, matrimonial and family law is extremely specialized. What you're paying a lawyer for is both knowledge of that law and negotiating skills. These things are vital because a settlement that your and your husband's attorney negotiate is probably the best chance you have of getting a good outcome at a price you can afford.[15]

But that's not always true, as Mercy showed. By second-guessing and supplementing her lawyer's expertise, she was able to win what she wanted from her divorce. Mercy was intent on getting the house so that she could live there with her four children. The lawyer she consulted advised that there was no chance. Not willing to accept that verdict, Mercy discovered an old law in the local library that required that anything a man owned could be used for the support of his children. When her lawyer used that law as justification for turning her husband's interest in the house over to her, he prevailed.

Mercy only had a high school diploma at the time and was supporting her family on her own as a housekeeper. Her divorce decree was just one step of many in her march up the ladder to a successful career.

✕✕✕✕✕✕

A Necessary Evil

For both widows and women who are divorcing, lawyers are a necessary evil. With rare exceptions, if you try to save money by hiring less than the best, you are taking a big chance that you will curtail your future income. Ideally, you want a lawyer who

- knows all of the special laws that apply to your circumstances;

- is tuned in to your situation;

- works *with* you in choosing each step in the process;

- lets you lean on him or her during your worst moments;

- has the skills to get you the income you deserve;

- doesn't charge an arm and a leg!

Finding such a jewel will not always be easy, nor will it always be comfortable for you to actively participate in the process. But delving into what may be an alien environment will allow you to stretch yourself. It will let you use the managerial skills you've gained in other parts of your life in new and challenging ways.

Sadly, even if your experience with your lawyer is a positive one, the results may not be what you hoped. Still, there is no cause to despair or become bitter. As dozens of women told me, *not* having sufficient money from their former or deceased husbands, while a shock at first, ultimately proved to be a blessing. For them, needing to learn how to make the most of their small incomes and how to earn their own money were important stimuli in their metamorphoses into self-sufficient single adults. The challenges of money will be the subject of the next chapter.

4

Gain Financial Expertise: Your Own and Others'

Without planning, it's nearly impossible to increase your wealth.
. . . Whatever your situation—whether you are trying to scrape
enough money together to cover your expenses or wondering
where to invest excess income—financial planning is the foundation of a sound economic future. The earlier you begin planning,
the more secure your future will be.
—The Beardstown Ladies' Common Sense Investment Guide[1]

✂✂✂✂✂

Women and Money

W hat a splash the "Beardstown Ladies" made! This assortment of some sixteen middle-aged women from Beardstown, Illinois, started out modestly enough. One of their founders, frustrated at how little her certificates of deposit were paying, had been turned down by two stockbrokers she approached to handle her money. But a third broker in nearby Springfield saw the potential in this untapped market niche. He helped organize the Beardstown Business and Professional Women's Investment Club. When the sixteen women began meeting in the basement of a church, they had a modest goal: wanting to learn about the stock market. Less than ten years later, the club won a national contest based on the 23.4 percent rate of return they earned on their 1991 portfolio of twenty hand-picked stocks.[2]

Suddenly the "ladies" were celebrities. (Please note that the word "ladies" does not appear in the formal name of the club. Perhaps it just sounded cuter than "business and professional women" to the publicists.) They were on television and in newspapers and magazines, and they produced two best-selling books and an instructional video. What was so noteworthy, apparently, was not *what* the Beardstown women were doing, which for the most part followed all the basic investment principles laid down by the National Association of Investment Clubs.[3] It was, I think, that middle-aged women aren't supposed to be doing it at all. Or winning prizes at it. Yet the women, investing only twenty-five dollars each per month in individual stocks, have averaged a 9.1 percent annual return on their money over a ten-year period.[4]

These women are now cited everywhere as proof that you don't have to be an economist, a financial wizard, young, or even a man to learn how to invest in the stock market. It would be great to think that the Beardstown women's success has changed other women's attitudes about taking charge of this aspect of their lives. Maybe it has. But given how ambivalent most women are about money—and the power it confers—it's likely that changing attitudes is going to take more than having the Beardstown Ladies as role models.

The brokerage firm Merrill Lynch confirmed this view. A study it sponsored of eight hundred people between forty-five and sixty-four showed that middle-aged men had almost twice as much money invested in the stock market as did middle-aged women (an average of $52,500 for the men, versus $25,700 for the women).[5] In order to show potential female investors how much more you can earn over the long term by investing in stocks, Merrill Lynch organized a series of seminars for a group of some three dozen affluent women.

What they uncovered was that the attitudes of the women weren't entirely rational. Although all were successful professionals, they expressed great fear about managing money. One woman, the vice-president of a chemical company, said, "No matter what I do with money, I feel I'm doing something wrong."[6] Even though they knew that having more money would give them security, they still did little to acquire a lot of it because, as one woman put it, that would mean "giving up the fantasy that someone is going to come along and take care of me." Another woman expressed great guilt about the money she did have.

To counter those feelings, Merrill Lynch turned the last few seminars into a kind of support group. A *New York Times* article describes how the women were asked "to come up to the front of the room and claim what was theirs: the right to learn, the right to have, empowerment."[7] Whether this approach to investment counseling succeeded in transforming these women into risk-taking stock buyers is unclear. For now, Merrill Lynch isn't saying.

It's possible that it didn't work because of the depth of many women's irrational attitudes about money. Amazingly, surveys show that one out of every two middle-class, educated women says that she harbors an intense fear of becoming impoverished.[8] That's certainly true for many women I interviewed. When I asked the women what was initially the hardest thing about being widowed or divorced, a surprising number—even those with little reason to think so—replied it was their fear of becoming a bag lady. It's a haunting image, being reduced to living out of a shopping cart, scavenging for clothes and food, constructing makeshift shelters for the night.

However, there is another image that many women apparently fear: the cold, unlovable, rich woman. Probing this curious fear of riches, Annette Lieberman and Vicki Lindner asked women to describe their image of a woman in their field who made a lot of money. The respondents described such a female as a pariah, unapproachable by both men and women, unlikable and "unfeminine."[9] No wonder the Merrill Lynch women were ambivalent about making money in the stock market. Who would want wealth if the price is that high?

Researchers from the National Center for Women and Retirement Research found a surprising level of passivity about their finances among the 352 divorced women over forty they surveyed. Describing the women, who were mostly middle class and educated and from long-term marriages, the researchers concluded:

> When it comes to money matters . . . most women are sorely uninformed. During marriage, nearly two out of three never discuss finances with their spouses; forty-two percent don't look at tax returns, checkbooks, or financial records. Divorcing, more than half have no idea what kind of property is jointly owned; sixty-two percent don't understand or aren't aware of investments; about a third didn't have a clue about bank and credit accounts.[10]

Women's lack of understanding about their finances, combined with their fear and guilt about money, leads many to compromise and accept basically unfair distributions in their divorces.[11] And it's a good guess that these same handicaps are one reason that women who find themselves newly poor after their husbands' deaths are unable to pull themselves out of poverty, even though they, on average, outlive their husband by eighteen and one-half years.[12]

We can feel pretty sure, however, that that won't happen with the Beardstown women. All these women needed was a lot more information about investing, knowledge of the relative risks of different types of investments, and the confidence gained from taking small risks and seeing them pay off. As serious students, they came to understand that stocks are no more risky than most other investments and outperform them over the long term.[13] It's encouraging to know that when and if these women become single-again, they'll be way ahead of the game.

⋈⋈⋈⋈⋈

Taking Other Paths Than the One to Poverty

A woman's ambivalent feelings about money can cause her initial steps down what the Older Women's League calls "the path to poverty" in her later years.[14] According to the U.S. Census Bureau, only one out of two women between the ages of sixty-five and seventy-four is married with a spouse present in the house.[15] And while the median annual income of all women over sixty-five in 1993 was just above the poverty level (about $8,500, compared to almost $15,000 for men), whether or not you are married can determine whether you are poor. Census figures show that wives are better off financially than widows— four times as many widows live in poverty. But poorest of all are separated and divorced women.[16] Those dismal statistics should spur any newly single woman into becoming a serious student of money management.

But if you're new at managing your money, you can't expect to go it alone, especially at first. You're going to need a lot of advice. Professionals who give financial advice range from accountants, to tax advisors, bankers, brokers, and financial planners.[17]

Whoever you choose, however, you're going to have to be the one in charge. In her book *Money and the Mature Woman,* Frances Leonard draws the distinction between *abdicating* responsibility for your finances—turning it over entirely to husbands, bankers, or financial advisors—and *delegating* it—exercising control over it while consulting with professionals and other knowledgeable people.[18]

Several women I interviewed had changed dramatically from being financial abdicators to being financial delegators. Once they became single, they understood right away that abdicating responsibility would be the path toward poverty. So they altered their course. And by doing so, they altered the outcome.

Take, for example, Sue Ellen—the woman who walked away from five lawyers until she found one who was aggressive enough to confront her husband head-on. Divorced at fifty-six, with a job that didn't pay very much, Sue Ellen quickly realized she didn't know much about managing her money. So she turned to a financial consultant for help, a woman she still uses as her accountant. Working with her, Sue Ellen says, "I learned all about what capital was. And we plotted what I was going to do with whatever I had."

The approach Sue Ellen took was to turn whatever assets she had into cash that she could invest in stocks and bonds for her retirement. She decided to sell the home she won in the divorce, buying a much cheaper townhouse and investing the money that was left over. After that initial entrée into investing, she began saving and investing with any other money she could get her hands on—including renting out part of the townhouse. She has done so well that now, fifteen years later, her government pension, Social Security, and the income from her retirement accounts give her an income of $3,800 per month. "I don't know what to do with it all," Sue Ellen enthuses. "Isn't that marvelous? Starting from nothing? I've been very lucky with money."

While I'm sure luck played a role, so did Sue Ellen's willingness to take risks and learn the rules of investing, with the help of a professional.

Matty is also reaping the rewards of the energy and smarts she has put into financial planning since she divorced her husband at the age of forty-three. Looking back, Matty sees her life as divided into twenty-year segments: twenty years growing up; then twenty married and raising a family; then single with a career as a meeting planner for the next twenty. She's entering her last twenty now, she says, and she thinks they may be the best.

Matty was able to retire at sixty-one because the pension she earned from the job she began after she divorced is supplemented by the income she gets from her investments. She took the leap into saving and investing because, even though she got alimony in her divorce settlement, she worried that she wouldn't have any money for retirement. So like Sue Ellen and others, she sold the house she and her daughter were living in and bought the smaller house she lives in now. Not only was there a rental property connected with the new house to bring in income, but she had money left over from the sale of her first home to invest in stocks. And when the new property appreciated a great deal, she refinanced it and put some of that money "out to work" in the stock market too.

To learn how to invest, Matty began to take courses in the evenings and joined the National Association of Individual Investors (NAII), receiving its monthly newsletters.[19] She also turned to two friends, a woman and a man, who gave her advice on "how to get my money to work." Matty confesses, though, that a lot of what passes for financial advice still goes over her head. So rather than spending the time it would take to buy individual stocks, she invests mostly in mutual funds.[20]

May, on the other hand, invests her savings in individual stocks, an avocation she has pursued since her husband died over twenty years ago. Initially, May recalls, she sought advice from everyone. "I went around and shopped for it. I talked to a whole bunch of friends. I visited brokers. I literally spent a lot of time doing that in the first few years. And I saved as much as I possibly could." In addition, she began reading as much as she could about finance—the NAII guides; *Kiplinger's* newsletter; business sections of newspapers and magazines, like *Working Woman* and *The Wall Street Journal*.

May says she spends "months and years now" making up her mind about what individual stocks to buy. She sticks to companies in her urban area because she can follow what's happening with their operations in the local papers. Her philosophy is to research the facts about the company's financial position. But she decides to buy based on the "feel" of a company—whether or not, for example, when you walk in, there is an agreeable atmosphere, and how the employees feel about it. That takes using intuition, she says, something not all people in finance rely on.

May has done so well that she has moved on from being mentored about financial management to mentoring other women. She often brings finances up herself, she says, because other people may be hesitant to. She wants women to read and think a lot about investing because "you need to know those things."

⁂⁂⁂⁂

If You Want It Done Right . . .

In learning about finance and investing, first you have to understand the jargon, which is much less intimidating than it seems

at first glance. Any introductory book on money management will translate those terms for you and give you the basic tools of financial planning. Then undertake as many of the following activities as you possibly can to fill in gaps in your understanding:

- Instead of automatically throwing it out, *take ten minutes to read the business page of your local paper.*

- *Take a course or read all the self-help material that's available in your local library.* Community colleges offer basic courses on financial planning and retirement and estate planning (which, though they may sound as if they are only for old people, do give advice that will help you at any age). And in some one thousand sites, AARP and a local co-sponsor offer workshops to women of all ages on basic money-management skills. [21]

- Armed with that basic information, *look for the professionals you need to help you with specific tasks.*

- *Watch for seminars on investing tailored to women,* offered by financial-services companies, mutual funds, and insurance companies. Prudential Securities, Oppenheimer Management Fund, Merrill Lynch, and Chase Manhattan regularly sponsor them, to name a few.[22]

Learn what you can from stockbrokers. But if you decide to use a brokerage firm to advise you on making specific investments, keep in mind that they earn a commission from any stocks they buy or sell for you. As a result, their interest *can* focus more on the buying and selling than on your long-term financial future. And be aware that surveys show that women often feel they don't get enough attention and advice from traditional stockbrokers.[23]

When you consult an expert, you should know exactly what information you're looking for, factoring what they tell you into what you already know and making the final decision yourself. Your aim is to find investments that are neither so risky that they cross the line into speculation nor so conservative that they barely keep up with inflation. Frances Leonard explains:

> The key is moderation—a prudent mix of risk, safety, stability, and liquidity.
>
> Here, we mature women have an advantage. We've managed our households for decades. We've been the principal buyers of a variety of commodities—from soup to nuts, and furniture to sheets. We know in our bones the principle of moderation. It's no wonder that investment clubs formed by women across the country have track records exceeding two-thirds of those made up only of men.
>
> Some, not too kindly, tell us that women were born to shop. Okay, then—let's go shopping![24]

It appears that an increasing number of women are viewing investing in this light—as more of a challenge than a threat. To become self-sufficient investors, women are joining one of the over seventeen thousand clubs that belong to the National Association of Investors Corporation (NAIC)—over 40 percent of them all-women groups—where they learn about investing. The one or two dozen members of each club contribute a small sum each month to a joint fund from which they purchase the club's stock portfolio. An NAIC study shows that women's clubs had a 13 percent average rate of return *per annum* over a fifteen-year period, outperforming the 12.3 percent earned by the men's clubs.[25]

Most of these clubs have a common investment philosophy and make their investment decisions without relying on an expert. They are heeding the warning of the NAIC that if there is "a perceived expert" in the club, "in all probability other members will lean on such an individual and know no more after years of membership than they did upon joining!"[26]

⋈⋈⋈⋈⋈⋈

Still Not Convinced?

If you find yourself still unwilling to seek out and master at least a minimal level of expertise about your own finances and financial planning, you should look long and hard at what's stopping you. Are you remaining stubbornly attached to a childish notion that someone or something else is going to take care of you? Without some basic understanding, you leave yourself vulnerable to all the mishaps that occur when others manage something of yours about which you know little or nothing. Ask yourself whether you'd be competent to select and assess a school for a child or grandchild without understanding the basics of a good education. Why should finding good investments for your money be any different?

5

Get a Job (or Keep
the One You Have)

XXXXXXXXXXXXXXXXXXXXXXXXXXXXXXX

*While many mid-life divorced women are twice disadvantaged,
having to cope with the emotional trauma and seek work for the
first time, the study [of 352 divorced women over forty] high-
lights that they also gain an unexpected benefit: **the intrinsic
value of working can heal even the deepest wound.** . . . Work
enables a mid-life woman to see that she can rise to new challenges. She meets new people. She is exposed to new ideas. Most
important, she can paint a new self-portrait.*
    —Christopher Hayes, Deborah Anderson, and Melinda Blau
      Our Turn: The Good News about Women and Divorce [1]

⊠⊠⊠⊠⊠⊠

Why You Need to Work

"Going Out to Work Was My Salvation"

Luckily for her, Beverly didn't know that she was considered washed-up at the age of fifty-six, when she divorced her husband of thirty-six years. Beverly had been an English World War II bride, leaving home at twenty with her dashing American soldier after a three-month whirlwind courtship. On her own and working since she left school at the age of sixteen, Beverly was experiencing a fantasy come true—sailing off to live in America, "the land of milk and honey."

But like all fantasies, hers faded, gradually at first and then irretrievably. As their three daughters became teenagers, Beverly found herself first depressed then increasingly angry. Her husband was a government scientist, and associating with his colleagues, who were all bound up in their esoteric, secret work, left her feeling alienated and inadequate. Beverly recalls those years:

> I would knit furiously day and night. I remember thinking to myself, "I've gone through a war and survived by myself. My parents died—my mother died right before the war, my dad was killed in the early months of the war." And I thought, "I don't have to take this kind of stuff." So I started speaking up. I used to say to my husband, "You know, I'm not the village idiot. You wouldn't have married me had I been the village idiot."

So when in 1980 her husband was offered a new job out of state, she knew she did not want to move with him. When a mediator they consulted suggested that they divorce rather than just separate, they both agreed. "I just couldn't live with him anymore. And it didn't matter whether he was in the same town or three thousand miles away," Beverly says. Through the mediation, she received a "very nice settlement" with alimony for five years. But immediately after the divorce was settled, Beverly's emotions became more complex: "There was almost a feeling of relief, but there was also a feeling of great fear: what am I to do?"

Beverly had worked as a secretary while her husband studied for his Ph.D. but after 1952 had stayed at home to raise their daughters. "My world was bounded by these four walls and my children. You tend to fall by the wayside," she says.

Calculating what she had to offer, she thought about her management skills. "I had always been a very orderly and organized person. I literally ran this house like a machine. The kids would make a joke out of it," she remembers. Beverly's assets included her attention to detail and her good math skills, demonstrated in all of the responsible volunteer work she had done, such as acting as secretary and treasurer of her bowling league. She pulled it all together into a resumé and set to work getting her typing back up to speed.

Although she wanted to wait a while before looking for work, her daughters urged her to begin right away. Two who were already employed in the city acted as her mentors. They insisted she search downtown "because that's where the money is." So Beverly took the subway into town in response to a newspaper help-wanted ad for a sales aide in the advertising department at the city newspaper. The personnel people at the paper tested her skills (she got 100 on the spelling), called her back for two more interviews, and hired her. Her starting salary was $14,400 per year, a source of real elation because it was "*my* money!"

Beverly has worked at the paper for thirteen years now, has been promoted several times, and earns enough to live on her own, even to travel every other year to England. Her retirement is vested, but her ambition is to stay for twenty years, until the turn of the century. (She would be seventy-six.) Nobody has told her she can't. "I love working. I dread the day when they have to carry me out of there," she says cheerfully.

Beverly reports that, because of her age, not in spite of it, she is a showpiece for the department. She has twice won the "publishers' award" for her department for outstanding service. Staff tell her that she knows everything there is to know about the advertising department, that she really runs it. Palling around with "a lot of the guys" meets her need for male companionship, with no harm done. "They're mostly married and I'm donkey years older than any of them so I'm not a threat to anybody." And she prizes her role as office mom, baking huge quantities of cookies for Christmas, as well as twenty-dozen scones with homemade jam for St. George's Day, the April 23 celebration of England's patron saint.

Looking back at her divorce, Beverly says that "going out to work was my salvation . . . the beginning of a totally new life for myself. I've never looked back." Her assessment is one shared by legions of widowed and divorced women.

This chapter is about the crucial role that holding a job can play in helping you make the transition from living as a married woman to having a fulfilling life on your own. It explains how work can help you move beyond your loss; offers tips on how women with limited confidence, work experience, and skills can find help with their job search; and describes conventional and unconventional ways women manage to find employment. The subject of how women move beyond holding a job to building a career is covered in chapter 11, "Step by Step to a Career."

BEING YOUR OWN WORST ENEMY

It all sounds so *right* when Beverly describes it: supermom transfers everything she learned as a homemaker to a job as super salesperson and office manager. But it's not something that happens every day and Beverly knows it. She says that since she was hired for her job by a thirty-five-year-old woman, they haven't hired anyone over the age of thirty for a support position.

That's not at all uncommon. In fact, employers who hire *any* older people are in the minority. Studies show rampant age stereotyping and discrimination against older job applicants.[2] In polls of employers, nearly two-thirds admit that they discriminate against older applicants. Most don't hesitate to say that in a secretarial position they prefer an attractive young woman to an older one.[3] A survey of four hundred human-resource executives revealed that they are doing less than ever to hire older workers. Many personnel managers believe older persons are "unwilling to accept new or additional tasks, cannot adapt to new working environments and resist using new technology."[4] And although polls or surveys may not reveal it, older women suffer a further handicap: offensive images in the media and elsewhere depict them as airheaded, annoying, too garrulous, intrusive, bossy, fairly useless individuals.

So why did anyone hire Beverly? Beverly believes it was because she had just the right mix of skills. They needed someone who would be good on the telephone with advertisers and other customers. "I was obviously very well-spoken, very literate, and I had no trouble articulating." Beverly also knew she would be good at the job, and her self-confidence must have been part of why she got it. And once she was hired, of course, she proved herself indispensable.

The sad truth is, however, that most mature women who find themselves divorced or widowed with no real work experience *have* absorbed the judgment that they are basically unemployable.[5] They are among the 1.1 million male and female "discouraged workers" over the age of fifty who are willing and able to do just about anything, but who believe that (a) there are no jobs out there; or (b) they're not qualified to do them; or (c) employers will find them too old.[6] Another survey of American job-seekers over fifty-five found that women were more likely to be discouraged than were men.[7] Their negative feelings lead to a vicious cycle of looking for work with less energy and confidence, which leads to limited success and eventually to almost total apathy.

Work as a Building Block

For mature women, the problem of finding a job, even an entry-level one, may be worse than for men because of the importance we all place on a woman's youthful appearance. But many women who become single recognize that holding down a job is critical in building a new life and so do whatever is necessary to find one.

One of these is fifty-eight-year-old Joanne. When her husband suddenly died after a thirty-year marriage, she promptly found a part-time job at a senior center in a Chicago suburb. Today, two years later, she is unruffled and full of Irish humor. But Joanne describes a time when her life was in sheer chaos because, right after her husband died, both her parents passed away.

Although she didn't have any immediate financial problems, she decided to seek a job in a supportive, low-key environment. It would, she hoped, provide some relief from all the unpleasant tasks she faced at home, keep her from becoming too isolated, and provide affordable health insurance coverage for her high blood pressure. The job she found as a database manager is just right for her—for now. Joanne was hired because even though her previous work with computers was outdated, she had recently worked as a volunteer to help set up a computer system in the local library. Joanne says her new job has given her back confidence in her skills and has been "ideal for getting back on my feet."

A job is important for you as a newly single woman because it

- buys you time to heal;

- furnishes you with structure and challenges;

- cuts down on your isolation;

- affirms your new status; and

- can lead to financial independence.

- *A Job Buys You Time to Heal*

Healing fully after the death or divorce of a husband can take more time than you'd like. Having a job makes it possible to move gradually toward the stage when you can make major decisions with the certainty that they are the right ones. Women I interviewed felt lucky to have a job to get them through the initial stages of disorientation. Their jobs gave them a point of stability in the midst of chaos, making it impossible for them to spend all their time grieving and fuming—a dangerous proposition at best. For one woman who was leaving an especially disorderly marriage, taking a job made her realize that life didn't have to be so chaotic, a concept she was able to carry over to the new life she was building.

• A Job Furnishes You with Structure and Challenges

One way a job helps is simply by getting you out of the house, where everything can remind you of your loss. It also gives shape to your day, providing new tasks—pleasant *and* unpleasant—when old ways of spending time don't make sense anymore. Any grieving has to be minimal so it doesn't get you fired. You must relegate the worst bits of your sadness and anger to early mornings, evenings, and weekends, which still adds up to a lot of hours of despondency.

A widow said that her job selling real estate, which meant she had to work on weekends, made it possible for her to avoid the times most associated with the happiness she shared with her husband. It also served as an excuse to avoid seeing their well-meaning friends who wanted her to continue in her former role as "wife of" instead of moving on.

Work can also help replace all the challenges that being married provided. When you're married, "You're problem-solving constantly. You're negotiating. You're figuring things out. You're juggling," said one woman. When you no longer have that role to play, work can be the vehicle that "piles on tasks" and challenges you.

• A Job Cuts Down on Your Isolation

One aspect of working that is especially beneficial, according to women I interviewed, is the emotional support you get from co-workers. Beverly immediately sought out friendships among her (mostly younger) male and female colleagues at the newspaper by literally feeding them and otherwise paying attention to them. In turn, they gave her a strong emotional base for her new life as a single older woman. Dozens of other women spoke about how important the network of new friends they made at work was in helping them through the initial stages of being unmarried.

Lynne Caine, the author of four books on being a widow, cites her own experience when she took a "miserably low salary" in publishing shortly after her husband died. She writes, "The job was good for me. I was busy all the time, and the work demanded a great deal from me. It also gave me the opportunity to meet people, and that was something I also badly needed."[8] Like Beverly's work, Caine's job opened a new life for her. But even when that doesn't happen and the job leads to a dead end, it can be an important route to getting back on your feet.

• A Job Affirms Your New Status

Going out to work sets out for public view your new identity as a single woman. Describing women facing the empty nest, author Lillian Rubin affirms how work can provide a much-needed prop:

> Women who have work from which they get substantial independent gratification **can** more easily avoid the pain by burying themselves in their work. They have other things to think about, other ways of relating to the world and to themselves. They have at least the beginning of another identity, an emerging sense of their own separateness. Like a newborn colt, that developing identity may not yet stand firmly, but its existence alone is enough to make a difference. It is demonstrable proof that a self lives apart from the children, clear evidence that a future exists.[9]

Substitute the word "husband" for "children," and her conclusion is equally valid.

• *A Job Can Lead You to Financial Independence*

When you're making the transition from married to single-again, the knowledge that you can take care of yourself financially also has special resonance. The paycheck from a job, even if it's not very large, confirms your self-worth when other measures seem up in the air.

Long Island therapist Alice Umbach, who was married for thirty-one years before she divorced, encourages her patients to face the need to support themselves right away. Even when they don't have to work, she says, "The truth is that working saves you a lot. It keeps structure in your life. You're getting rewards from the job. And you can't just sit around and focus on yourself all the time." It took one of Umbach's patients six years to go from no job to a job that paid enough for her to leave her husband. When she did leave, she told Umbach, "If I hadn't had my feet firmly planted in a job, I don't think I would have made it."[10]

Work as an Emotional Cocoon

Carla has come a long way since her fifty-six-year-old husband suddenly died, leaving her, at the age of forty-five, stranded in Indonesia with five children, aged eleven to twenty. Carla's husband was an international economist. Their family had been posted all over the world for two- to three-year stints, leaving them with nowhere to call home. She had married when she was twenty-three, just out of school in England—so young, she says, that "I actually absorbed a great part of his values, tastes, and such, because I didn't have any of my own." After his death, "I had to grow a new arm and a leg to compensate."

But where would that be possible? Carla knew she would have to create a place, the more sheltered the better, preferably not in a city or the suburbs. And she would have to find a way to earn enough money to support her teenage children. Their family had become Quakers some years before. So Carla thought of a tiny community that boasted an excellent Quaker school. She had earned a master's degree in history in England before she married, and that credential was enough to persuade the school's headmaster to hire her as a history teacher. Her job also made it possible for three of her children to go to school there tuition-free.

For five years, until her youngest child went off to college, she and her family were taken in and supported by this close community. Carla says that although their family had always been close, it became closer and stayed that way. It also "changed shape." Whereas when her husband was alive, it was hierarchical, with him gone, "It became a circle." Her children thrived, growing up to become motivated, self-sufficient adults. And the time was a big plus for her too, both because she had to get out and do for herself and because it allowed her to grow the "new arm and new leg" she needed.

Carla's new appendages have, it turns out, transformed her into a virtual gypsy. And she has worked up a series of wonderful jobs to support her freewheeling lifestyle. She lived and worked for a while both in Indonesia and, with her son, in China (where they collaborated on her first magazine article); wrote for two years in France; and then began her current arrangement as a writer part-time in the United States, part-time in France.

Carla thinks the secret of her continuing success in the working world is simple: her old-fashioned British education. It gives her an advantage, she believes, over younger writers because she knows more about topics like history and geography than they do. What she forgets to mention, however, are her writing skills, dependability, and penchant for hard work. The last two are characteristics we all can imitate.

Is Volunteering an Adequate Substitute?

One obvious question is whether, if you can get along without the paycheck and benefits, and have plenty saved for your old age, you might get the same kind of satisfaction from an interesting and challenging volunteer position as you would from paid work. In some cases (such as Joanne's library volunteering), when the volunteer work is engaging enough to provide the same types of rewards as paid work (obviously minus the paycheck), volunteer work can be a good substitute. **But the main difficulty is that challenging work for volunteers may not be any easier to locate than are challenging paying jobs.** Most volunteer jobs are poorly structured and are not integrated into an organization in a way that will allow you to feel connected and valued.

For that reason, a number of women who did a lot of responsible volunteering before they went into the paid workforce told me that they might never go back to the volunteer world, even after retirement. They said that volunteer work is just not as valued as paid work. Others, however, as we'll see in chapter 12, "Pursuing Your Passion," were able to transform volunteering into a career that was the centerpiece of their lives.

⁂

When You Need a Leg Up

What Are You Qualified to Do?

Many women don't have the luxury of deciding whether to work or not. They *have* to work because they no longer have a husband to support them. And often they have no substantial work or educational background. In the 1970s, Tish Sommers and Laurie Shields coined the term "displaced homemakers" to describe these women.[11] There are over 3 million of them between the ages of forty-five and sixty-four, according to one analysis of the 1990 census.[12]

While Beverly fits our definition of a displaced homemaker, she was able, with just her daughters' coaching, to find a job she loved. Others with less self-assurance and ability to sell themselves are not so fortunate. Without help, these women are likely to end up unemployed or severely underemployed. A startling 40 percent of them live in poverty.[13] Most never prepared themselves when they were young for careers they could resume later, assuming that they wouldn't ever go back to work after they had children. But often they do go back, dipping in and out of the workforce over the course of their lives. Usually they never even consider better-paid, nontraditional female jobs, nor do they stay long enough at any one job to build up a salary, expertise, or pension.[14]

Still, that doesn't explain why women who do re-enter the workforce don't earn salaries commensurate with their skills. (Women over fifty-five earn only 54 percent of what similarly educated men do.)[15] One obvious reason, discussed earlier, is the age and gender discrimination they face. But analysts also speculate that another reason is how they approach their job search:

> If [middle-aged] women have received lower wages after work interruptions, it seems more likely that a lack of recent references, a lack of information about the job market, or a lack of confidence in their own abilities are more likely explanations than a deterioration of their basic job-related skills.[16]

In simple terms, then, women trying to re-enter the job market after a number of years away from it are likely to be floundering. Someone who has concentrated her energy on being a wife and mother is naturally going to have difficulty coming up with a clear idea of strengths that are transferable to the job market, not to mention what kind of work she wants to do. Even if she uses every trick in the book, how does she get over or around the barriers of age and gender stereotyping? In addition, her self-perceptions may be way off the mark, ranging from thinking she has no skills when she has many, to anticipating a well-paid job immediately when the best she may be able to do right away is to get a low-paying temporary or entry-level position. Without a lot of help, she can't surmount these external and internal barriers.

GETTING THE HELP YOU NEED

If you find yourself facing some of these same obstacles, **experts advise you to attach yourself to other people in the same boat. Join a support group for job seekers, for example. Or set up such a group on your own,** using as a resource a book like the American Association of Retired Persons' (AARP) free booklet *Returning to the Job Market: A Woman's Guide to Employment Planning.*[17] Even better would be to **join a group led by a specialist in job hunting.** For that, you'll need to find an ongoing course or program, preferably one tailored to women, or, best of all, to women facing the same problems you do.

Fortunately, there are over thirteen hundred programs that specialize in meeting the needs of women trying to re-enter the job market, including displaced homemakers. Affiliated with the Women Work! Network (formerly the Displaced Homemaker Network) and funded by federal, state, local, and private funds, these programs are run by organizations like community colleges, the YWCA, and women's centers. (See chapter 5 in the Resources section.) For low-income women, services are often free or at a low cost. Women who enroll (some four hundred thousand per year) receive at least one workshop and access to referrals. When adequately funded, the programs may offer counseling, skills assessment, support groups, referrals for psychological, financial, or legal help, even job training and help with job interviews.[18] Sometimes they can even help out with the costs of going back to school, child care, and transportation.[19]

One excellent example is the "Keys to Success Pre-Employment Program" offered by Women Employed (WE) of Chicago. The Keys program is three weeks of training that covers the basics of the job market today, what a resumé is, skills assessment, and the like. Most of the students are in their mid-thirties to their late fifties, with backgrounds that range from well educated to relatively unskilled. Few have any history of recent paid work.

Once a woman finishes a Keys workshop, she works in collaboration with a job developer to search for job openings. But according to Keys director Sheila Rogers, **when a woman succeeds in getting a good job, it's usually the result of her own motivation and follow-through—often despite her age or her lack of recent work experience.**[20] That's why an essential component of Keys is training that helps you transform some basic attitudes that can interfere with finding work. To be successful, Rogers and others say that you need to develop these approaches:

- *Become more assertive about what's best for you as a single-again.* Many women put others first, often to their own detriment. Learning to say no to demands on your time and energy means you must let others know that you won't be available to them in ways you have been in the past. Rogers tells the women, "In order to maintain a job, you have to have a balance."

- *Build on who you are right now by transforming what you feel are handicaps into assets.* Rogers tells her students:

  > Say what living on earth for fifty years has done for you and how it can relate to helping that company. Don't shy away from that. . . . You know how valuable [homemaking] is because your family would have fallen apart if you were a bad manager. You have to educate that employer about what skills you

have honed as a manager and how they can be trans-
ferred to that job.

- *Learn how to sell yourself—something you may have done
  only rarely in the past.* Rogers think that our society programs women to be modest and stay in the background,
  which shows up when you present yourself to an employer.
  To help women become comfortable talking about themselves, "We start out by having people vocalize a particular
  trait they may have, their strongest personality trait, and put
  that in a positive sentence." Then in order to start believing
  it, the women repeat that sentence over and over, saying it in
  front of a mirror until it becomes natural.[21] Another technique is to write in a diary every day about something you're
  proud of having accomplished—a daily affirmation.

ADDITIONAL SOURCES OF HELP

The Keys program and others like it are doing what they can,
given their numbers and resources. But they are not the only services that exist. Your local library and even the telephone book
are places to start looking for other sources of help. In different
communities, job counseling and support groups are offered
through technical schools or colleges, the U.S. Employment
Service (under state government in the telephone book), the Job
Training Partnership Act (JTPA, under the state department of
labor), the state board of education, city and county commissions
on women, and women's organizations. Some forward-looking
private temporary agencies are so intent on supplying good
employees that they have even begun to offer job counseling and
training. (See the section on "Temping" later in this chapter.)
Unpaid internships also offer a chance to explore job possibilities
in a particular field, while providing on-the-job training.

And a growing number of localities now offer special job
counseling and support for people over forty.[22] Although some

of these are oriented more toward people (mostly males) who have been laid off at midlife or who want to change careers, not all of them are. One interesting model is the LifePlan Center in San Francisco, which offers "comprehensive planning for later-life transitions." Aimed at people over fifty who want to review their priorities and set new goals for the future, the center offers individual counseling and mentoring (paid and volunteer), workshops, and support groups. In the center's newsletter, executive director Gladys Thacher exhorts members "to change our own attitudes first before others, employers and the younger generation, will perceive us as we really feel we are: experienced, capable, creative, doers, and contributors, not imminent economic and social liabilities."[23]

Faced with growing unemployment among its members (who are fifty and older) as a result of corporate layoffs, the American Association of Retired Persons is offering job-search skills through a program called AARP Works. They now have about ninety sites, and the course is also offered on Mind Extension University on the educational cable television network.

AARP and nine other national organizations also operate sites as part of the federally funded Senior Community Service Employment Program. SCSEP places poor unemployed people over fifty-five in temporary, minimum-wage nonprofit and government jobs.[24] AARP says that about half of these people are successful in using these jobs to move into permanent nonsubsidized jobs.[25]

While funding may be tight in all these programs, it still exists. Sixty-two-year-old Olivia, for example, could only find temporary secretarial jobs after she relocated to Atlanta. She did a lot of digging to find help, coming up empty-handed at first. She finally hit pay dirt when a phone call to the National Urban League led her to a source of JTPA funds—one that will pay for literate older people to attend any college of their choice. Olivia was excited, when I talked to her, to be starting college that night to become a paralegal.

⚜⚜⚜⚜⚜⚜

Find a Job on Your Own

IT'S NOT EXACTLY ROCKET SCIENCE WE'RE TALKING HERE

If you feel up to it and want to start a job search on your own, the process isn't all that complicated. You've solved a lot more difficult problems. The aisles of any good bookstore are loaded with advice on what you should do to find a good job that suits you. A short version of the process follows.[26]

1. *Discover what your strengths are and how to talk about them with others.* Richard Bolles does a great job of describing how to do this in his classic *What Color Is Your Parachute?*[27] The overall idea is that you try to see yourself as others see you, or as you'd like them to, and articulate that vision as clearly as you can.

2. *Figure out what subject area fascinates you and look for a job in that area.* Bolles suggests imagining that you're at a party, pursued by several people who want to talk to you. One is extremely interesting, and the others are boring. What is the fascinating person talking about? *That* topic is the one you should try to focus on in your job search.[28]

3. *Prepare a resumé.* You should tailor yours to the kind of job you're after—making sure the qualities you stress are important in the job you're seeking. One study by Purdue University researchers found that "it's the little things that really set an applicant apart from the crowd"—things like elected offices to show responsibility or high math grades for an accounting job.[29]

4. *Find out where the jobs are.* What kinds of places hire people who do what you want to do? Look at small- and medi-

um-sized organizations because that's where the job growth is. But also include state, local, and federal government jobs in your search. In addition to your library, you'll have to call around to potential employers to find out what they do and if they have any jobs. If you have computer skills, more and more jobs are being listed now on the Internet. If necessary, be ready to move in order to find or keep a job.

5. *Develop a network of people who can hire you or recommend you to others who will interview and hire you.* Networking is the subject of the next section.

6. *Plan what you will say at an interview about your skills and accomplishments.* Mock interviews with a friend are a good idea, as is trying out your responses in front of a mirror. Bolles says that in an interview you should talk half of the time and listen half of the time, which means you have to come prepared with some intelligent questions for your interviewer. He also says that you should find a way to stand out from the crowd.[30]

7. *Setbacks and rejections are no excuse to stop looking.* Be persistent.

Psychologist Mary Lou Randour, who has worked in the area of women and employment, thinks that women often go back to school without a clear idea of where the jobs are. She suggests that if you're interested in a certain kind of work, "Go to the company that does that and ask them what kind of people they hire." If school or training is important, you can decide at that point to take the necessary courses, not sooner.[31]

But keep in mind some facts: overall, college graduates earn 85 percent more than high school graduates; and persons with computer skills earn 20 percent more than those without such skills.[32] Not only that, almost one-fourth of the forty thousand jobs that opened up in 1997 were in technology-based occupations.33 Taken together, it's clear that education and skills are nearly a prerequisite today if you want to find a job that pays adequately.

NETWORKING: IT'S EASIER THAN YOU THINK

To expand upon the advice in step 5 above, you should understand that most jobs are found not through formal means like advertisements or employment agencies but through informal networking.34 It's not as torturous as you might think. Begin by contacting the friends and acquaintances you've built up over the years—family, friends, school acquaintances, professors, colleagues of your husband or their spouses.

Even though you may think that's not time well spent, you could be wrong. Unless you try, you'll never find out whether someone you know might be able to point you toward a job opening. And your telephone calls can serve a dual purpose. They can help you re-establish contact with people who may want to remain friends with you but haven't taken the first step because of their own uneasy feelings about what happened in your life. Your call will let them know that you aren't mad at them, that you're working to get yourself back on your feet, and that you'd welcome any help with your main priority—finding a job.

A second source of people for the network you're building is casual contacts—people you meet each day—people like your doctor, or dentist, or banker, or lawyer, or neighbor, or someone you meet through your children or at church or at a party. You need to be able to tell them what kind of job you're looking for, in just a few words, and see if they have suggestions about other people you might contact.

In the end, even if you don't think you know how to network, it isn't all that difficult. An article in the *Washington Post* says this:

> Everyone has a network. They just don't know how to define it. . . . A network consists of everyone the job

seeker knows, plus everyone those people know. . . . [S]o
if a job seeker believes he knows no one, he must alter
his belief system immediately.[35]

WHAT TO WATCH OUT FOR

You're primed and poised to job-hunt. So what can you
expect to find? It's no secret that almost all of the new jobs that
are being created in the United States are in the service industries, which include retail trade, education, health care, government, and finance.[36] Although many people assume those jobs
are mostly low-paying and dead-end, a recent analysis by the
Hudson Institute concludes: "The reality is that many of the
largest service industries involve relatively high wages and
advanced technology. . . . [They] require extensive knowledge
and training, and pay premium wages."[37] As a result, the institute projects that there will be more joblessness in the future
among unskilled workers but more jobs will open up for the
"educationally advantaged."[38]

For a job-seeker, then, the idea is to convince a potential
employer that you are indeed "educationally advantaged" (as
Beverly did with her British accent and perfect spelling test) and
that you're computer literate (even if you've only completed the
introductory course) and that you are as flexible and adaptable
to their environment as any eighteen-year-old (and you will be).
But don't go too far with your oversell, or they may say you're
"overqualified."

Being told you're overqualified is only one possible warning
sign that an employer is discriminating against you when you've
applied for a job.[39] Other signs (most of which are against the
law) are when a potential employer

- indicates a preference for younger people or persons with
  less experience (or tells you that their customers prefer a
  youthful image);

- asks your age, or your marital status, or about dependents, your health, or your stamina;

- lists physical job qualifications that are unrelated to the job;

- will not let you substitute volunteer experience for paid;

- indicates that it would cost too much to hire you or that you would be absent too often or unable to meet the job's physical demands;

- hires someone less qualified who is younger or a male;

- is enthusiastic about your qualifications but cools after seeing you face-to-face;

- offers to pay you less than a male or someone younger for similar work; or

- denies you benefits because of your sex or age.[40]

Doing something about any employment discrimination you encounter is another matter, however. Rarely is it possible to get any kind of justice, even when evidence of discrimination is clear and can be documented. The Equal Employment Opportunity Commission (EEOC), the agency that oversees two federal laws against job discrimination—because of age and because of gender—does not have the resources it needs to do its job. But since you must take most complaints to the EEOC before you can go to court, their local office is where you must start, within 180 days of the incident.

When it looks as if they will close your case (which usually happens even if you have a well-documented complaint), you can turn to a private lawyer.[41] Be forewarned, however, that finding a lawyer to take your case on a contingency basis is unlikely because the private bar is reluctant to take all but the tiniest fraction of complaints.[42] And even if you have very deep pockets to pay for legal help up-front, plus an enormous sense of outrage and lots of proof, there's no guarantee you'll win if you wind up before a judge. An analysis by the Women's Legal Defense Fund of midlife and older women who had pursued multiple charges of age and sex discrimination into the courts found that the judge sided with the employers 59 percent of the time, with the women prevailing only 41 percent.[43]

Not being hired at all or getting a job at wages lower than the going rate are just two ways women are discriminated against. Another way is by depriving them of benefits like health insurance and pensions. Next to a salary, these benefits are the main reasons why single women need to work. But a strong trend now is to fill what used to be staff positions with people working on temporary contracts, providing no job security once the contract is up, as well as no benefits.[44] A Senate subcommittee hearing on this "disposable workforce" disclosed that labor and civil rights laws don't even cover contract workers. The flexibility that gives employers and the money they save means they are increasingly turning full-time permanent jobs into contract work.[45]

Perhaps an even worse trend is one toward part-time jobs. Not only is the quantity of work expected disproportionate to that done by full-time employees, but it can be virtually impossible to survive on part-time wages alone. And once again, benefits are usually nonexistent or, at best, pro-rated.[46]

For women who have no alternatives except to work as contract or part-time employees, these jobs do have one clear advantage: they offer a foot-in-the-door to an organization that might eventually hire them for full-time jobs with benefits. But for now, if you take one of these jobs, you should be fully aware that you're on hazardous ground. As Ellen Bravo, the head of 9 to 5, the National Association of Working Women, told the Senate subcommittee:

Not so long ago, employers would simply have hired

women and people of color for less money. You can't get away with that anymore. But there are no restrictions on inequity for part-time and temporary workers— where women and people of color tend to be overrepresented.[47]

LIE ABOUT YOUR AGE?

Innovative as ever, single-again women have found ways to get hired in spite of the prejudices against them. Sheer vanity and the wish to attract young lovers are not the only reasons that hair dyes are such big sellers. Women have learned that they can become "ageless" to potential employers by creating the appearance of youthfulness—at least in the right kind of light. That, however, can be fairly expensive and involve a lot of effort. An easier trick is to remove from your resumé very old dates, such as your graduation date, as well as deleting work done a long time ago if it isn't relevant to the kind of work you're seeking now.

Another less ethical way is to follow Nancy Reagan's lead and conveniently "forget" how old you are. That's what one older woman I talked to claimed she did when her job search at the age of forty-nine yielded absolutely nothing. With three of their five children in college and a husband whose government job couldn't cover costs, Sue Ellen set out in 1974 to find a job to supplement his income. "I hit the street for six months," she recalls. "And nobody wanted me."

Waxing enthusiastic, Sue Ellen only had her tongue partway into her cheek when she told me she always has very specific advice to give mature women trying to get into the job market: "I always tell women, 'Lie through your teeth. Do anything you have to. And then get in there and prove yourself.'" Unethical, perhaps, but it can and does work.

But now that the U.S. workforce is growing older, lying about one's age may become less and less necessary. One newly separated woman I spoke to expressed amazement that she had been hired as a flight attendant at American Airlines in spite of being forty-six years old. The reason, she concluded, was that the people doing the interviewing and hiring were all midlife women. As she described the daylong series of interviews she underwent, it became obvious that not only did they *not* hold her age against her, but they rated highly her mature, balanced approach to problems and challenges. She was amazed to be hired on the spot, but even more amazed that she was not the oldest one in her group hired.

Successes like these give us all reason to be hopeful about finding work at midlife. There may even be a new trend emerging, with businesses starting to look for mature women for some of their operations. Employment counselor Sheila Rogers says that she is starting to see more slots being filled by mature women in companies that decide they want to avoid turnover. They look for someone older because she is more likely to be settled and have good work habits.[48] (And in some cases, they prefer the older employee because she won't present them with child care and pregnancy problems—discrimination of a different order.)[49]

Temping: One Way to Sidle into a Job

More often than not, single-again women trying to find a decent, well-paying job don't find it through a frontal assault, which requires a lot more expertise than they are able to demonstrate. They find it via a nontraditional route, slipping in through a side door when the front door seems too intimidating or unwieldy.

One such route to a permanent job is through a temporary job, such as those temporary minimum-wage positions offered to low-income persons over fifty-five by the Senior Community Service Employment Program (SCSEP, described in the preceding section on "Additional Sources of Help" and in chapter 5 of the Resources section). Another way to find temporary work is through the burgeoning number of temporary employment agencies that place employees in temporary professional and clerical jobs, taking a portion of the hourly rate charged as their fee. One recent survey found that the temporary personnel business was the top U.S. job creator from 1990 through the middle of 1995.[50]

As Diane Thrailkill explains in her book *Temp by Choice*, **if you are looking for a permanent job but can't find one, a temporary employment agency can serve an interim function. It can even lead to permanent employment.** Thrailkill advocates the use of temporary agencies for re-entry workers like widows and divorcées as "a way to get a view of what many types of jobs are all about. You can ease back into the workforce, and your maturity will work in your favor. . . . Mature temps are highly regarded because of their experience, wisdom and work ethic."[51]

According to economist Audrey Freedman, "The temporary help industry essentially is a big hiring hall. It's the best way to become employed in this economy." The article in the *AARP Bulletin* that quotes Freedman goes on to say that as many as one-third of the 5 to 7 million people who worked in temporary jobs last year found permanent jobs as a result. One agency, Kelly Services, has even set up a separate KellySelect line for temps who want full-time jobs.[52]

Some temporary agencies specialize in re-entry workers or have special divisions for them. Some even provide training in the skills that are most in demand by the client companies. Manpower Temporary Service, for instance, has trained some five hundred thousand workers in computer skills like keyboarding and software use.[53] And although not many agencies provide health benefits, they all must comply with state laws that require coverage for unemployment, disability, and worker's compensation.

But the work is certainly no bed of roses. Regular temp workers complain about being isolated from the office social life, feeling disoriented because they don't know where anything is, and being given incredibly mundane and boring tasks. "If they were good jobs, temps wouldn't be doing them," one temp is quoted as saying. "Sometimes I feel like a piece of furniture," says another.[54]

Although temping is certainly not for everyone, it's probably worth a try. Thrailkill even recommends it as a long-term job of choice, if you value diversity, flexibility, and the ability to earn a living without a more permanent commitment. Every temporary agency has its own method of screening candidates who want to register, although the tests and interviews they give are similar. Thrailkill suggests that you practice applying first at an agency with a poor reputation, since you won't want to register with them anyway. If you do poorly on one test or another, then you can take a quick remedial course in that skill before you apply seriously at another agency. Ultimately, if it's feasible, she advises registering with four or five agencies, so you can be assured of choice assignments when you want to work.[55]

"Passport to Adventure": The Peace Corps

Another temporary "job" that can demonstrate your capabilities to potential employers is with the Peace Corps, an assignment that two women I interviewed completed with great success. Caroline Bird also interviewed a number of older women who had been in the Peace Corps for her book *Lives of Our Own* and concluded:

> The Peace Corps can be a poor woman's passport to adventure. For older women who qualify, it offers physical, emotional, and social challenges, a chance to help others, and, because of its age-equal policies, a chance to do professional work that private employers hesitate to give to older beginners.[56]

Some 550 of the current 6,900 Peace Corps volunteers in the field are over the age of fifty. The Peace Corps screens applicants carefully for physical and mental health and only takes one out of four. And while skills like language proficiency or a background in education, the environment, health, or economic development are considered assets, so too is a candidate's wish to make a difference.[57] Once accepted as a volunteer, candidates are not required to undergo physical training. And older persons are easy to place in the ninety-three host countries, with no higher dropout rates than those among younger volunteers.[58]

But even though having completed this kind of professional-level assignment is a one-of-a-kind education and should be impressive to potential employers, Bird found, as I did, that when volunteers return home, they could not find work of the same caliber as their assignments overseas.[59]

⋈⋈⋈⋈⋈

A Job Can Be the First Step

Some single-again women who have a reasonable income from their former or deceased husbands—and therefore don't have to fear the money-hungry wolf at the door—aren't forced to look for ways to support themselves. So very often they don't. And oddly enough, those women may be all the poorer for being so well off.

Because a job, after all, serves a vital function in helping women make a successful transition to independence after years of marriage. In her book *Coming Back: Rebuilding Lives after Crisis and Loss*, psychologist Ann Kaiser Stearns points out an important trait of people who become "triumphant survivors" of huge losses in their lives: they let go of false hopes that things will return to the way they were. Instead, Stearns says, triumphant survivors strive toward self-sufficiency and "make an early decision to go forward and reinvest in living."[60]

A job is obviously not a one-size-fits-all cure for everything that ails a new widow or divorcée. It's only one piece in the new jigsaw-puzzle life you're putting together. But it can be one of the most important pieces in the section of the puzzle where you begin to take charge of your life—even when you seek a job but don't find one, or find one and hate it, or get fired after you're hired. It can be an important symbol—not just to the world but to yourself—that you are indeed going forward.

6

Turn to Wise Friends —Where You Can Find Them

It is only when the woman can move to thinking about the true quality of her connections and to improve or change them rather than thinking of first pleasing another and conforming to his desire and expectations that she can even begin to know herself.
—Jean Baker Miller
Toward a New Psychology of Women[1]

Being married usually makes a woman feel secure and cared for. That can be true even when a husband has been a less-than-ideal protector and provider. So when you're on your own after years of being married, especially if it's your first time ever, you may feel pretty isolated. Friends you had when you were married may not be there for you as they were in the past. Having children still at home may help, but even then, being newly single may feel as if you have no one or nothing to turn to when you're lonely or upset.

This chapter is about creating a circle of support through friendships. Like other approaches in this book, friends, by themselves, will not make everything immediately okay. But they can be a big help, as well as an essential safety net, during your transition into singlehood.

The Pros and Cons of Friendships

WHAT FRIENDSHIPS CAN MEAN

Having good friends is second only to having good health in determining whether women feel satisfied with their lives.[2] This is especially true for women who have been single for a period of time and who know how important it is to have a well-functioning network of friends to meet a variety of needs.

When gerontologist Jacquelyn Mattfeld asked women in their seventies and eighties who lived alone in urban areas about their close relationships, most replied that they were more significant than they had been at any other age. For example, a single older woman facing an incurable illness said:

> Of course, I'm not really alone. The fact that I'm loved and important to my "little family"—that takes in a lot of things. It helps me over a lot of rough spots. Being cared about and in turn giving care, too. That's the

important thing to me. I'm just thankful that I have close friends, that we care about each other. And that's it. That's what life's about.[3]

In her book *Secret Paths: Women in the New Midlife,* author Terri Apter tells of the hunger that midlife women have for friendships with other women. Friendships serve, she writes, as "a form of resistance—against feeling marginal, against a machinelike dedication, against self-doubt, against social images of midlife."[4]

Friends may play an even more important role when you're on your own than when you're married. When you have that sinking feeling that no one cares, friends can make you feel special by assuring you that they miss you when you don't check in, that you and they have a unique connection, that they share a worldview with you. When everything seems especially bleak, friends are there to listen, letting you tell them how scared and upset you are until you start to feel better again. When a problem seems insurmountable, friends can start you on a path that will solve it. And when you have a crisis, or even just a mini-crisis, they're there to lend a hand. As an eighty-eight-year-old woman in Mattfeld's study put it, "[A] close relationship is an exchange where you can still give of yourself, and where some of your most important needs are met. You can't say that about much else in your life when you're this old."[5]

Friends can be as important when you're newly single as when you were a teenager. Just as your close friends then provided a mirror for you to figure out who you were and where you wanted to go, now friends can sanction your search for a new identity.[6] In her book *Necessary Losses,* Judith Viorst sums up their significance:

> Close friends contribute to our personal growth. They also contribute to our personal pleasure, making the music sound sweeter, the wine taste richer, the laughter ring louder because they are there. Friends furthermore

take care—they come if we call them at two in the
morning; they lend us their car, their bed, their money,
their ear; and although no contracts are written, it is
clear that intimate friendships involve important rights
and obligations. Indeed, we will frequently turn—for
reassurance, for comfort, for come-and-save-me help—
not to our blood relations but to friends. . . .[7]

The National Academy of Sciences Committee on Health
Consequences of the Stress of Bereavement sees "social support"
after a loss as essential to personal growth and as a necessary
part of bereavement. The committee concludes:

Four aspects of social support—enhancing self-esteem
and a feeling of being loved, problem-solving, networking, and providing relationship resources for meeting
life cycle transitions—are thought to modify the effects
of traumatic loss and to facilitate recovery from
bereavement. . . . Perceived social support seems to be
important in deciding the course of grief and the likeli-
hood that the individual will return to effective func-
tioning.[8]

WHEN FRIENDSHIPS AREN'T HELPFUL

As we all know, there are friends and then there are friends.
While most friendships are beneficial, it is the quality of the
friendship that is important. Recent studies suggest that **when a
woman's close friendships involve her giving much more than
taking, those relationships can place a heavy burden on her and
reduce her happiness, not increase it.**[9] So at the very least, there
can be as many disadvantages as there are advantages when a
woman has numerous close friendships.[10]

Even when a friendship is *not* more burden than blessing, the
help a friend gives you isn't necessarily helpful. Because after all,
friends are not disinterested parties. Your change in status has
disrupted a delicate balance in the relationship. Dealing with
someone who is so upset is unnerving. Very often, as author

Douglas Manning describes it, long before you are ready, a friend finds "subtle but effective ways to take grief away."[11] Intentionally or not, friends may want you to forget you're a widow or divorcée and just return to the way things were.

Another reason friends may be unavailable to help you grieve, or may give you self-serving advice, is that they too are upset by your divorce or your husband's death. Lucille found this to be true. Looking back to the aftermath of her divorce sixteen years earlier, she advises, "Everyone you know is affected. Your friends don't want to take sides. Your family is too traumatized. It affects your in-laws. It affects your church. It affects everyone. Don't look to them for support." Instead, Lucille turned to AlAnon and Alcoholics Anonymous (AA) for help.

Paradoxically, friends who *are* able to provide support when you are down may try to sabotage any sign that you are growing and changing—again because of its potential to disrupt the familiar pattern of your relationship. A support group one divorcée started broke up when some members objected to others discussing their budding romances. The women who complained were uncomfortable with women in the group who were ready to move on.

※※※※※

Cobble Together a Platform of Friends

MAKE SPACE FOR DIFFERENT TYPES OF FRIENDS

Given the pros and cons, by all means go ahead and seek out close, sustaining friendships, but be aware of some pitfalls. One of these is the illusion that perfect friendships are possible. Connections, like people, are always imperfect. Accept the reality that even the best of friends are what Judith Viorst calls "friends in spots"—wonderful for some things, but not for others.[12] Realize that no one is always suitable and available when you would like and that even the best friendships can be filled with competition and envy.

Realize that you most likely are going to need more than just one or two friends to fulfill all your needs. As writer Barbara Holland puts it, "That's the advantage of friends; no real lady should have more than one husband or lover at a time, but we can cobble together a whole platform of different friends for different purposes."[13] With a platform of friends to stand on, we can feel relatively safe, even if we know there's an abyss below.

A tumultuous life transition gives you a chance to change your approach to making friends. It involves initiating a methodical, clear-eyed hunt for a network of friends who can act not just as a platform for you today but also as a springboard to your new life.

Rethink what kinds of friends you want. You have a chance to redefine what family means and to either transform your relations with your current family to meet that definition or make yourself a new "little family." And even more important, you have a chance to reform how you relate to others—increasing what you get from a friendship and finding ways to be more true to yourself.

In constructing your platform, make space for different types of friends. While all close relationships share reciprocal feelings of caring, warmth, affection, or love, gerontologist Mattfeld's interviews with single older women reveal that friends typically fell into one of four categories:

- *work- and playmates*—sharing values, interests, and time together;

- *help providers*—giving each other money or services;

- *confidantes*—able to talk together about anything without fear of criticism; and

- *kindred spirits*—friends who probably were all of the above, plus who shared "an inexplicable affinity . . . that allowed each person to be completely herself and at ease with the other."[14]

If you're both dogged and lucky, you'll find friends that typify the first three categories. And if you hit the jackpot, you'll find someone who's a "kindred spirit"—the kind of friend that Holland claims "appears only two or three times in a lucky lifetime, one that will winter us and summer us, grieve, rejoice, and travel with us. These are the diamonds in our porridge."[15]

What You Need in a Friend

Evelyn Vuko was quick to notice her friends fleeing when she was diagnosed with cancer, and she warns others to "prepare yourself before you tell them your news." Danger signs that friends are deserting, she says, is when they react to your terrible news by a monologue about a recent problem of their own; or when "a friend talks to you with beseeching eyes and gentle words, as though she's always silently praying that you won't gasp your last while you're together, hip deep, in the sales rack at Saks."

But you'll also be quick to know when someone's on your side, Vuko continues:

> If he quietly puts his arm around you and says, "What's our plan?" put him in your hip pocket. If, despite the cancer, she still treats you like the same cantankerous, repressed rock-and-roll star you always were, nail her shoes to the floor beside you.[16]

These are the kind of friends you need now, as you try to get back on your emotional feet as a single-again. In your case, the friend you want is someone who not only treats you the same, but who offers to help you move or watch out for your children. When Jocelyn's husband of sixteen years died of cancer, three women friends came to her rescue—one a lawyer, one a financial planner, and one an accountant. They figured out what Jocelyn's situation was, sat her down, still in shock, and told her what she needed to do. These experts and her other friends "really carried me through that first summer," she recollects.

One chief requirement, of course, is that friends stick around. The value of just having someone you can feel free to call on, or who checks in regularly to see how you're doing, can't be overestimated. Psychotherapist Audrey McCollum's study of women in search of new friends after a move found a number of other qualities women wanted, namely:

- *mutuality*—a friend who shares your concerns, has similar values and dreams, and who "wants to share the special moments of everyday life";[17]

- *authenticity*—knowing that a friend's response is genuine and can be depended on;

- *trust*—knowing that you can expose your inner self and still be accepted;

- *spontaneity*—responding to you on the spur of the moment or when you need her; and

- *reciprocity*—giving and taking go in both directions.[18]

One psychiatrist who believes firmly in the importance of these kinds of mutual, reciprocal friendships is Jean Baker Miller. She writes: "We observe that women tend to find satisfaction, pleasure, effectiveness and a sense of worth if they experience their life activities as arising from, and leading back into, a sense of connections with others."[19] When a relationship is "growth fostering," Miller believes, each person feels a greater sense of "zest" and self worth, has a more accurate picture of herself, and is motivated to act and to seek out other new relationships.[20]

When a woman already has a network of this kind of friends, they can make a huge difference. They did for psychiatric nurse Donna Damico Mayer, who told her story to the world on

National Public Radio.[21] Everything collapsed for her when her husband of twenty years decided it was over. "He wanted more, something intangible, something that I apparently couldn't provide," Donna remembers. Heartsick, she couldn't eat, lost "fifteen pounds, half a shoe size, and one bra size." At first, she was afraid she was going to die.

> I barely slept. Some nights, even though I was exhausted, a terrible vigilance and watchfulness took over and it was as though I had to stay awake to guard against any other awful things that might happen. I roamed my house from room to room, looking, I suppose, for comfort. I didn't find it. . . .
>
> But my friends did both ordinary and extraordinary things that made life bearable. Right at the very beginning, one friend looked me squarely in the eye and said, "You won't die." And another said, "You don't need sympathy, just company," and offered to sleep on the floor next to my bed. Another friend walked miles with me around my neighborhood into the night while I sobbed and kicked fences and street signs. My best friend from childhood came east from Oregon, and my sister and niece came from England.
>
> People showed up unannounced, called constantly, threw me a surprise party, sent flowers, books, CDs, and letters. They invited me out and into their homes. An old friend that had been divorced years ago and is now happily remarried took me out for coffee one night. "There is a strong wind blowing through your house right now," he said, "and there isn't a thing you can do to stop it. But I promise you, the wind will eventually die down and things will look different. But it will be OK."[22]

Donna's friends had all the essential qualities of supportive friends: mutuality, authenticity, spontaneity, trust, and reciprocity. And they helped her grasp that the world really hadn't come to an end. Donna still misses her husband and their "day to dayness" terribly. But her friends had pulled her through the worst part:

> I realized I would make it when I was driving home from work the other day and I heard the Rolling Stones on the radio. I made a u-turn, headed for the record store and bought a double CD of the Stones. My husband hated the Rolling Stones.[23]

CULTIVATING YOUR CURRENT FRIENDS

Some women I talked to said that their *current* networks of friends and family weren't much help. But others had a very different experience. And although common wisdom holds that widows get a lot more support after their husbands' deaths than do women who are divorcing, I didn't find that distinction always true. While the widows I talked to generally felt supported by friends and family, so did a lot of divorcing women who, like Donna, already had well-established friends.

Sally, for example, had organized—some thirteen years before she was faced with divorce—a group of two dozen women friends that called themselves "the farm ladies." The women went off together to a nearby farm for a weekend once a year just to relax and talk, away from their families. They had gone through all of their own and their children's growing pains together.

In hindsight, Sally says that organizing that group was "the best thing I ever did for me." Because when Sally's husband left their thirty-year marriage for another woman, they all reached out to her. She accepted every invitation to lunch and dinner, she remembers, "mainly not to be alone and just to keep going, because I was determined I was going to get through this." And she told them to call and just leave messages on her answering machine:

> Because it's just devastating to walk into an empty house by myself. I can't tell you how reassuring it is to

have somebody talking to me [on the machine], even though I can't answer because I'm not capable of it. . . . I couldn't reach out to them. I couldn't take the initiative.

One happy surprise was that the friendships remained reciprocal even though Sally was in more need than her friends were:

As I talked to people and shared my pain, and was open with them, what was terribly rewarding was what I got back. I learned things about friends, people I had known for years, that they never would have shared with me in any other way. And so it deepened friendships right away.

The importance of having a number of friends also became clear to Sally, "because nobody can take the extent of the depression, and anxiety, and all the horror. . . . Each person has something different that they can give or offer, and things that they can't do."

Tapping into your family and current network of friends may not be as surefire as it was for Sally and Donna, however. One way you can go wrong is that in the initial, fragile stages of becoming single, you can assume that friends don't want to be bothered with your problem. So, anticipating that they will reject you, you take the initiative and reject them first by pulling away. May says she did that with couples who were their friends before her husband died, only to learn later, to her dismay, that her friends had wanted to help. But they had felt that she was unreceptive, even rude, to their overtures.

In addition to not giving your existing friends a chance to come through for you, another possible mistake is assuming that the way the friendship has always worked is immutable, that you can't change it to meet your current needs. That may sometimes be true, as Evelyn found out when she and her husband of fifteen years divorced when he came out of the closet. A self-employed graphics designer with a five-year-old handicapped son, she says that a number of her friends dropped her "because for the first time in our relationship I had needs of them."

But it's still worth trying to make a relationship more reciprocal before you give up on it. Like Sally, Pearl found that talking about her separation and divorce brought her friendships to a deeper level. "Telling other people what you're going through is like breaking the ice. When you begin to talk about it with others, it's like a dam breaking. You learn things about them because they open up too."

Mothers, fathers, sisters, brothers, and various other relations came through as friends for these women, providing a sense of continuity and stability as they walked the tightrope. After her divorce, Antoinette got back the sense of family that she missed so much by moving closer to her twin sister and her family. They don't have to spend a lot of time together to feel connected, she says, and they are there for her to celebrate holidays and important occasions.

Sometimes a little "retraining" is necessary to turn friends into the kind of friends you want. Jennifer loves and admires her mother, but when she was first getting divorced, she had a difficult time talking to her because of all the advice her mother wanted to offer. Finally, Jennifer told her mother that what she needed was for her just to listen. Now, in their once-a-week-Friday-night telephone sessions, her mother listens so well, Jennifer says, that "she should be a professional." Jennifer succeeded in turning her mother into a friend by telling her exactly what she needed, an approach that can be useful in making any kind of relationship into a mutual friendship.

Another source of support can be friends from your past. To their amazement, a number of women found that bonds they had made growing up or as young adults were still intact even though they hadn't tended them for years. Jocelyn discovered, when she went to a college reunion after her husband died, that the reunion was a turning point. Jocelyn says it was the first time she remembers thinking "I am going to have fun again in my life. It is going to happen." Now those college friends, whom she neglected for years, are so important to her that she gets together with them every summer.

Old friends who represent your roots can be especially healing. Anna, who comes from Poland, says she felt totally shunned by the friends she and her husband had made during their twenty-two-year marriage in the United States. "There is something in the American society that repulses me. Your husband divorces you. No one invites you anymore. . . . I was not invited by one couple that we knew. And I was the one who kept the friendships." She speculates that wives worried that she would take their husbands away. "That's the last thing you'd think about. You don't want a man after a divorce. You just want to be comforted by people."

Her husband had disliked all her Polish friends, Anna says, but they were the ones who "rallied around" her. Among them, she sought out especially those who were single. Six of them, all professionals and all but one single, became very close. Eight years later, they still meet once a month. "We have so much fun. Men would never believe women could have so much fun. And we don't even talk about men," Anna teases.

⣿⣿⣿⣿⣿

Making New Friends

ACCIDENTAL VERSUS PREMEDITATED FRIENDSHIPS

If you're like a lot of women, the idea of actually setting out to make friends will be intimidating. Friends you've made in the past may have just "happened" because you were thrown together in school, or at work, or in your neighborhood, or through hobbies or your children. In the course of getting to know each other, you decide whether you like each other, and if you do, you move on to becoming friends. If there is no common bond, probably no one's feelings will be hurt.

But now that you're single-again, you might need to change your approach to making friends from accidental to premeditated, becoming proactive in a way you may never have been before. Many women, however, don't like to take the initiative to make friends. They dislike what Audrey McCollum calls the "intentionality" of it all. In her study of women who had relocated with their families to a new city, McCollum found that setting out to make friends made women worry about being too pushy. They also feared rejection. "It's hard to be planful and calculating about making friends," she quotes one woman as saying.[24]

Don't let any discomfort and anxiety you may feel about taking the lead deter you. Try to follow the lead of women like Melinda, who are just naturally good at making friends. In every class or function she has attended since her husband died, Melinda approaches and begins to cultivate a potential new "soulmate." Her daughters have told her how extraordinary they find what she does. They say they don't know anyone else so willing and able to make new friends.

Melinda may be braver than most, but the network of close friends she has developed by her boldness easily compensates for any risks involved. Writing about the growing need for close friends as you age, Betty Friedan admits, "Intimacy in age, maybe more than in youth, has to involve pain, mistakes, uncertainties." But these missteps are worth the aggravation, she believes. "The ties of intimacy, the bond of truly shared self ('confidants') are the crucial source of the fountain of age."[25]

SEEKING OUT PEOPLE IN HER SHOES: MAY

Making new friends once you are single requires seeking out people who fit two profiles: the person you are, and the person you want to become. That was the approach taken by May, a charming, energetic, fit, capable seventy-year-old with a statewide and national reputation as an advocate for issues concerning older women. Since she retired several years ago from her job heading a senior center, May has focused much of her energy on lobbying on behalf of older women. But she also travels, manages her own investments, and cultivates a large array of women friends.

Before May's husband became terminally ill, however, she had never worked for pay. She was only vaguely aware of what an advocate did and had never managed more money than was in her checking account. Her travel and friends were limited by the eighteen moves she and her husband had made in their twenty-plus years of marriage. That all changed in her early forties when her husband was diagnosed with cancer. Facing up to it, she started to plan for life on her own.

When her husband died six years later, May had found the work that would lead to her career. Even though her husband's illness left her with a pile of unpaid medical bills and no assets but their house, she had already begun to save money and invest it, committing herself to living on the minimum possible. And she had started the process of patching together the quilt of friends that would sustain her.

A wise woman friend helped her one afternoon to face her panic about her husband's death and finally begin to accept it. She went home, sat on the floor beside his bed, and told him how scared she was, finally giving him permission to die. He did—the following week.

Going to work became indispensable for May because of the structure it provided and because of the nurturing environment of a mostly female staff. Outside of work, May took the suggestion of one of her married friends that she start to look for a new circle of friends—cultivating the people she was meeting through her advocacy. Some were males or married, but most were female and single. "I think there's a certain commonality you have with people in your own shoes," she counsels. "I've come now to value female friendships. I didn't appreciate them as much when I first was widowed."

With too little savings to attract a good financial consultant, May began to befriend people who knew about money and investing and who were willing to give her advice. Another whole group of friends came from her travels. The first was a cousin who, when May telephoned to tell her that her husband had died, invited her to travel with her to Indonesia the following year. For that whole year, the trip gave May something to look forward to, and when it was over, her self-image had changed. "It's like you have grown up," May muses. "The minute you do it, you've grown up. You're on your own."

Now she takes trips every year with someone, often more than once with the same person. "With friends, you get to know them better and then you have common memories. . . .There's a bonding I've made with many women by traveling with them. You get to know people in a different way."

May learned that you don't always have to be the strong one in a relationship, the one who mentors and gives more than she gets. She asks her friends for help when she needs it, but in subtle ways that leave a friend the option of not responding without having to say no.

May has friends all over the country now—fellow amateur capitalists, travelers, and rabble-rousers for change. They all provide the juice to keep her full of life and optimistic about the world. "I do believe that I can change the world," May enthuses. "I am absolutely convinced that you can make a difference."

EXPECTING TO FIND A SOULMATE: VIRGINIA

It was rare to find someone who had not made new single friends since becoming single herself. **Most women decide that having single friends is just more practical. Their lifestyles, needs, and availability are similar. Having single *female* friends is especially rewarding.**

Making those new friends is not a simple matter, however. Transforming a casual acquaintance into a good friend can be a tedious, time-consuming, self-exposing exercise, involving a lot of missteps along the way. If you haven't had much practice at self-consciously setting out to make friends, you might need some inspiration from women who make a practice of it.

Virginia is a woman whose spectacularly successful career has been balanced by a spectacularly difficult personal life. Now a very vital seventy, she has been divorced for twenty-four years, almost as long as she was married—to a classmate she met while studying for a Ph.D. Their marriage was rocky, and some years before they divorced, her husband had a complete nervous breakdown that left him unable to work. Not only did Virginia have to cope with his increasingly erratic behavior, but she also had to be sole support for two daughters and two orphaned nieces. She finally gave up and filed for divorce, having him evicted from their university housing.

One day while she was at work, her husband came with a mover and took most of their joint belongings away. He also burned all her papers and photographs. At that time, her mother was dying of congestive heart failure, and her teenage daughters were experimenting with drugs. Longing for a perfect marriage, Virginia had two serious affairs, both of them ending very badly. "It couldn't have been a more hellish time," Virginia remembers.

In the meantime, however, Virginia's career in college administration was taking off, culminating in a job as president of a prestigious women's college. But each new job entailed moving to an entirely new setting. Virginia, an attractive, midlife divorcée, also found herself excluded from the socializing that took place among faculty couples—treated, she says, "like a rare entity or a scarlet woman."

Even with these handicaps, however, she always had a few close friends. It was really a matter of focus, she explains. "I constantly expected to find good and intimate friends in every job. And I always found one or two that have stayed good friends over the years." Not only are her adult daughters her friends, but she also has friends between their age and hers. "I'm always looking for soulmates. Some are men and some are women and some are thirty years younger and some are ten years younger."

Virginia says that making friends after each move was comparable to her habit of cultivating a garden wherever she lived. When it was time to move on, she could just begin to see the results. But "unlike a garden, making close friends is like a chemical bonding." Even though she only sees her friends about once a year, that bond enables her to remain close by telephoning each of them every few weeks. "In fact, the weekends are really taken up, now that I'm retired, by being in touch with people I love all around the United States."

CHOREOGRAPHING A FRIENDSHIP

Working hard to both make and keep friends is an important reason for Virginia's success. Audrey McCollum calls what she does "the choreography of friendship."[26] Here are a number of steps you should take in choreographing a network of friends:

- *Act "as if" you're interested in other people, are feeling positive about life, and aren't bitter about your situation, even when almost none of it is true.* Widow and author Lynne Caine says that this kind of "playacting" not only got her the support she needed, but made her begin to think more optimistically about herself and her new life.[27]

- *Make cultivating friends a priority and mobilize your energy and resources for the task.* That means both initiating activities with possible friends (something you may have to do most of the time at first) and being available to them when and if they ask. And that may mean spending money on socializing despite the fact that you have scarcely enough for the basic necessities.

- *Risk being ignored or rejected when you let people know who you are and what you need.* Rejection stings, but it doesn't ache like the loneliness you feel when you want to share something with a friend but don't have anyone to turn to.

- *Create special occasions or moods or spaces for you and your new friends that will allow you to fashion common memories.* May did this with her travels and Sally with her "farm ladies." Betty Friedan believes that these special occasions or rituals among friends can "deepen the touching and shared disclosure that is the true glue of intimacy."[28]

- *Recognize that friends' advice may not always be the best, but it is given in the spirit of being helpful.* Listen to your friends (and expect them to listen to you in return), and then make your own decisions.

- *Don't make any one person in your network of friends so essential that you risk a major blow if you lose him or her.* Psychologists Carol Anderson and Susan Stewart found that midlife women who were living successful lives on their own had put together a network of diverse friends: "In this diversity, there is great strength. No one relationship meets all of their needs; no one tie is so crucial that its destruction would cause their network to fail."[29]

- *Give a relationship time.* When you're in need of friends, you may want to rush the friendship from one stage to the next. But you can frighten off people if they sense you're too needy. Start with small overtures, gauge the response, and then move ahead. Don't always expect a positive response, and try to be patient. Don't forget: they may be risking as much as you are.

- *Keep your relationships healthy.* Psychologist Michael Yapko recommends you do this by letting the other person know your personal boundaries and any rules for the relationship.[30] Setting these ground rules can help you avoid excessive demands, which you may be inclined to comply with because of your image of how a *good* woman should behave.[31]

- *Learn to do and to enjoy things on your own.* When you've always had a companion, setting out alone can feel awkward and even riskier than making friends. But learning to like your own company will make it possible to approach friends with the confidence that comes from knowing you'll be all right even if they reject you.

Occasionally, McCollum says, the "choreography of friendship" is nearly perfect, proceeding smoothly "from the first 'click'—the recognition of mutual interests and values and concerns—to felt intimacy . . . [and] a gradually deepening trust." But that isn't generally true. In most cases, the dance is "erratic, marked by advances, pauses, retreats, and by some painful falls."[32]

Disturbing as those falls may be, the rewards from a densely woven safety net of friends make them all worthwhile.

7

Tap Into Religion

When I was married, my husband was very large and strong and vibrant and protective. I felt very safe. When that was suddenly removed, I felt like one of those bugs that crawls out from under a rock. A bird could swoop down and eat it.
     —Susan, widowed after twenty-one years of marriage

Life crises have always caused spiritual crises. And long before psychiatry existed, the main source of help for a crisis was always religion. Of the women I interviewed, those who held strong religious beliefs turned to them right away. Some of them held beliefs connected to a traditional religion, while others were highly spiritual but did not adhere to any organized religion. A number who hadn't been particularly religious said that the loss of their husband was a wake-up call. As one woman put it, her divorce was "how God got my attention."

Career guru Richard Bolles believes that your faith can be an important way to find out who you are. He advises those in life and job transitions to turn to their faith and "reexamine it and activate it. Many of us have [our faith] hanging in the closet like a suit of old clothes, useful when there's a wedding. But we need to dust it off and use it for everyday wear."[1]

Women who have relied on their religion in the past for comfort and counsel are able to use existing beliefs or develop new ones to come to terms with their loss. Their beliefs are helpful in a number of ways:

- *in finding solace;*

- *in searching for the meaning of what happened;*

- *in exploring who they are and who they want to be;*

- *in tapping into the spirituality in everyday life; and*

- *in tapping into the power within themselves.*

In Search of Solace

For many women, church is a place they can turn for comfort, where they are accepted as themselves, where both the religious ritual and the community of people serve as refuge from

life's chaos. Jean's faith in God was very important to her when she divorced, but just as important was the "sense of belonging" she got from attending her church. That church continues to be a place where she spends a lot of time and where she was recently ordained as an Elder. Like Jean, divorcée Teresa thinks that "church has been an important family for me." She has good friends there and uses them and her faith as a source of strength and comfort on a daily basis.

A sense of community was also what Lee was searching for after she divorced and her twin daughters went away to college. She tried a suburban church, but felt excluded there because of its orientation toward couples and families. She found her niche in an inner-city church that was more open and inviting, with members of all ages and backgrounds. "They actually made an effort to introduce themselves to someone they'd never seen before," Lee recalls. Now her new church community gives depth to a life that was previously made up just of her daughters, her work, and a few close friends.

Jill found balm for her emotional wounds in a Unitarian church she joined after she separated from her husband. She remembers why the church attracted her:

> I had really been yearning for a spiritual community. . . . It was a very nurturing, nourishing place. The music was beautiful. The environment was beautiful. Each time I went it felt like they were talking directly to me. . . . It felt like a very welcoming, warm, real place. You didn't have to pretend to be happy when your world was coming apart at the seams.

Celita's church was also an important part of her initial recovery from her husband's death. She explains, "I am a Roman Catholic and in all the chaos and emotions I was going through, that was the one place I could go." She found the rituals to be an island of stability, "the one thing that hadn't changed. I could sit there and I knew what was going to happen next." Because

Celita viewed her dependence on her family as a crutch, she didn't want to use the priests that way, but found them "as helpful as I let them be. I wanted to figure things out for myself."

Divorcée Grace, on the other hand, did let the priest in her Catholic church help her figure things out. Not only did he counsel her whenever she asked, but he also gave her the tuition she needed for her daughter's private high school. At first, the members of her church seemed reluctant to accept her as a divorced woman. But eventually they warmed to her and began to play a "big brother" role for her son, even allowing him to be an altar boy. The church now offers a support group for divorcées, Grace reports.

The minister in Jocelyn's Baptist church was also very important to her both as her husband was dying and after his death. Although Jocelyn considers herself an agnostic, this "thoughtful, fatherly man" prayed with her and her husband every day in the hospital. Afterward, he confronted her lack of faith, counseling her about faith and about the afterlife. "He really got me through in many ways," Jocelyn acknowledges.

Women with strong nontraditional religious beliefs are also able to turn to them to find some relief from the chaos in their lives. Isabelle says that she doesn't belong to any organized religion but believes that she is in harmony with God, a kind of universal energy. Her resulting view that "the universe will take care of you" has enabled her to move rapidly ahead into a new identity.

Antoinette says she used spirituality "to gain comfort" after her divorce, even though she wasn't able to find a church that met her needs. Reconnecting with warm memories of a God-like figure from her youth, she says, brought her a sense of companionship. And books on spirituality helped by giving her "good nuggets of thoughts." Those books don't have to be strictly about religion, of course. Psychiatry, psychology, philosophy, poetry, and even science can provide similar "nuggets" of solace and perspective.

One woman, Laura, began to study Buddhism after divorcing

her husband of thirteen years. She found it empowering. Buddhism teaches mental techniques, such as meditation, to achieve "happiness," a term that has a very different meaning in that philosophy. As psychiatrist Mark Epstein, who has trained both in Western medicine and in Buddhism, explains it:

> We confuse [happiness] with a life uncluttered by feel-
> ings of anxiety, rage, doubt, and sadness. But happiness
> is something entirely different. It's the ability to receive
> the pleasant without grasping and the unpleasant with-
> out condemning.[2]

Epstein thinks that by helping you accept both the good and the bad, Buddhism makes it possible to live with painful events without becoming angry or anxious. That philosophy, says Laura, has worked for her in the ten years since she divorced her husband and became an active lesbian. Even though she isn't a practicing Buddhist, learning about detachment and holding dualities has made it possible for her to resolve many of the apparent conflicts between her Mormon upbringing and her current way of life.

But of course religion and spirituality don't bring solace to everyone. Some widows found that once their husband's funeral service was over and a few months had passed, their priest, minister, or rabbi was impatient for them to "just get over it." A few widows and divorcées said that the religious service dredged up an intolerable amount of pain and bad feelings. And others who associated churchgoing too closely with their former husbands needed to find alternate supports and outlets that they could call their own.

⌧⌧⌧⌧⌧⌧

In Search of Meaning

Some women return to their religious roots in a quest to make some sense of what happened. That's what Susan did when her successful, athletic husband of twenty-one years died in an air-plane crash. In her early forties, Susan was in mid-career as a medical writer, but had to stop writing for a while. "I didn't think I'd survive. It was a very close marriage. We didn't have children and we did everything together. There was a real bond there," she remembers.

She moved in for a while with her parents and thought about going to see a therapist, but was turned off by the idea:

> There was nothing wrong with my head. I was perfectly okay there. I had just suffered this horrible insult. . . . My world had been all blown into bits and thrown into chaos. What I really wanted was gone. I needed to make some sense of the world in some spiritual fashion. I needed some sort of deeper meaning to my life. I needed some kind of reason for living.

So although Susan hadn't been a regular churchgoer before her husband died, she started to go to the Episcopal church around the corner, where she had belonged ever since she was a little girl. "Just to be there, I found that very comforting. And the people were very generous and kind in their attempts to be solicitous, but not overly so. They made me feel welcome."

In addition to finding a sense of community there, Susan also began to tap into a "deepened religious awareness, a sense of the ephemerality of life and of the fact that you cannot control anything. . . . I felt that I could not count on any person or anything, that I had to turn to a spiritual base for my life."

To fill the time, Susan decided to become more involved in the church and its volunteer activities. When a bereavement group was starting up, she joined it. Like her, most of the men and women in it were early middle-aged (which is somewhat unusual for a widowed persons' group, she later learned). A social worker led them for the first eight weeks, after which they continued on their own. Looking back, Susan concludes:

> The main thing I got out of it was knowing that I was

not weird and strange, that I was not the only one feeling these horrible things. And I decided that I wasn't going to fall apart and just be a complete basketcase, a catastrophe who could never really do anything.

Two other important things came out of the group. The first was a booklet on bereavement that they all wrote, Susan edited, and the national Episcopal church published. By working on this booklet, Susan felt she was doing something useful to educate people about how to deal with their own and others' grief. (Later, Susan also wrote a very poignant article on this topic for a local magazine.)

The second thing was Susan's meeting and eventually marrying a widower from the group. Initially, both said that they would *never ever* get into another marriage. But they became attracted to each other in the nonthreatening environment of the weekly group meeting. That kind of atmosphere is essential, Susan believes, because at first the world feels very dangerous, and you feel completely alone and vulnerable in it. (Hers is the quotation about feeling like an unprotected bug at the start of this chapter.)

Susan took her time getting back into life but eventually moved out of her parents' home, resumed her career, and made a new life. Five years after her husband died, she felt strong enough to decide to remarry.

But she has not turned away from religion. If anything, Susan is even more involved now in her own spiritual development. She is taking courses in the Bible and theological principles, with the goal of turning her writing career in that direction. The studies are mainly for herself, however:

I think this [religious study] helped me to grow a lot, spiritually. It deepened my understanding of human nature. It helped me to understand why some people act the way they do and how we can react to them in a positive and loving manner, as opposed to an angry or critical manner.

Susan's search for meaning through religion after her husband died has become a continuing quest that enriches her life.

⊠⊠⊠⊠⊠⊠

In Search of Yourself

Religion can play a crucial role in helping you explore your **new identity as a single woman.** Matty turned to it the day her husband moved his things out of their house. She was forty-two and had been married for twenty years, with three children. By chance, at the grocery store that awful day, Matty ran into a friend who invited her to join an ongoing Bible study group. She immediately accepted.

Matty stayed in the group for a year. "We became a very close, bonded group of women. . . . That was one of the big changing forces in my life, when I started to grow personally and find out who I was." The group offered equal portions of religion and support. They began each session by going around the room and saying in a few words how they were feeling. One woman then took the lead in reading and discussing a lesson from the Bible. Afterward, they provided each other with support, praying with people who were hurting and giving each other practical advice.

Expressing her anger and distress before the group was a revelation, Matty remembers. During her marriage, she had always put her husband and children first, never really thinking about her own feelings. "These were things I really didn't identify in myself—whether I was feeling guilt or joy or shame over something. . . . Just to be able to identify those feelings, rather than sublimate them, was very beneficial to me." Learning to express her emotions taught her to recognize and work through her feelings apart from the group.

From that beginning, Matty's church became the mainstay of

her emotional, spiritual, and social life. She joined a Christian singles' group and occasionally organizes book discussions for its members. She also joined another Bible study group, made up of four couples and two single women. They are a "sharing group," with the men in the group often acting as her mentors— although she has to work hard not to be a threat to their wives. They even took a cruise together. And she was elected to be an Elder in the church.

Matty's faith has continued to develop over the years. "Whenever I am personally lacking the ability to handle something well, if I turn to my faith, it's there. I have the strength I need to accomplish it." Matty used that growing sense of self-confidence to build a successful career as a meeting planner, saving and investing so that she was able to retire at sixty-one. Now she enjoys her family and first grandson, dating, her friends, classes she takes for pleasure, a volunteer position with the Red Cross, and, of course, her church.

In Search of Spirituality

Some of the most religious people I talked to were women who are actively involved in developing a spiritual life apart from any traditional or formal religion. These participants in what is often called "New Age" religion usually believe in some kind of higher power. But they also celebrate the healing power of relationships, as well as the power of intuition, imagination, and their own inner wisdom.[3] Three women I interviewed even went on to become nontraditional spiritual leaders. Finding themselves single-again, each began to search her soul and to develop her own belief system, later moving on to help others develop theirs.

Although the "others" they help are not exclusively female, they are mostly so. They are part of a burgeoning number of women who find in each other the path to continuing spiritual development.[4] Because they celebrate the power of the female, the groups have their roots in the women's consciousness-raising groups of the 1970s. What is new is the emphasis on spiritual connections—with each other, their psyches, their bodies, and nature.[5]

It's easy to dismiss these groups of women, with their kooky-sounding names like "Wild Woman Circles" and activities like drumming and chanting. But women who participate in them give them rave reviews, even women who also hold traditional religious views. Matty, for example, is now taking a course on "women as goddesses." She loves it because it lets her see where *she* fits in in the panorama of goddesses from the past, helping her in the process to be more self-approving.

In Search of Serenity and Power

Many women offered a glimpse of the larger role that religion continues to play—one that is central in their search for happiness, peace, and ongoing growth. Author Germaine Greer, herself middle-aged and single, also speaks of religion's significance in making a new life. In the final chapter of her book *The Change: Women, Aging and the Menopause*, Greer describes the "serenity and power" a woman can achieve through spirituality, once she lets go of the desperate need to be young and eternally beautiful. She writes:

> Even the woman whose mind and soul have been ignored by everyone, including herself, has within her the spiritual resources to make something of her new life, though she may have some difficulty in getting at them . . . .
>
> Religion is one of the easier ways that the aging woman can unlock the door to her interior life. If she

has been an unreflective Christian or Hindu or Muslim or Jew or Buddhist she may find it easiest to find her interior life by entering more deeply into the implications of her religion. . . . Women who do not adhere to a particular creed will nevertheless find that in the last third of their lives they come to partake of the "oceanic experience" as the grandeur and the pity of human life begin to become apparent to them. As one by one the Lilliputian strings that tie the soul down to self-interest and the short view begin to snap the soul rises higher and higher, until the last one snaps, and it floats free at last.[6]

With that vision in mind, ask yourself if you might find serenity and spirituality in a religious environment, and then give it a try.

* * *

A sustaining belief system can be a superb aid in helping you through periods of feeling lonely and isolated. But for many women, these and other self-help approaches aren't sufficient. Overwhelmed by their feelings, they need to discharge their emotional overload so they can move ahead. How they use support groups or a therapist to help them do that is the subject of the next chapter.

8

Discharge Your
Emotional Overload

XXXXXXXXXXXXXXXXXXXXXXXXXXXXXXXX

It was a psychological devastation and I hit the skids. I just fell apart. I had a total loss of identity. I didn't know who I was if I wasn't married to this man. . . . And I realized I didn't have the power to help myself.

—divorcée Judith

Some women go through the chaos of a divorce or the death of a husband with everything they need to bounce back. They have good self-esteem, a roster of friends who love and stick by them, and plans for the future that take into account their going solo.

For others, however, friendship networks are inadequate, especially if a woman doesn't have a job or most of her friends are married couples. And when becoming single coincides with other terrible life events, or when her loss is particularly traumatic or sudden, the shock of changing gears from a married to a single life can be staggering. Symptoms can run the gamut from anxiety attacks to insomnia, feelings of helplessness and hopelessness, eating problems, drug or alcohol dependency, nightmares, even full-fledged depression.

Many women get the extra support they need during this difficult period by joining a support group. When that doesn't entirely fill the bill, some also turn—instead of or in addition to a support group—to a professional therapist.

⬚⬚⬚⬚⬚

Support Groups as a Bridge to Your Future

THE BEGINNING OF A TOTALLY NEW LIFE: ROZ

Roz believes that her divorce was the catalyst that enabled her to take charge of her life. And one important turning point in learning how to do that was joining a support group for newly separated and divorced people. "That really was the beginning of a totally new life for me," Roz says.

When her husband suddenly left her after thirty-one years of marriage, Roz floundered at first. Excluded from her former social life as a foreign service wife, her parents deceased, and her grown children far away, Roz, then fifty-three-years-old, realized how shortsighted it was to have integrated her former life so totally with her husband's. But that was the model she had for a good marriage. "I thought that was what I was supposed to do in my marriage—link up with my husband and become part of this family unit and not have anything separate. . . . Then when you are suddenly single, you don't have a lot of yourself left."

Roz felt isolated. So when she heard at church about a group for newly separated men and women, she tried it out. The group of about twenty people met in members' homes and a facilitator led a discussion of a topic like "rejection" or "sexual expectations in the 90s." Roz found the atmosphere nonthreatening, and she was able to open up and make her first nonmarried friends, even men. "I had my first male friends in my adult life. You get this whole new perspective. It's very helpful to you when you're living alone," she remembers.

After six months, she decided to get training as a facilitator. "That was a big step for me—to feel like I could facilitate a meeting, that I didn't need to be there for myself. It was a wonderful thing to go through this training and then be the one guiding the discussion." She says she was nervous for the first six months, but the group was supportive. "Nobody really wants to hurt anybody else. It really encouraged me."

She began to attend singles' evenings at a museum, then to go to dances, and eventually to date. When she needed to buttress her desire to have a relationship with a man without getting married, she formed her own support group of four "women of very strong character." They still meet every other week "to deal with issues of dating in a forum where we can say anything." And they call each other night or day to talk about current problems. "I can't remember ever having this kind of thing in my life. It's very special," Roz muses.

How Support Groups Can Help

Psychiatrist and grief expert Colin Murray Parkes would approve of the way Roz used her first support group—as a bridge to a new life. She crossed that bridge in stages, first as an observer, then as a participant, then as a leader, finally moving on to a new identity and a network of different friends. Writing about groups for widowed women, Parkes says that **support groups "should be seen as steps towards other forms of activities rather than as ends in themselves . . . [as] an organization for transition rather than a perpetual refuge."**[1] Used in that way, he believes, these groups may prevent people from becoming stuck in bad feelings or becoming ill.

There is not much question that support groups can work. Women I interviewed talked about how effective support groups were in helping them with their feelings of isolation—knowing there were others in similar straits, some in even more dire circumstances. They chose from a range of types of groups,[2] each type serving different needs:

- *Special groups for singles who are divorced or widowed (sometimes even mixed) let you vent your feelings among likeminded people.* They can be a big help in assuaging your pain and anger. They also help with the practicalities of adjusting to your new situation. Going to meetings of Parents Without Partners (PWP), for example, gave Felicia a chance to compare experiences with others, as well as to practice going to a gathering as a single person—something she initially found intimidating. The widows' support group Debra joined discussed practicalities like how to deal with an empty bed (for example, changing to another bedroom, moving the furniture around, eating in bed) and what to do if you dream about your husband.

- *Groups for women provide support, consciousness-raising, and expertise on a whole range of topics.* Many tapped into a women's group for the short term and ended up staying involved with women's issues. When she was widowed at the age of forty-five, Celita joined a support group for divorced and widowed women. The group served as "a coffee klatch" for her, Celita says, giving her a place to vent her feelings of danger because "the big wall holding me up was gone." It also gave her the courage to make decisions without asking someone else for permission.

• *Twelve-step programs like Alcoholics Anonymous, AlAnon, and Adult Children of Alcoholics can provide a new perspective on yourself and your former husband.* When Stephanie's marriage broke up after she entered treatment for her alcoholism, she used her women's AA group as the backbone of her recovery. She thinks AA's twelve-step philosophy is essential because it teaches that bitterness puts you into a negative place, while letting go helps spiritually. Sue Ellen says AA helped her get rid of rage against her ex-husband. "You take the steps. You have to forgive yourself. Then you forgive the other person."

The common denominator among support groups is the sympathetic ear they provide for your concerns. They provide places where you can let down your guard without fear of harsh judgments that you should or could be different somehow. Therapist Alice Umbach, herself divorced, believes support groups are a good idea and belonged to one for a while. Umbach says:

> I think every woman who is going through a divorce ought to go to a support group. For one thing, you have a lot to deal with—a lot of anger and a lot of fears—and you really need to be talking about it all the time. And, let's face it, your friends can't listen to that forever.[3]

And Jean Ellzey, who runs support groups for divorced and widowed women, thinks that they do more: "They can help you stretch your limits. . . . **When you give voice to your own concerns and acknowledge them out loud, you are more likely to empower yourself and others to take action.**"[4]

WHAT TO BE WARY OF IN SUPPORT GROUPS

That certainly does *not* mean, however, that support groups are always beneficial. Just like families, these "substitute families" can be a mixed blessing, depending on how well you fit into them and how well they function. So if you are interested in joining a support group, go ahead. **But in order to be an informed consumer, be aware of the potential downside to these groups:**[5]

- *Groups that place an overwhelming emphasis on being supportive make it almost impossible to tell the truth or express any criticism,* however mild, about co-members. In such groups, truth-telling is frowned upon even when a criticism is justified and might help someone in the long run. Taken to its extreme, it is what one critic calls "a world in which all opinions are equally valid, stories have happy endings, commandments are replaced by suggestions, and 'judgmentalism' is the cardinal sin."[6]

- *Although people often join groups because they want to make new friends with similar life experiences, group members often feel no real obligation to each other and can leave whenever they feel like it.* His experiences as a participant led religious scholar Robert Wuthnow to conclude in his book on support groups that the connections made in these groups are often more shallow and less enduring than those supplied by friends, families, and neighbors."[7]

- *Focusing exclusively on venting bad feelings can encourage passivity and infantilism rather than problem solving and taking charge of your life.* That can sometimes happen in women's groups, even though the research shows that women usually do better when exposed to consciousness raising and examining what's wrong with *the system*, rather than what's wrong with *them*.[8]

- *Groups that mix men and women can leave women feeling dejected if the group's primary interest is matchmaking, not self-development.* Even women who just want to make male friends can find that that's not possible if the atmosphere is too much like a "meat market."

- *Labeling everyone in a group as having the same problem or illness can lead members to adopt that negative label as their primary identity—a self-fulfilling prophecy.* All group members may or may not have that problem, or some may have a very different one. And when everyone is equally ill, they are also equally restricted to only one path to a cure.[9]

- *Perhaps most risky of all, support groups can offer a false hope of feeling better to people who are in need of more than self-help.* One divorcée I interviewed, Harriet, put enormous energy into self-help groups that only delayed her getting effective help for her severe anxiety. Some weeks, she attended eight or nine meetings of different groups. Only when her symptoms got worse and she went to see a doctor did she get the treatment she needed to recover from the cumulative effects of a terrible childhood and divorce.

Harriet was an exception, however. For many women I interviewed, support groups proved beneficial, even essential.

Support Groups as a Lifeline: Jennifer

Jennifer did not resolve her sadness and anger about divorcing her husband of seventeen years easily. It took her ten years to finally get over what her friends thought of as a perfect marriage:

> I didn't feel like a human being anymore. My best friend was gone. Half of me was missing. What did I have to look forward to in the morning if I couldn't tell my best friend everything? . . . I would look in the mirror and I hated myself because I couldn't keep the man I loved.

She entered therapy, but that only put a small dent in Jennifer's wish to have her husband back. Although she was a regular churchgoer, "the sadness from the breakup caused me to get hysterical in the middle of mass." Worse, no one in the congregation even approached her to try to help, a slight that still hurts. She had to deal with a daughter and son who were wildly upset because they adored their father. But even when her son developed an obsessive-compulsive disorder, her husband would not agree to a regular schedule for seeing the children.

Feeling suicidal, she decided to attend a group for separated and divorced Catholics run by a "renegade priest." At her first meeting, she remembers being so upset that "if I didn't have that group to go to, I don't know what I would have done. It really saved my life." She became close to two men and two women in the group, socializing outside the group, telephoning night and day.

During the months before all their divorces were settled, the group members were more important to her than anybody: "Nobody could have the kind of time or emotional strength to pull a friend through like that. We needed each other. I call that my lifeline." The group, plus her therapy and friends, served Jennifer well. They allowed her eventually to get back on track, earn her teaching certificate, find a job teaching home economics in high school, and establish a long-term relationship with a man.

What Kind of Group Is Right for You?

The women I talked to participated in a wide range of types of support groups, each with advantages and disadvantages. Some, like Roz, even started their own groups. In picking or forming a group, the women had to decide whether they wanted a group

- where participation is expected to be short term *or* where you are expected to participate for an extended time;

- that is solely for women *or* that also includes men;

- that includes both divorced and widowed people, *or* exclusively either divorced or widowed people, *or* people with a whole variety of concerns;

- whose approach is based on the twelve steps used by Alcoholics Anonymous (or variations of them), *or* is not based on the twelve steps;

- that has a leader *or* is leaderless.

Finally, the women had to find a group that filled their most pressing immediate needs—such as finding a way to express and get support for their feelings; begin a new social life; deal with the practical uncertainties of being single (such as legal and financial problems); search for answers to spiritual issues; or harness their energy into advocacy for needed changes.

One place to locate a support group that will fit your needs is the American Self-Help Clearinghouse. In order to match you up with a group that can help, the clearinghouse publishes a directory with information on hundreds of national groups, on what support networks are popping up online, and on how to start your own group.[10] (See the Resources section, chapter 8.) Or begin your inquiries at your local women's center or commission on women, church or synagogue, community college or university, hospice, or mental health center. **Don't be afraid to shop around to find a group that suits you and to trust your own instincts about ones that don't.**

Support groups—just like self-help techniques, religion, and friends—are far from a perfect solution. But when you're feeling particularly dizzy on your tightrope, and your own resources just aren't enough to help you keep your balance, a support group can offer a temporary bridge over the chaos you're facing. Choose it with care and put your trust in it, and it should help you safely across.

⚙️⚙️⚙️⚙️⚙️

Professional Counseling—
Luxury or Necessity?

HITTING THE SKIDS: JUDITH

Judith just showed up one day, dead drunk, at the home office of her neighbor—a psychotherapist—and asked for help. As she recounts the story now, some fifteen years later, it's hard to imagine that this stylish-looking, relaxed, successful sixty-year-old novelist was ever so desperate. But Judith says she was—that her husband's desertion after a twenty-two-year marriage knocked her off her pins.

They had been college classmates and soulmates in the sixties, she working as a waitress and stewardess, both of them involved in protests against the Vietnam War. They married in their early twenties and settled into domesticity in a spacious old row house in a modest urban neighborhood, where Judith still lives. They took up separate careers—he as an attorney and she as a writer. While their three children were small, she wrote freelance for local publications and taught English at three colleges.

Judith and people who knew her believed she was quite self-confident—maybe even a little cocky. She had her work, had traveled on her own, and had even emerged unscathed when her husband left for an affair ten years before. That experience was just grist for the mill for her first novel. But she went to pieces when her husband left for good. She remembers:

> I thought I had been cut off from the universe. Suddenly the world that we had inhabited together became off bounds. And I literally had no identity left whatsoever. I was way out there, way out. I shocked everybody by falling apart. They thought I was going to buy purple high heels and a red hat and go off swinging. Instead I was breaking windows and ramming cars. I went crazy.

She reached out for help from her friends, but says, "I ultimately drove most of them away with my behavior—my carrying on, my crying, my drinking, my raging. . . . Even my parents couldn't take it. It was too brutal. It was too battering. I clobbered everybody." In addition to alcohol, she turned to drugs and promiscuity.

Although her husband gave her the house, she couldn't afford the mortgage payments. So she began to rent out rooms, even as the place was falling down around them. It was sheer filth and squalor. She went six months without changing the sheets. Judith thinks her twelve-year-old son, the only child still at home, got the worst of it: "He was alone in this ramshackle slummy house with his drunken mother on drugs."

Judith eventually "hit bottom and bellied up," she says. "I realized that I didn't have the power to help myself." So even though she was drunk and barely knew the woman, Judith walked the block to her neighbor therapist's house and asked for help. The one hitch was that she couldn't pay, so would the therapist work on credit?

Astonishingly, the woman agreed, but only if Judith would stop drinking entirely. Instead, she put her on medication, requiring Judith to take it at her office three times a day. Then she took hold of Judith's life in a way Judith was unable to do for herself. Judith came for therapy every morning, five to seven days a week. And the therapist planned how Judith would spend her days, giving her a schedule that said things like "play tennis" and "clean up your room."

As Judith gradually resumed control, the therapist got her to return to work teaching English part-time. Judith remembers very well the act of buying "two hideous dresses" to wear to work—because of how strange it felt to have someplace to go. While teaching a writers' program, Judith says, "suddenly I remembered I was a writer. I had just forgotten."

"And then I started to write. That was the blessing in disguise because I had so much to say. I worked like a dog." At her vintage computer, she vented all her rage through humorous fiction about the breakup of a marriage. "I loved writing that book. It gave me a sense of control. I was on top of it. I formed that book like clay. That was my triumph over the divorce and a personal statement about myself and my friends."

The novel was a best-seller. Not only did Judith, at the age of fifty, get revenge, but she still gets income from that book and has written several more. Although she doesn't want to remarry because she treasures her solitude, she has a boyfriend. But she says her greatest pleasure is her grandchildren, who find her exotic and wonderful. One wrote an essay on her, saying she was divorced, smokes cigarettes, wears wild clothes, and has frizzy hair from the beach. "They make me feel like Rosalind Russell, like the kind of lady I might have liked to have been. I'm really kind of conventional. . . . But they think I'm wild. . . . The relationship I have with them is the most profound thing I've had since my divorce."

Judith believes her recovery would never have happened without her therapy. She knew she had healed enough to discontinue it when after three years she had a dream that she had bought a new set of kelly green luggage. "And I was ready to go," she explains. Looking back at her life now, she says it was wonderful "except for five years of hell. But it was a tunnel and I came out the other end wonderfully, with some damages done." Acknowledging that her therapist's hand guided her step-by-step through that tunnel, Judith has since paid her everything she owed.

How to Know When You Need Therapy

As stressful as losing a husband can be, few widows and divorcées have the kind of breakdown that Judith did. Still, many of them turn to therapists for a period of time. Women who enter therapy fall roughly into two different groups: those who, like Judith, really *need* to see a therapist because they are stuck in a range of exaggerated reactions and in danger of becoming worse;

and those who *benefit* from professional therapy, but who most likely could make it on their own if they had to.

Therapists point to a number of symptoms that would indicate *the need* for professional help. They include

- feeling helpless, hopeless, out of control, or as if you're losing your mind;

- severe anxiety attacks;

- a desire to "give up" through drugs, alcohol, or suicide;

- loss of all perspective;

- disturbing behavior patterns; or

- trouble eating, drinking, or sleeping.

But these symptoms don't always indicate a grief-gone-wrong. Many of them would be considered a normal reaction to a terrible life event unless they are distorted, exaggerated, prolonged, or preclude living a normal life.[11]

So even though you're terribly upset, that doesn't necessarily mean you *need* to seek professional help right away. Judith needed and sought professional help to get her unstuck. **But for some women, just knowing and recognizing the stages of grief and the pain that many women go through after the death of a spouse or a painful divorce can help. Assess whether you seem to be moving, however slowly, through the various "stages":**

- *Stage One.* **Denial,** characterized by shock, numbness, and disbelief, interrupted by flashes of anger and despair;

- *Stage Two.* **Intense pain, distress, and agitation,** marked by crying spells, yearning, anger, and protests;

- *Stage Three.* **Despair** from realizing that the loss is irrevocable, feelings of hopelessness, despondency, and other symptoms typical of depression;

- *Stage Four*: **Recovery** (also referred to as "adaptation" and "adjustment"), indicated by gradual acceptance of the loss and feelings that a new life is possible.[12]

As pointed out in chapter 1, the problem with using these stages to gauge your progress is that there is no such thing as a straightforward path through them. British psychiatrist Colin Murray Parkes explains it like this: "Grief is not a set of symptoms which start after a loss and then gradually fade away. It involves a succession of clinical pictures which blend into and replace one another."[13]

One way you can tell if you're stuck and need professional help is by noticing whether you get periodic relief from your feelings or are constantly obsessed by them. Writer Barbara Holland uses this analogy: "Grief comes and goes, flickering like heat lightning." But depression is different, she says: "Depression doesn't flicker like grief. It settles down over our days like a bad smell—perhaps a dead rat in the wall—and seeps into everything."[14]

If you don't feel stuck in your bad feelings or consumed by them, those are good signs that your reaction hasn't "gone wrong." **To determine if you will continue on a track toward feeling better, you need to assess how you've handled other stresses and losses in your life.**[15] If you have a vulnerability to depression, which is often a lifelong trait, you should think carefully about finding a therapist. Michelle, for example, had struggled with depression her whole life and so turned to a therapist even before she was divorced. It was, for her, a necessity, not a luxury.

Another way to determine if you may need professional help is to assess whether you have concurrent pressures that could put you at risk of becoming ill rather than just grief-stricken. These include factors like how traumatic becoming single is for you, how ambivalent you feel about your marriage, whether your life is chaotic and full of other stresses, and whether you have a good support network.

You only have some control over one of these risk factors: your support network. However, the catch-22 is that being depressed works against finding the energy to cultivate the friends you need. That's probably both because you may be too demoralized to try and because people generally don't like to be around depressed people. Understanding that caused Nina, who felt abandoned by her married friends after her husband left, to consult a therapist for help *until* she could build a new network of friends for herself.

THE BENEFITS OF THERAPY FOR NORMAL UNHAPPINESS

Even if you don't formally qualify as someone who *needs* professional counseling, there are still a multitude of other reasons why you might want to see a therapist now—provided you can afford it. For one thing, there's the old saw about the Chinese character for "crisis" being the same as the one for "opportunity." Feeling as if your life is a jigsaw puzzle that has come apart may be extremely disorienting right now. But consulting with a good therapist might help you put the pieces together in a new way, creating a picture that in some ways you may like even better than the old one. It lets you admit your failures to someone who won't judge you. It provides you with your own private sounding board to probe how you're really feeling and what you'd like to do next. Therapists can also help by noting old and outdated assumptions you may be laboring under because you have grown so accustomed to them.

When Corinne left her husband and children behind (temporarily at first) to take a new job across the continent, she didn't doubt her ability to make it on her own, "probably because my mother raised me on her own, having been a divorced woman herself." But as her marriage unraveled, she became disoriented and lonely and chose to enter group therapy rather than just talking to a pastor or friends.

I asked her why. "If there's a serious problem, you need professional help—some disinterested person who doesn't know you, who's not at all like you, and who's not really saying much. They're just listening." What she got out of therapy, Corinne says, was "hearing myself talk. Hearing my own voice and saying 'That sounded really dumb,' or 'That's full of holes,' and being shocked at my own feelings, when I thought I knew myself."

Psychologist Mary Lou Randour agrees with Corinne, saying that although friends try to be helpful,

> they give advice and I don't think advice usually works. They also have lots of emotional investments in different ways. And they have points of view, which is fair because they're your friends. Therapists try more to help you figure out what your point of view is, rather than give their own.[16]

Although a great many emotional problems like depression and anxiety diminish without treatment, therapy often can shorten their course and prevent them from getting worse.[17] In a 1994 survey, *Consumer Reports* queried its readers about their experiences with professional therapy. Almost four thousand of them (about half female) said that they had used a mental health specialist, 43 percent reporting that when they entered treatment their emotional state was either very poor or fairly poor. An article reported the results:

> Overall, almost everyone in *Consumer Reports'* survey who had sought help experienced some relief, improvements that made them less troubled and their lives more pleasant. People who started out feeling the worst reported the most progress. Among people no longer in treatment, two-thirds said they'd left because their problems had been resolved or were easier to deal with.[18]

Felicia is another proponent of therapy for normal unhappiness. Felicia and her husband went into marriage counseling when their thirty-five-year marriage was on the rocks, "to figure out what was going wrong so we could avoid the divorce."

When her husband stopped going regularly, Felicia ended up seeing the counselor on her own, first individually and then in a group. "That was extremely useful," Felicia comments, twelve years after her divorce. "I certainly consolidated my sense of myself as a valuable person. And I developed my own theory of therapy, which is that life is a journey anyway and therapy is an intensification of things you've been moving on."

Felicia realized in therapy, she says, that during her life as "wife of," she had adapted to "a life that wasn't happening." Therapy showed her how to express her anger, to grieve that things hadn't turned out as she expected, and to become "infinitely more assertive." Eventually she was able to resolve her resentment at her husband and to recognize that she could retain the good and interesting parts of their marriage, that she hadn't lost them when she divorced. And in therapy she found the courage to enroll in graduate school in her late fifties, eventually becoming a therapist herself.

Felicia's recovery from a nasty midlife divorce is almost a textbook case of an impressive comeback. But could she have done the same thing without professional help? It's hard to know, but if resources are available, therapy can be a good investment.

MAKING THE CASE FOR THERAPY

Almost everyone I interviewed who saw a professional therapist was happy with the results. A few, like Sally, were adamant that it was indispensable.

Sally lived a very privileged life until she faced divorce at the age of fifty-three. She met and married her husband when they were both in graduate school. After they married, Sally immersed herself in the life of a well-to-do suburban wife, mother of three, and "professional volunteer in all the right things." In her mid-forties, she began to study to become a psychotherapist, "with the idea of having something that was mine when my kids were grown that I could be very involved in." Still, she described her role as "wife of" and caretaker for her children and ailing parents as "the most important things in my life."

Sally's choice of career turned out to be a fortunate one. When her husband shocked everyone by announcing that he was in love with someone else and wanted a divorce, she had already begun psychoanalysis as part of her training. Sally's reaction was fierce. For a year, she was full of rage and despair, crying constantly and pacing the floor all night. What she went through, she asserts, was worse than being raped or diagnosed with terminal cancer. She would have preferred it if he had died. "When you divorce, you have to deal with the shock plus the deceit, not being able to hold onto what you thought was good. And he's still there, and is being a much better father in a lot of ways—courting his children."

Although she was seriously unhappy, Sally had probably everything she needed to get over her loss: good self-esteem; enough money to be comfortable and get a good lawyer; satisfying work; and a group of loyal, supportive friends. Still, to get through it, she went into daily psychotherapy. She thinks that it, along with the support of her friends, was absolutely vital. "I don't think you can get through this in a positive way—growing—without awfully good therapy. Because for me absolutely every part of my life suddenly had to change. Everything."

Sally says that therapy "grounded" her, serving as a kind of ongoing meditation, as "an inner journey, a chance to turn inward and find what's important, to struggle with that." It helped her deal with all her anger and resentment, not letting it make her bitter:

> Analysis really helped me get through this because I had to go in and have someone who knew exactly how to deal with me in all these stages, when to push and when to be supportive. . . . The therapist has constantly been thinking of *my* growth . . . helping me find myself in what is my way. . . . I've gotten through this faster than I ever would have, by a long shot, and I've had to work

through a lot more than just the result of the divorce. I've worked through many early things, my own neuroses, that I never would have touched if he hadn't left.

Sally was still in therapy when I talked to her, partly to increase her skills as a practicing psychotherapist. But she was mainly in pursuit of her goal to be "freed of my own inhibitions or neuroses, the things that keep me from growing." When she's finished, she says, "I want my husband not to be a factor, in my dreams, in my life, at all. . . . I want to get over the results of all this trauma."

The kind of therapy that Sally pursued—an intensive self-examination—is rare because of both the emotional and the financial investment required. It *is* a true luxury, but not something that everyone who could afford it would want to pursue. Even for Sally, it was a mixed blessing. Living full-tilt on her own now—with her own salary, her travels, a newly purchased and remodeled house, loads of single and married friends, even a boyfriend—this tall, attractive fiftyish woman paused when asked whether she feels better off now. In one way, yes, Sally replies. She has a more positive sense of herself now than when she was married:

> But I have to tell you that I didn't know I didn't have that. I thought I was positively independent and I had a very good life. And I was effective, and I offered a lot. . . . I think I can say that I'm better off now, but I sure as hell would rather have not had to do it. . . . No real growth comes without pain, but who wants the enormity of the pain? I would have much preferred to be able to work on the marriage and struggle through.

Despite her ambivalence about the changes she went through, Sally makes a good case for the benefits of therapy. Other women I talked to spoke of ways therapy can help. They said that therapy helps you to

- legitimize your strong, sometimes conflicting emotions about what happened;

- vent your sadness and anger and begin the process of purging yourself of it;

- get in touch with ambivalent feelings about your marriage;

- examine past roles you played, as well as mistakes you made, so you don't have to repeat them;

- identify your strengths and possibilities for new roles;

- challenge destructive patterns of thinking and acting that can hold you back;

- define what your most important problems are and how you might approach them;

- come to terms with your new status;

- question self-restrictions and have confidence in steps forward, even tiny ones;

- be empowered to do what's best for you, not cave in to others' wishes; and

- find structure and direction when you are unable to create them for yourself.

The *Consumer Reports* survey found three ways that their readers reported that therapy was important for their well-being. Therapy

- eased the problems that brought people to treatment;

- helped them to function better, improving their ability to relate well to others, to be productive at work, and to cope with everyday stress;

- enhanced what can be called "personal growth"—people in

therapy had more confidence and self-esteem, understood themselves better, and enjoyed life more.[19]

What Kind of Therapist Should You Look For?

If you're thinking about seeking professional counseling, it's a good idea to look for the best possible therapist, rather than for a specific kind of therapy. For one thing, little adequate research exists to shed light on what type of therapy works best for what type of person or problem. For another, most therapists, even if trained in one specific therapeutic discipline, become pragmatic after a few years and incorporate more than one method into treating their patients.

But decide in advance whether you are seeking short-term or a longer-term therapy (although you can obviously change your mind as you get into your search). Short-term therapies (anywhere from a few to twenty sessions) are good for solving immediate problems.[20] It's pretty clear, however, that if you want, as Sally did, to make major alterations in your view of yourself and the world, short-term therapy won't fill the bill.[21]

Consumer Reports (CR) found that although health insurance usually limits mental-health coverage to short-term therapy, respondents reported greater gains the longer they stayed in treatment. People who were in treatment for more than two years reported the best outcomes. *CR* contrasts its finding to one from a Northwestern University study that found that "recovery followed a 'dose-response' curve, with the greatest response occurring early on. On average, 50% of people felt they had recovered after eleven weekly therapy sessions, and 75% got better after about a year."[22]

The qualifications of a good therapist can vary widely, because the practice of therapy is still as much art as science. But you do want someone who specializes in mental health—whether it's a psychiatrist, clinical psychologist, or social worker. These were the therapists rated highest by *CR* respondents.

Rated somewhat lower were marriage counselors, who may have different credentials from state to state. Those with the worst track record in the *CR* survey were family doctors, who relied more heavily on medications, without counseling.[23]

Certain mental-health specialists use the title "psychotherapist." The term can be confusing because, in many states, it is not defined by law, so anyone who claims to be able to help people can hang out a shingle and charge for their services. This can lead to some pretty far-out, and probably unhelpful, therapies. Psychiatrists, psychologists, and social workers are licensed in most states. In addition, other professionals like family therapists and addiction counselors may be certified in some states. Unless you are confident that you can spot a quack, make sure that the therapist you see is licensed or certified by the state or commonwealth.[24]

More important than the type of mental-health specialist is how competent he or she is and whether she is a good "fit" for you and your issues. To determine both of those factors will take a little digging:

- Order the guide that the American Psychological Association has published to help people find the right therapist.[25]

- Get recommendations from your friends, minister, priest, or rabbi.

- Tap the same sources you would use in seeking a medical doctor, such as your physician, a medical school or teaching hospital, local medical or psychiatric society.

- Contact local psychological associations, schools of social work and psychology, community mental-health centers, and women's or senior centers.

Psychiatrist Frank Pittman III believes that you should search for a therapist who is warm and optimistic, with a sense of humor. But you shouldn't pick someone who will try to protect you too much or blame everyone else for your problems:

> Psychotherapy is a process in which people in pain and/or turmoil purchase the time and expertise of a therapist who helps them: 1) define the problem; 2) figure out what normal people might do under these circumstances; 3) expose the misinformation, the misplaced loyalty, or the uncomfortable emotion that keeps the customer from doing the sensible thing; and 4) provide the customer with the courage (or fear of the therapist's disapproval) to change—that is, to do what needs to be done.[26]

Before you select a therapist, Pittman recommends that you schedule at least one session in which you conduct an interview. Pittman writes:

> Find out what sort of person the therapist is and hire a therapist who leads a life that seems desirable to you. Read anything he or she has written. Ask questions, even personal ones, about whatever you consider relevant. . . . about the therapy being proposed: how long it takes; how much it costs; and what happens if you want to drop out.[27]

Although Pittman suggests that you insist on getting answers to personal questions, that is not always realistic. Certain types of therapy necessitate keeping a therapist's personal life segregated from the therapy.[28] Other than that, Pittman's advice strikes me as sound. **Hiring a therapist is one of the most important decisions you'll make because of its potential for helping you make order out of chaos and find your way to a new life.**

Overall, Pittman recommends that, rather than looking for someone of a specific gender or religion or race, you seek someone who is sane and wise and who has "values that work." Most important is to select someone whose values you admire and whose general approach—whether it leans toward being warm

and supportive or toward being more authoritative and direc-
tive—makes it easy for you to work together.

Two therapists I interviewed believe that their effectiveness is
enhanced because they are women who have "been there too"
and so understand all the ins and outs of what their patients
have been through. Therapist Alice Umbach thinks that her
divorce is an asset because she realizes that "getting a divorce is
not a failure. It really can be an enormous step in growth."[29]
That belief makes her better able to support others who are in
the throes of a divorce. Psychotherapist Edie Irons believes that
being a widow helps her deal with the taboo topic of death. It
enables her to be "real" and "not shy" in talking about it.
"Death isn't easy to talk about, but you do need to talk about it.
There's a lot less tiptoeing around." And she thinks she can be a
model for her widowed patients. "Just by virtue of their seeing
someone who has survived, there is hope. It's like waving a flag
to show that it's possible to get through."[30]

An essential aspect of whom you select as a therapist, of
course, is whether or not you can afford him or her. Several
women who had little or no money to pay a therapist were still
able to get therapy. May, for example, used the counselors at the
senior center where she worked, and Grace got free counseling
at the community college she attended. Antoinette turned to long
telephone consultations with psychiatric nurses who were former work colleagues. And don't forget Judith, who was able to
pull off the phenomenal feat of getting therapy on credit.

But if you have to pay, you'll probably find that health insurance is pitifully inadequate. Most plans cover only 50 percent of
the cost of a limited number of visits, after "capping" bills at an
amount that is less than the therapist's actual fee.[31] Getting
access to mental-health services through a health maintenance
organization (HMO) is only feasible if you are super proficient
at getting through all the gatekeepers, and, even then, coverage
is minimal.[32] If you're stuck with all or most of the costs, as is
likely, ask if the therapist's fee is negotiable or if there is any kind

of "sliding scale" for fees (in which persons with lower incomes pay less). Many therapists offer that.[33]

ⵣⵣⵣⵣⵣ

Making It Across

Using a support group or a therapist, or both, to discharge your emotional overload might ease your journey across the tightrope to the other side of the abyss. You'll know you're there when, little by little, you can accept what has happened and start to glimpse the possibilities ahead.

How women who reached the other side were able to chart courses to new identities and lives on their own are the subject of Part Two of this book.

Part
Two

charting your own course

9

What Kind of Life Do You Want?

※※※※※※※※※※※※※※※※※※※※※※※※

In our time we have heard a great deal about people's lack of authenticity. What we cannot hear so clearly is that, for half of the population, the attempt at authenticity requires a clear and direct risk. For women to act and react out of their own being is to fly in the face of their appointed definition and their prescribed way of living. To move toward authenticity, then, also involves creation, in an immediate and pressing personal way. The whole fabric of one's life begins to change, and one sees it in a new light.

—Jean Baker Miller
Toward a New Psychology of Women[1]

※※※※※

Entering Uncharted Waters

It takes a while (for some much longer than others) after a divorce or a husband's death to get over the initial disorientation, a period one widow described as "swimming in molasses." Eventually, a widow or divorcée navigates her way out of the molasses into clear water. Like many other mature women, married and unmarried, she realizes that she has a chance to start over, to seek a more autonomous, adventurous life. But in deciding that, she is entering uncharted waters.

Part Two of this book provides a set of maps and travel tips that divorcées and widows have devised to navigate these waters, charting courses that enabled them not just to survive but to enjoy the voyage. This chapter (9) delves into how they decide what kind of lives they want. Resolving that question enables them to choose homes that keep them both safe and connected to the world (chapter 10). Knowing who they want to be empowers some to seek a career (chapter 11). Others pursue their passions for the arts, or help others, or confront the status quo (chapter 12). And such self-knowledge provides the wisdom to solve, at least temporarily, the dilemmas of sexual intimacy and whether or not to remarry (chapter 13).

Designing a life that will fit the kind of woman they want to become means, first of all, uncovering who they are—the "elusive self" that hides underneath the roles they play to be acceptable to others. To find that self, women dig deep into their pasts and recapture pieces of themselves buried along the way. They use techniques like writing autobiographies to get access to their feelings and wishes. They discover the importance of making strategic plans for their lives and work. And they unearth cores of untapped creativity and playfulness with which to express their joys and sorrows, hopes and dreams.

✕✕✕✕✕

Who Am I?

A WOMAN'S "ELUSIVE SELF"

Just like the "grief work" you need to do initially, discovering what you are going to do with the rest of your life usually involves a lot of what many therapists call "identity work" — something psychologist Lillian Rubin refers to as a "search for self." Rubin believes that women in particular can have a hard time with this identity work, especially when it entails breaking long-held habits. She writes:

> A lifetime of doing what they're supposed to do, of putting the needs and wishes of others before self, gives a particular urgency to the question, Who am I? No easy question precisely because for so long women have mystified themselves and others as they sought to comply with socially prescribed roles, sought to obey external mandates about who they are, how they should act, what they should feel.[2]

Even when a woman no longer must follow the "socially prescribed" role of wife, other "external mandates" may arise. Depending on whether she is divorced or widowed, and on physical traits like age and attractiveness, she receives specific feedback from others about how she is supposed to act, or often how *not* to act. While those expectations may not mesh with her own wishes, the need to twist herself to meet others' expectations is hard to resist.

But not all the constraints on determining her identity are external. A woman who has mainly devoted herself to being a wife and mother can be sadly lacking in self-knowledge and self-esteem, as Rubin explains:

[T]he years, the demands of family life, have taken their toll—paid in the erosion of self-confidence; in the fears that she is undisciplined, incapable of commitment, without real interests; even in her failure to know whether she "adds up to a whole person."[3]

Acknowledging her own capabilities can frighten a woman, Rubin says, because she has to come up against "the prohibitions of a lifetime—powerful prohibitions that forbid women to come into serious contact with their ability to achieve, to be powerful, to be masterful."[4]

Therapist Alice Umbach sees a lot of that fear among widows and divorcées she counsels. It explains the strong resistance she encounters among newly divorced women to examining who they are and what their lives are all about. "Women are either too scared to think about it, or they figure they're going to be married in a couple of years and they're not going to have to think about it," Umbach explains. Because of their fears, she says, "Prince Charming fantasies abound"—even among lesbians.[5]

Psychologist Andrew Morral describes another compelling internal constraint on some widows and divorcées: preconceived notions of what a divorcée or widow should feel and how she should behave. Even though a woman may have formed that image long ago, and it may have little or no relation to real-world widows and divorcées, it can still exert a kind of stranglehold. For instance, a widow who might yearn to go on a date, or laugh at a funny story, might stop herself with the thought "It would be unseemly for a widow to do" or "It would seem like I don't miss my husband or didn't love him enough." These overly conventional ideas are ways a woman tells herself that her spontaneous impulses are somehow wrong or improper, keeping her from getting in touch with what *she* is experiencing and what *she* wants for herself. Morral speculates that these fixed notions can be just as detrimental to discovering who you are as any leftover beliefs about being rescued by a Prince Charming.[6]

THREAD YOUR WAY BACK TO CHILDHOOD

One big task in your self-assessment and life-assessment is looking at the past with fresh eyes. What kind of child were you before you began to mold yourself to conform to others' expectations? Lillian Rubin believes that all of us have repressed basic parts of our natures because it was too risky to display them. Uncovering what you buried is part of your identity work. Divorcée Corinne describes it this way: "You discover that undeveloped girl you were that your husband loved in the first place. Sometimes it's that undiscovered self that's your salvation."

Psychoanalyst Helene Deutsch describes what is required in her classic work *Confrontations with Myself: An Epilogue*, written in her late eighties:

> Only when women confronted what life had laid at their feet and began to question where they themselves stood in the configurations of their life, did they become aware that they had pictured themselves happily embedded in enduring relationships. With these images shattered, they began to realize that investing in relationships without articulating a sense of self could not ensure against change, damage or loss.
>
> A woman who could respond to the disintegration of old assumptions by threading her way back to childhood and catching hold of a girl she could draw strength from and rely on matured.
>
> Women who had no such childhood self to retrieve succumbed to defeat.[7]

As the women in this book took long walks, or wrote in their journals, or read, or bared their souls to each other, they got in touch with what they had wanted for themselves when they were still growing up. Therapy was another common route to forgotten parts of themselves. Others conducted their explorations by meditating regularly, or joining a support group, or going to college, or taking courses on life planning. Some uncovered hidden parts of themselves through their work. Still others found it through creative expression, a topic we'll explore in chapter 12.

However you do it, the goal of this soul-searching is to get in touch with your interests and passions—to begin to know the real you. What you're after will not be revealed quickly. It will likely be a lifelong quest. But only by digging in and beginning, most experts agree, will you be able to use that self-knowledge to change the course of your life.[8]

AUTOBIOGRAPHY TO REWORK THE PAST: IRENE

Writing regularly in a journal is one technique for venting your feelings and charting your progress over time. Often these journals are simply diaries—full of secrets meant for no one else's eyes but your own. As useful as they may be, what happens when you take a step beyond a private journal to a narrative intended as a public chronicle of your life—a no-holds-barred autobiography?

That's a step Irene took after she had been widowed twice, first after a thirty-three-year marriage to "the love of my life," and again when her second husband died after twelve years of marriage. An important part of her life now is creating her own memoirs, intended as a legacy for her children and grandchildren—and helping other women do the same.

Irene's autobiography is the most recent step in a self-transformation that began after she and her second husband moved to California. When, after a few years there, her husband was diagnosed with Alzheimer's, she began to prospect for some meaningful activity that would give relief from her constant caregiving duties. Responding to a notice in the paper seeking mature women for volunteer counselors, she was accepted for a twelve-week training course in peer counseling. That experience, Irene claims, "just truly changed my whole life."

That was eleven years ago. Today, Irene has found a niche for herself that combines her lifelong passion for teaching with a natural aptitude for helping others. Apart from providing individual counseling to clients referred by the center who trained her, she participates in an ongoing program of courses, lectures, and weekly supervision. Immersion in this program has provided her with the prerequisites to develop and change, she explains: "I recognized that I needed to change. I wanted to, and I have. I became aware of many things about myself that I had not been aware of before. The awareness comes first, and then the desire to change."

Her capacity for change also stems from a journal group she initially co-taught with a young art therapist. The course was designed to demonstrate the idea that mature people can use autobiography—exploring and documenting their inner lives— as a technique for growth. Conceived by UCLA professor James Birren, the theory behind the course is "You don't know where you're going unless you know where you've been. Writing about the past frees you up to deal with the future and expand future relationships with other people."[9]

At the end of the first series of eight classes Irene co-taught, she began to teach on her own. She now has a group of twelve women who meet once a week to read from and discuss their journal writing:

> I don't think any of them anticipated what this would become—I certainly didn't. I didn't think it would end so beautifully in this wonderful group I have. I think of it as a writing group and as a therapy group and as a bonded group of women. For some of them—like a woman who has leukemia—there is really nothing as important in their lives.

Irene describes the purpose of the group as twofold: "to learn more about ourselves and to leave a legacy for our children." The women feel free to write about everything, warts and all, because in that way, they let their families know that "we're human. . . . We go way back into our selves and lives." An article about Irene and the journal group quotes a recent widow as saying:

> All I could see in screaming blinking lights was the word "widow," which, for me, meant my life was over. The people who I thought would be supportive reacted like I had a plague and I was busy making them feel comfortable. But the journal group came through for me, even when I said negative things about my husband.[10]

In addition to leading the group, Irene participates in it by sharing her own writing with the members. She credits her participation as one reason why "I have changed more myself the past ten years than during my whole life." Being able to be more open about herself has meant that her relationship with her grown children is not just "different, it's wonderful. Before, I wanted my children to think of me as the perfect mother. My relationship with my children changed completely when I was able to let that go, and let them know that I was letting it go."

WRITE ABOUT YOUR MARGINS

By combining elements of memoir writing and group therapy, Irene's group has made a big difference in its participants' lives. But even when the therapy component is absent, **writing about yourself and your life can be important in your identity work.** Irene points out why:

> Now we all realize that the more we write, the better we write, and that writing triggers memory. Our primary purpose is to learn more about ourselves; as we uncover the past, we glean a better understanding of the present and future, thus recognizing increased value in ourselves and in our lives.

Writer Tee Corinne, who also teaches a class on memoir writing, agrees with Irene about its main value. Corinne says her community education students come in with clear ideas about what and for whom they want to write. Still, she pushes them to write first and foremost for themselves, to use writing as a way to understand their lives:

I'm looking for ways to give my students permission to write about their own margins, the things they think they can't say or that no one wants to hear. I ask them, "What is it that you want people to know about you that they won't know unless you tell them?"[11]

Another writing teacher, Janet Lynn Roseman, became involved with women writing their autobiographies after she continually heard belittling comments among her female university students about both their writing and their lives. So Roseman started an autobiography writing workshop with the specific goal of empowering women through writing. In Roseman's book *The Way of the Woman Writer,* she writes, "I believe that writing one's life not only serves as a personal guide to understanding one's past, but frequently can point the way to one's future."[12]

Accessing All Your Parts:
Hannelore Hahn and the IWWG

Another woman who stumbled upon the importance of writing autobiography—by writing one of her own—is Hannelore Hahn. Not only did the process of writing her memoirs help Hahn find herself, she also cites it as the main reason she founded, in 1976, the International Women's Writing Guild (IWWG).

Hahn is now executive director of the IWWG, which counts some three thousand women writers as its members.[13] But when she took the initial steps to set up the guild, Hahn says, she had "no real blueprint" for the organization or for the role it would play. Instead, she recalls, "Everything I did, I did because I needed it. . . . And what I needed most was to see who I was."[14] In communicating with other women writers and setting up meetings and workshops, she always chose themes dealing with autobiography, memoirs, or a journal—or any other writing she believed was aimed at "trying to find a sense of self."

It was a self she had been searching for since she and her family fled Nazi Germany of the United States when she was ten years old. In her twenties, after attending college in California, Hahn settled into married life, bearing one daughter before she divorced in her early thirties. Although she says, "I always had a feeling I was somebody," she remembers feeling especially confused just before her divorce about who that somebody was. She even asked a friend, "But who will I be when I'm not Mrs. Stoumen?"[15]

Some thirteen years later, while feverishly vacuuming a rug, Hahn had a sudden flash of anger at a small incident from the past. "That's when I exchanged the vacuum cleaner for the pen," she writes in the guild's newsletter, *Network*. She sat down and began what was to become her autobiography, a writing process that took ten years. During that time, she founded the IWWG, settled on a new identity as a writer, and in 1982 published her memoirs.[16]

Hahn's belief in the importance of writing autobiography has given two ideas salience in the IWWG. One is that everyone's life is a worthy subject. When a woman writes about her life, Hahn says, she gives value to her personal experiences and engages in "a process of reflection, re-examination, re-evaluation and a re-setting of herself vis-à-vis life." The second idea is that through writing we can integrate hidden parts of ourselves and become whole. She writes that "we access, through writing, all of our parts—the used, the less used, the atrophied and the buried—and in becoming whole, transform ourselves, and possibly, the world. . . ."[17]

<hr />

Translate Your Dreams into a Plan

What You Can Gain from Planning

"Most women spend more time planning a two-week vacation than they do planning their own lives," says Joan Kurianski, a former executive director of the Older Women's League (OWL).[18]

A number of women I interviewed, however, both widowed and divorced, believe strongly that planning was important in their ability to turn their lives around. When Grace, the mother of three children, decided to divorce, she was in dire straits. She had only a poverty-level income and a high school education. So Grace decided to earn a college degree. She set that goal even though she had never set any goals for herself—in order to feel in charge of her life.

Grace describes her college graduation day as "the highest point of my life. If you could just imagine what I felt like when I walked across that platform." With that success, she made goal-setting part of her life. Even though it seemed a little overwhelming, she set simultaneous goals—for making money (with a vengeance), for physical and emotional self-improvement, and for having her social needs met. Grace gives this advice to others who are single-again:

> You've got to have goals for every area to maintain a balance. You set the goals and they just kind of happen. Regaining control is by setting goals. You just don't set them for today or tomorrow. You set them for down the road. You give yourself plenty of time. And you always allow yourself to be able to change them.

When I met her, Grace had made a phenomenal trip up the ladder in a male-dominated profession. But at fifty-seven, one of the oldest in her company, she had hit the glass ceiling. So she was using a career development course to identify her goals for the rest of her working life. Happy and self-assured, she seemed confident that this round of new goal-setting will lead to as much success as ever. I have no reason to doubt it.

WHAT DO YOU LOVE TO DO?

Any system of career planning or time management can work only if you know your values and are willing to make your priorities reflect them. A time management course I took, for example, began by teaching all the simple rules, like breaking down larger tasks into manageable portions. But then came the hard part—assigning all your tasks a priority. Before you could do that, you had to identify what was most important.

Entrepreneur Rebecca Maddox recognizes the difficulty women have with this prioritizing and has written a book on the subject, *Inc. Your Dreams*.[19] While on the surface the book is about whether you should go into business for yourself, it is really about discovering your dreams and pursuing them. Maddox is a strong believer in having whatever you do reflect your core values and interests. She has put together a range of techniques like writing a journal, imaging, and other exercises in self-exploration for discovering those values. Women especially need to do these exercises, Maddox writes, because

> No one ever really taught **any** of us how to make decisions. Certainly, no one shared with us a process for finding out what we love to do. We have been taught to look to the outside to find the answer, to quickly grab hold of any likely alternative **out there**.[20]

There are other tried-and-true approaches for uncovering what you're good at and love to do. One proposed by Richard Bolles in his classic *What Color Is Your Parachute?* is called "mirroring."[21] You start by listing the people you value, writing down what qualities you like best about each one. Then put one check beside those qualities you'd like to have more of, and two checks beside those qualities you already possess. That will give you a good idea of who you are and who you want to be. Mirroring is a process that works, Bolles says, because people taught not to boast and brag may find it easier to think about what they admire in their friends than in themselves.[22]

Another simple technique is called "Fifty Things to Do Before I Die." The idea is to put together a list of fifty things you absolutely don't want to miss out on before your time is up. At first, making the list may feel like a lark. But as it begins to take form, you realize that it reveals a lot about what you believe is important.

Writer Wendy Swallow Williams relates how the act of making such a list helped her sort out some priorities. Later, when she looked back on the list, Williams writes, she learned "some startling things." Although some items on the list, like learning to rollerblade, weren't all that important, she found others, like publishing a novel, to be quite "intimidating":

> because they mean a serious commitment of some sort. . . . These things won't fall in my lap. If I'm going to accomplish them, I need to start building for them now. . . . The list has items I've thought about for years, dreams I've carried with me since I was young, or things that resonated when I first heard about them.[23]

Williams is now a convert to the idea of articulating her dreams as a way of "preparing the ground so that life [can] work in mysterious ways." She quotes a friend who has accomplished amazing things as saying, "If you want your ship to come in, you must build a dock."

Making Your Choices

Exercises to find your values are helpful, but after the lists are complete, you still have to make choices. That can be both difficult and anxiety-provoking simply because when you select one path over another, you will probably have to give up hope of traveling down other paths—at least in *this* life!

Because choosing your future direction is so hard and so personal, only you can know how you should go about it. One woman who invented a technique that served her well over the course of her life was Leona, an impressive seventy-one-year-old who has been divorced for forty years. Leona's story of working to support herself and her daughter as a young divorced African American in the segregated South of the fifties and sixties was full of hardship and pathos. But her honesty, hard work, and entrepreneurial spirit brought her through. Her mantra as she talked to me was "It was rough. But I managed."

To manage on her own for so many years, Leona describes a kind of ritual she uses whenever she has a hard decision to make. Her initial step is to clear her mind. To do that she first goes to sleep. Then at two or three in the morning, she gets out of bed and meditates or reads spiritual books. "And once I'm clear and focused, I'll put everything down, drop everything then and there, and try to figure out a way to do it. Sometimes I am up and down all night." She alternately prays, reads spiritual books, and focuses on her problem, "until God or whatever spiritual being is out there gives me the idea or the insight to go forth and do what's best for me."

Leona's method of turning inward to make important decisions has served her well. She was able gradually to move from working as a nursemaid, to doing payroll in a garment factory, to being top salesperson for a cosmetics line (which allowed her to send her daughter to college), to holding increasingly responsible secretarial jobs with the school system. Along the way, she began to invest in run-down real estate, fixing it up and renting it out, then eventually selling it for a profit.

Now semi-retired, she works weekends as a computer operator at a medical center and is an active member of a number of volunteer organizations, including the Atlanta chapter of OWL. Recognizing real quality when they see it, OWL has trained Leona, who was operated on ten years ago for breast cancer, as a volunteer counselor to teach other women about detecting breast cancer.

When Not Planning *Is* Planning

To begin planning your new life on your own, first set a broad, fairly long-term goal—to get a better job in three years, for example. Then, begin to work toward your goal. Break it down into several objectives, each achievable within a shorter time frame. Make a list of tasks that would lead to each objective, and assign those tasks to certain months and years.

This is classic planning technique, and it's also common sense. A lot of women who took charge of their lives were just following the basic technique, even if they didn't know it. Sally, for example, picked out a whole range of tasks that would be "firsts" for her. Even though she didn't say so, they were all aimed at one goal: becoming more independent. Each task she chose, like taking a trip on her own, she would be doing for the first time all by herself. "I had a list of firsts in my mind. Getting over the divorce has been an enormous process of doing and checking off one thing at a time. All the things I did for me on my own for the first time were turning points." The direction in which they turned her was toward a new, more autonomous life.

Not only were women doing basic planning when they didn't call it that, but I believe that quite a few *were* planning when they claimed *not* to be—like May, who made a highly successful career after her husband died when she was forty-nine. May says she never sets firm goals or objectives. But she does admit to taking advantage of opportunities when they came her way.

Lucille is another one who claims it was not necessary for her to make a conscious effort to change when she evolved from a frightened ex-wife with a drinking problem to an autonomous professional who teaches, writes, and counsels about wellness. For her, the way to move ahead is "just get out of the way and let it happen."

But I don't really buy it—that these women were as fatalistic as they claim, waiting around for something to fall in their laps that they could take advantage of. **The successful women who say they never planned their lives all have a very good notion of who they are and what they want in their new lives.** They have developed confidence in their own self-efficacy and built the dock that Wendy Williams described. But they didn't just sit and wait for a ship to come into port. They sent out tugboats to actively search for ships they could steer their way.

DARING TO DREAM

Many women I interviewed were quite happy with the way their lives had evolved as singles and wanted them to stay basically the same. But there were others who startled me by describing some fairly ambitious dreams for their future.

Take Sue Ellen, who claimed that everything had just happened to her. Sue Ellen is an enthusiastic woman of sixty-nine, who describes herself and her past with a delightful mix of humor and gravity. Married for thirty-five years to her first husband before he walked out on her, she is "living in sin" with a man—thrilled at having found her first exciting sexual relationship. In the throes of moving to a house they are building in the country, her life is full of excitement—socializing with her family and her grown children, traveling all over the world (she's been to over fifty countries), working on projects like helping women invest in Kurdistan. "None of that would have happened if I'd stayed with my husband," Sue Ellen comments. "I'd be off doing things *he* enjoyed."

Asked how she sees herself five years from now, Sue Ellen replies, "Sitting on a movie set." She tells me a tale of a bizarre trip she took that summer in Russia with a "bodyguard"—really the brother of a Russian friend—who fought with her continuously until they became fast friends. She wants to write a movie script based on this experience and has already pitched the story idea to a young director she knows. Her idea would be to write the script in her new home looking out on the Blue Ridge mountains. Making a movie is a dream she's been working on since her retirement, Sue Ellen confesses.

It's not exactly what I expected—this ambitious, possibly even far-fetched scheme for her future. But maybe that's because I'm not immune to the stereotypes about women of that age—which would preclude them from dreaming in such a grandiose fashion (unless, of course, they're rich), let alone trying to put those dreams into action.

Another woman who made me realize I had some fixed notions was Dorothy—but in this case the stereotypes were about what's an appropriate dream for single women with little or no money. Like Sue Ellen, Dorothy is also lively and articulate, talking about her experiences with humor, common sense, and intelligence. Sixty-six now, Dorothy left New York and her husband of thirty-two years when she was fifty-two, because, she says, he retired too early and "he just got on my last nerve." Even though he was a good provider and they had a brand-new house, they had begun to argue and bicker. Realizing that her mother had lived until she was ninety-four, she said to herself, "I might live another fifty years. Let me get out of here."

Dorothy had worked as a temporary secretary while she was raising her three children, which gave her very good skills, as well as self-confidence and a good deal of flexibility. So when she arrived in Philadelphia, where her daughter lived, she found a job right away, becoming a permanent secretary at a university after working only three weeks as a temporary. She settled into a house there with money from the divorce settlement and was very happy "because they have a lot of activist women there. I just had a ball."

But Dorothy's mother needed her in Atlanta, so she moved once again. She was dismayed to discover that being African American in the South wasn't all that different from what it had been like when she was growing up there. She finds Atlantans to be "weird" and life in Atlanta to be so different from life in New York and Philadelphia, where people of different classes mix and are "faster on the draw."

To compensate, she started a class to learn Spanish, joined activist organizations like the National Caucus on the Black Aged and OWL, and found a couple of friends to accompany her to casinos and yard sales. Still, she wants more of a challenge, as well as a way to find a niche for herself in this somewhat alien environment.

Dorothy is working on a dream: to set up and run a mortgage

company that would specialize in loans to young women with children. The company would acquire inexpensive houses, then resell them to working women with children, giving them classes on how to manage money and deducting their mortgage payments directly from their paychecks. She has taken a course at the Small Business Administration, but knows that to go any further she will need investors or donated funds. Although she has begun looking, she says, so far "it's like a brick wall."

I didn't probe very far into Dorothy's dream when she described it to me, probably because I wasn't expecting to hear such an ambitious, entrepreneurial scheme. But my (and others') stereotypes about Sue Ellen and Dorothy haven't prevented them from dreaming and scheming. Eschewing what an "appropriate" role would be for a mature single woman, they and others are taking full advantage of being able to do what they want and aren't terribly afraid of failure.

⚏⚏⚏⚏⚏

Simply for the Joy of It: Claim Your Fantasies

AN ALTER-EGO AS INSPIRATION

Prince Charming is only one of the myths women absorb— from nursery rhymes, popular songs, and movies. Ridding yourself of all that brainwashing is a formidable task, one to which scholar and feminist Carolyn Heilbrun is devoted. Heilbrun maintains that only recently have women come to recognize that these myths, which she calls "narratives," control their lives. But by questioning those narratives, Heilbrun believes, women can begin to write new ones for themselves.[24]

In her book *Writing a Woman's Life*, Heilbrun describes how in 1964 she began a new narrative for her life when she took the pen name Amanda Cross in order to write detective novels. Heilbrun hid this identity as a writer of pulp fiction to protect herself from being denied tenure at Columbia University (which she eventually got—the first female to do so). But in hindsight she perceives that she was also exploring an "alter ego"—a different identity for herself. That alter ego took the form of the private-eye heroine of the series, Kate Fansler, who like Heilbrun is an English professor at a big city university. Heilbrun describes Fansler this way:

> I created a fantasy. Without children, unmarried, unconstrained by the opinions of others, rich and beautiful, the newly created Kate Fansler now appears to me as a figure out of never-never land. . . . I wanted to give her everything and see what she could do with it. . . .
> [C]reating Kate Fansler and her quests, I was recreating myself. . . . Amanda Cross could write, in the unimportant form of detective fiction, the destiny she hoped for women, if not exactly, any longer, for herself: the alternate life she wished to inscribe upon the female imagination.[25]

Heilbrun never lived out her fantasy in the sense of totally reinventing herself. She stayed in her long-term marriage and continued as an academic for many years. But both the footloose, fictional Kate Fansler and the women's movement had an impact on her. She began to take risks and to reveal much about her personal experiences. Then, in 1992, she resigned her teaching position in protest against the dearth of women in Columbia's English department.

Now Heilbrun speaks around the country to women's groups, urging them to question everything they feel they have to do—the narratives that control them—and not to be afraid to live unconventional lives. She tells them, "The point is to have an adventure, to do something else and realize that the struggle [itself] is the point."[26] It's worth noting that Heilbrun did *not* have to become single first to undertake those adventures. She can serve as inspiration for all of us, married and unmarried, who would like to look for new directions in our lives.

MAKE YOURSELF HAPPY

Another way women get in touch with their fantasies is by doing something for the sheer joy of it. A number of women spoke of the enormous pleasure they got from dancing. Lucille found a whole new side to herself after she got up her nerve and enrolled in a ballroom dancing class. Not only did she get to dance with everyone, but she met her next husband there. Felicia was all seriousness with me until she began to describe her "wild enthusiasm" for her new passion, contra dancing. She surprised me, as did several women who took up ballroom dancing with a vengeance: Roz who "danced like crazy all winter"; and Lucille, who met her husband-to-be in ballroom dancing classes and now competes as his partner in amateur contests.

Several added a passion for music to their lives. Fifty-seven-year-old divorcée Isabel took up singing at open mikes at area clubs and restaurants and began Italian lessons so she can sing Neapolitan songs. She hopes eventually she'll get to Italy so she can sing at bars there. Carol took advantage of her earlier education in music to learn to play the mountain dulcimer. Performing and teaching the instrument now provide their own intrinsic rewards, including a good part of her social life and opportunities to travel.

As we'll explore in chapter 12, "Pursue Your Passion," other women discovered gratification through the arts. Evelyn began playing the piano and painting again—things she didn't have time to do when she was married. "I realized I needed to stay in touch with what makes me creative, because being creative is really centering for me," she explains. Jeanette rediscovered her love for acting when she auditioned for a little theater role after her husband died. She had acted in college, and so when a friend invited her to go, she thought, "Why not?" The audition was so much fun, Jeanette says, that she told her friend, "I could go on auditioning for the rest of my life."

Once on their own, many women unearth a totally new desire for learning. Returning to school, they are often surprised at how much pleasure they get from their classes—even when they had neither liked school before nor considered themselves smart. An article in *The Washington Post* describes two widowed sisters, Jessie Dodge and Beulah Walker, who stumbled into a lifelong quest for learning after both their husbands died in 1978. Every semester since, these rural Virginia housewives have taken an average of three college courses. For eight of those years, they even drove sixty miles round-trip to attend William and Mary College.[27]

Sometimes interests become consuming passions. One widow's interest in genealogy developed into a hobby that led her to master the computer. She happily uses that computer several days a week now, writing a newsletter and compiling guides to local genealogical records. Two widows, Julia and Edith, shared a lifelong passion for weaving and textiles. They met while studying those topics at a local museum and have both become volunteer docents and important resources for that museum.

INDULGE IN TRAVEL

For dozens of women, travel is another passion. Many had to force themselves to take their first trip after they became single. But after one or two trips, exploring new parts of the world began to play an essential role in expanding the scope of their lives. May is one. She carefully puts aside enough money for one trip out of the country every year.

Asked what travel does for her, May answers, "It just makes my whole life richer. I feel a greater sense of responsibility for the whole world." She adds, "I figure that travel is part of my investment for my older age. I'll have all these memories and I can sit and think about them. I think memories are very important."

May also explains why she likes to travel with another woman:

> I think that women are willing to travel a little more simply. You don't have to have the best hotel accommodations. You don't have to eat the most enormous meals. You might spend more time getting acquainted with the country and sightseeing.

In her book *Travelers' Tales: A Woman's World*, Marybeth Bond concurs:

> As I became aware of other women's travel experiences, I also began to be aware that women travel quite differently than men do, that we look for different things, we stop for different reasons, our goals and style are different, and what we take from our travels is different. . . .
>
> When we travel, we pause more to listen, assimilate, to move in and out of the lives of those we meet on the way. Where women go, relationships follow, from encounters with nature to special moments of connection and friendship with others.[28]

One way that women are able to travel on their own safely and inexpensively is by spending time in the homes of people they know around the world. Sue Ellen, for example, is able to travel on a small budget by taking advantage of all the hospitality she and her ex-husband had offered visiting foreigners who belonged to the same Catholic action group. (One year there were 250 visitors in her home.) Now, Sue Ellen says, "I can go anywhere in the world and visit families—Argentina, anyplace. I've been in over fifty, maybe sixty countries."

Single-again women can also find camaraderie and stimulation by combining travel with education or voluntary service in sites all over the world. They go to places that tourists never go, live with the natives, and participate in projects like archeological digs. The organization Earthwatch, for example, sponsors trips to more than fifty countries to assist scientific expeditions in areas like rain forest conservation, marine studies, art, and archeology. (Information on contacting Earthwatch is included in the Resources section, chapter 9.)

Divorced writer Elsie Bliss is also an advocate of solo travel. She believes that people find a woman traveling alone to be admirable, even fascinating. In fact, one seatmate on a plane to London eventually proposed to her. (She turned him down.) She also enjoyed the company of an American man in Paris when the hotel assigned them to the same room on the assumption that they were both Americans and wouldn't mind. But she advises that the extra cost for a single room is "the best money you'll ever spend."[29]

Complement Identity Work with Identity Play

Women on their own often discover for the first time the value of doing something for its own sake—or, put more simply, of playing. Asked what had been important to them in rediscovering themselves, they told me about kayaking, camping, mountain climbing, making a movie, investing in the stock market, taking exotic classes, weightlifting, you name it. A few took up some fairly wild hobbies, like Jill, who ventured into whitewater rafting. I wasn't that surprised to learn that Fiona had taken up beading and antique collecting, but found not exactly predictable her involvement with the Fortean Society, a group that collects and reports anomalies—things that can't happen but do, like circles that appear in the carpet and then magically disappear.

Widow Julia took to her hobby of pottery with a vengeance, leaving her chaotic life behind while she went off for six months to take lessons at a resort in Mexico. And after she saw a friend wearing a clown costume, Tilly picked a hobby that delights herself and others. She got a clown costume of her own and wears it to visit patients in the hospital, as well as to bazaars and her grandchildren's parties. Behind the mask, Tilly says, she loses all her inhibitions, singing and dancing with abandon.

Social scientists who study play define it as something you do for the pure pleasure of it—"the outward expression of some deep, presumably joyful urge."[30] Dutch anthropologist Johan Huizinga was one of the first to describe the play state, which is quite distinct from other states in several respects. According to Huizinga:

- Play is absorbing and exists outside of ordinary life.

- It is safe but has elements of uncertainty, or illusion.

- It is limited by rules of time and space.

- It provides both pleasure and relief.

- It allows you to step outside yourself for a while, "to goof off," even to make a fool of yourself.

- At play, you have higher-than-normal levels of confidence with which to experiment with roles and tasks you might not otherwise try.[31]

Play is important, then, not just because of how much fun it is or the relief it gives from stress and worries. **Doing something simply for the joy of it allows you to try out parts of yourself that will give new meaning to life on your own. So add to the "identity work" you should do the idea of "identity play."**

In her article "Single Bliss," author Elsie Bliss makes a strong case for single people taking the initiative to make this kind of play happen:

> I believe that you should indulge yourself, love yourself, do something wonderful for yourself. Liberate yourself from fear, from sorrow, from frustration. Create a memory for yourself by yourself. Plan a beautiful day, weekend, or week for yourself, instead of waiting for someone else to suggest it. Nobody cares as much as you do, yourself, how happy you are and how you feel. . . .
>
> Carrying out plans like these is easier for the single person because he or she does not have to consult with

anybody and consider other priorities to be able to spend for such a seemingly frivolous thing as FUN.[32]

When women take time out to play, their enthusiasm is often stoked by thoughts of "It's now or never" or of needing to make up for lost time. Some make fun a priority to ease the pain of loss and carve out a fulfilling life as a single person. Others feel that after years of putting themselves second, they can finally give themselves permission to transcend former self-images and to find fun and satisfaction in the process. Obviously, having fun is something you can also choose to do when you're married or unmarried, with or without a partner. Either way, it's a fine idea.

In her book *New Passages*, writer Gail Sheehy examines the need to do identity work to reach a level of maturity she calls "Second Adulthood"—a stage she defines as "a stable psychological state of mastery, where we control much of what happens in our life and can often act on the world, rather than habitually react to what the world throws at us." Reaching that state, Sheehy says,

> requires a new focus, energy, discipline, and a whole set of strategies. It must be done consciously. . . .
> [I]n order to participate in the potentials and rewards offered by a Second Adulthood, we must construct our own new second adult identity. Sooner is better than later. It means throwing off all the old stereotypes, letting go of outgrown priorities, and developing real clarity about what is most relevant in our lives for the future.[33]

While creating a new identity is optional for married women, it is a necessity for newly single women if they want to break out of the limited roles our society assigns to them as appropriate to their ages and status as widows or divorcées. The women I describe in this book found a range of original ways to do that identity work. They can serve as guides for other single-again women who want to chart a course to a new life.

10

A Nest
of Your Own

*Where we come from in America no longer signifies—it's where
we go, and what we do when we get there, that tells us who we
are.*

—Joyce Carol Oates
"American Gothic"[1]

When you are married, deciding where you and your family will live involves some compromises—something married women know a lot about. When you become single after many years of marriage, you confront a decision you may be making alone for the first time in your life: where to live?

For most of us, our home represents much more than just a residence. It is a place where you can feel safe, warm, cozy, emotionally sheltered, where you can let go of pretenses and be yourself. One common fear among women—of becoming bag ladies—encompasses not just a fear of poverty but also a fear of having no place to call home.[2] Your surroundings reflect your sense of yourself and of whom you want to become. And they exert an influence of their own by their fit or lack of fit with your internal evolution.

This chapter covers the advantages and disadvantages of the various choices women make about where to live when they are single-again. These choices include

- staying put, at least for a while;
- pulling up stakes;
- changing homes a number of times;
- living in nontraditional families or retirement housing; and
- living alone.

Whatever you choose, you'll know it's right when it provides a good mix of independence and support for your evolving life.

⁂⁂⁂⁂⁂

Stay Put to Get Your Bearings

BALANCE FINANCES AND EMOTIONS

For many women making the transition to being single-again, whether to move from their current home is not even an issue.

They are not willing to uproot themselves from the homes or neighborhoods where they feel comfortable and nourished. Their lives are already in chaos, and they don't want any more stress. So they decide to stay put in the same houses or neighborhoods.

That's what magazine editor Michelle did when she bought a home in the same neighborhood with her share of the proceeds from selling their home after her divorce. She bought a smaller house nearby, she says, because she had a child at home and "that allowed me to keep the same support system. Because when you're in an emotional state and your finances are a question mark, just the fact that you're going to the same grocery store every day is a support."

Most experts would say she did the right thing. Decisions made during a highly emotional time do not always work out. New widows, for example, trying wildly to take charge of their lives, can sell their family home and move in with their children. But that decision is not necessarily in their best interests financially or emotionally, and it is often irreversible.[3]

Most experts warn against making a major decision that cannot be rescinded during the first year or two following a major upheaval like death or divorce. In a crisis, financial interests often receive less attention than emotional ones. When things calm down and a widow or divorcée realizes she has lost considerable income from a precipitous move, or she misjudged how the move would affect her emotionally, she can have major regrets.[4]

Consult an accountant or financial planner. He or she will look at the pros and cons of various living arrangements from a purely monetary point of view—taxes, market conditions, and the like—adding a practical, hard-headed perspective to the emotional wrestling that precedes a decision about where to live.[5]

Stability as a Double-Edged Sword

Jocelyn, a psychotherapist, has remained in her home since her husband died of cancer eight years ago. At forty-two, Jocelyn had been married sixteen years when her husband's death left her in charge of two teenage children from his prior marriage, two pre-teenage children from their marriage—and a shaky financial future. "I went very quickly from being in a marvelously happy, shared-work, shared-sense-of-responsibility marriage to being on my own," Jocelyn remembers.

A quirk in the state law denied Jocelyn her husband's pension, but she was determined to stay in the house where her two children were born—to keep their lives stable and to preserve the sense of belonging she feels there. "I'm held up by this community," Jocelyn explains. She used the proceeds of her husband's life insurance to pay off the mortgage on the house. Now she works very hard to make enough money to meet their other expenses and to pay college tuitions.

Jocelyn has no regrets about the decision. "I've loved the continuity. . . . It's a source of enormous strength to all three of us," she says. Although the house needs repairs, it reflects their family history and connects them all to their husband and father. She especially loves all the shelves and furniture that her husband built himself: "In many ways, that's enormously comforting and joyous to me."

Jocelyn's life is very much the same as before her husband died. She is doing the same work, only much more of it, and her friends are also the same—their joint friends have continued to include her in everything they do. There are only a few things wrong with her new life, she says. The main thing is that she still misses her husband "enormously." Vivid dreams about him continue to awaken her, momentarily providing the illusion that he's not really dead. And because she socializes with the same married couples, she rarely meets anyone single. She is so comfortable, Jocelyn says, that she hasn't needed "to reach out and make a new world for myself."

Margie also stayed in her home after she and her husband

divorced, but with a different outcome. Margie is sixty-eight years old, divorced for eighteen years after a twenty-seven-year marriage to a minister. She lives in the same house where they lived together for many years—a cozy, well-worn suburban ranch, comfortably furnished and full of knickknacks and souvenirs accumulated over a lifetime.

When her husband left her, Margie decided to stay. By working long hours in her job counseling and teaching at a community college, she managed to get by as well as pay off the mortgage. But after she retired, she found she couldn't make ends meet. She had only a tiny pension from her teaching, no claim on her husband's pension, and no benefits from Social Security because of complicated offset rules that would have cut deeply into her pension.

So Margie had to go back to work part-time. She rents out her basement to a tenant, someone she sees rarely and who has little in common with her. Not only does her work mean she has little time to enjoy her house and lovely perennial garden, but she finds that, unlike Jocelyn, she doesn't feel connected to her neighborhood. She describes it as a kind of "yuppieville" made up of mostly younger working people with families. She is thinking seriously of selling the house and moving on.

Margie's support is elsewhere, among the women she teaches and mentors, other women friends, and her grown children. She loves her work because the women think so highly of her. And by encouraging other women to take big steps and expand themselves—go beyond their fears—she is also encouraging herself to do the same.

Jocelyn and Margie were seeking the same things—stability and community—when, despite the financial burdens, they decided to remain in the same homes once they were single. But the contrast between their lives couldn't be sharper— Jocelyn finding support from staying put and Margie feeling alienated. Still, Jocelyn's decision to keep her lifestyle the same as when her husband was alive may be one of the reasons that she finds herself now, eight years after her husband died, continuing to grieve. Margie, on the other hand, was forced—initially by her estrangement from her husband and then by feeling distant from her neighborhood—to seek a new life. She has succeeded in putting her married self behind her and has moved on to showing other women how to make their own life transitions.

CLAIM YOUR TURF AS YOUR OWN

If you, like many women, initially decide that moving out of your current home would be either too stressful or too expensive, you may choose to stay put for now. And while remaining in your old milieu, you will likely come to a point in time when you take hold of what was once joint property and make it your own.

Roz decided to redecorate the house she and her husband had shared "from top to bottom—absolutely everything. I just wanted it to be my house now." The brighter, cheerier decor reflects her optimism rather than her husband's somberness. Her husband thought it was important too. When he saw the remodeled house while attending their daughter's wedding, he agreed with Roz that it was time to make the divorce final.

Another divorcée, Evelyn, describes going through a similar process after she and her husband separated:

> The first thing I did was to completely change the whole house around. I had to make it my own. I washed all the walls to kind of wash him out of the house. I changed my bedroom around. I bought new linens. I love my house. I just wanted to make it more my own, to make it reflect my choices. I did some kind of wild things I knew he wouldn't approve of, or he would have argued with me about.

FIND WAYS TO AFFORD IT

If you are determined to stay in your home for emotional reasons but can't afford it, explore a few options that might make it possible.

- *Rent out space.* If you're an extrovert, like Darleen, it can add real spice to your life. Darleen rents to five boarders at a time, mostly people who come from a medical school and research facilities that are within walking distance. She especially likes the diversity of her housemates. They eat communally and take turns shopping and cooking. This setup works because Darleen is not uptight about her belongings or about everything being exactly where it should be. And although she loves getting to know her boarders, Darleen can also have privacy when she wants it because her office and bedroom can be shut off from the rest of the house.

- *Add a separate apartment unit or two.* The women who are able to do this own homes with some equity in them (the difference between your debt on your house and its current value) and finance the renovation by taking out a new mortgage or a home equity loan. In the course of adding rental space, they can also make the house safer and easier to keep up. The rent then covers the new mortgage payments. An accountant can tell you whether this approach will work for you.

- *If you're over sixty-two and have a great deal of equity in your house, obtain a reverse mortgage.* Once fairly exotic, reverse mortgages are now moving into the mainstream as a result of becoming available through branches of the Federal National Mortgage Association (Fannie Mae). Rather than your paying a lender, a reverse mortgage gives you monthly payments, based on the value of your home, up to a limit. You don't have to qualify on the basis of income or credit, and you need not pay the loan back until you sell the house, move out, or die. [6]

⬡⬡⬡⬡⬡

Move as a Declaration of Independence

A New Home = A New Life

There are often good emotional and financial reasons why it makes sense for you to remain on familiar turf. **But sometimes, staying on just reinforces your sense of being victimized by your situation. That's what many single-again women conclude when they signify—to themselves and to the world—their intention to begin a new life by pulling up stakes and moving on.**

Joy immediately understood the meaning of "having the rug pulled out from under you" when her husband asked for a divorce after twenty-six years of marriage because he had found someone else. Although she was knocked off her pins by her husband's announcement, she immediately refused to stay in their big house in Virginia with their youngest child, a fifteen-year old son, while her husband went off to his "little bachelor pad." She found an apartment for herself and, to her husband's dismay, signed a one-year lease and moved out, leaving her son in her husband's care.

The new apartment was Joy's declaration that she wasn't about to become the victim of their divorce. Moving into a small apartment, after years of living in big homes with her family, was not a hardship. What was hard for her was the initial emotional adjustment to being on her own, which showed up first when she found herself in a grocery store trying to shop for one.

A lot of women really enjoy moving into smaller, more manageable quarters, ones they can easily put their own stamp on. They talk about the pleasure of having their own nests, usually for the first time in their lives. The emotional part of a move can

188

be difficult, however, when it entails giving up supports they took for granted in their former homes.

Psychotherapist Audrey McCollum found when she studied women (mostly married) who had moved to a new community that many of them suffered intense feelings of loss, disorientation, confusion, and loss of control. The women were often dismayed by the strength of their feelings. "Moving is like dying," one woman told her. Only one-third of the women she studied had adapted to their new surroundings at the end of the two-year study.[7]

If moving is that difficult for married women, how could it be any easier for those who are unmarried? It isn't, and for an obvious reason. As gerontologist Jacquelyn Mattfeld concluded from her study of older women living alone in urban areas

> for almost all of these old women, close relationships with select family members and friends were tremendously important, more important than those at any previous time in their lives. Older women need to keep this in mind when considering relocation that could disrupt or greatly reduce those aspects of their close relationships that they most prize.

Mattfeld's word of caution can apply to women of all ages, not just older ones. **When moving, try to make choices that will allow you to maintain as many important friendships as possible.**

FIND SURROUNDINGS TO FIT THE NEW YOU

Two women I interviewed, one a widow and the other a divorcée, concluded early on that they no longer fit in the suburban settings where they had spent their married lives. They headed in opposite directions to wholly new lives—one to the city and the other to the country. In making those moves, they both had to resist pressures from well-meaning friends and relatives who thought the moves too risky, or inappropriate, or whose own interests conflicted with the best interests of these women. Trusting their own instincts about what they wanted and needed in their surroundings, each found a satisfying new life on her own.

While many of the women I interviewed who had made major moves were still relatively young at the time, being older does not have to be a deterrent. Doris Grumbach, a novelist and critic, took a giant leap just as she was turning seventy—from city life in Washington, D.C., to rural life in Maine. She apparently took it all in stride, turning her experiences into grist for two more books, *Extra Innings* and one on her experiences living completely alone.[8]

Another older woman, widowed for fourteen years, moved from her home of sixty-seven years to another state to be nearer her daughter and two grandchildren. Writing to *Modern Maturity* magazine, she enthuses, "I'm 72, full of arthritis, walk with a cane, and am a very happy person. Everyone has trials and tribulations, but you can't sit around feeling sorry for yourself. Get up and get moving!"[9]

In her book *The Fountain of Age*, Betty Friedan tells about people who moved a number of times until they found a home that could be an "enabler" of their struggles to remain vital as they age. She concludes that although some moves only serve to show what a person really needs from a home, precipitating another move, eventually you will find a place that permits you both to stay yourself and to change.[10] And this is all part of healthy aging. Friedan writes:

> To move or to stay—we keep having to make that choice as we age. There is no guarantee, ever, for any of these people, or for any of us, that we will never have to move again, or that we can completely insure ourselves against illness, pain, death, or losing control of our lives. We keep having to move, and stay, and move again. . . . [P]aradoxically, we can choose with more and more freedom and sureness of what we want—liberated now

from irrelevant considerations that have stopped or driven us in the past—though we face obstacles surely as we move into this unknown territory of life.[11]

⬚⬚⬚⬚⬚

The Joys of Living Alone

IT TAKES A WHILE

For some women, living alone is a good fit. But for women who have never wanted to be on their own or who are still struggling with the heavy weight of grief and anger from their loss, living alone is not without its risks. **In the early phases of divorce or widowhood, a woman may find that living alone can cause not just disorientation and distress but even severe anxiety or depression.** Her physical move mirrors a more drastic psychological one—from a life in which she defined herself mainly by relationships to one in which she is living primarily for herself.

One divorced author, Barbara Holland, who has lived many years on her own, believes that because women are used to defining themselves in relation to others, too much solitude can trigger an identity crisis:

> Even today a solitary woman may feel like the tree falling in the empty forest; alone in a room, nobody's daughter, wife, lover, mother, or executive assistant, her ectoplasm thins out until the furniture shows through. Let someone walk in and she solidifies in relation to the visitor, but alone her outline fades.[12]

Living alone can provide so much free time that it can feel like chaos and lead to feelings of helplessness and danger, or at the very least to the sense of operating in a vacuum. Women programmed all of their adult lives to respond to the wishes of those around them may have difficulty getting in touch with their own needs and doing something to fill them. Some don't even feed themselves properly because there is no one else around demanding to be fed.

Even women who take good care of themselves and who claim to enjoy living on their own complain about not having anyone to help with repairs and emergencies. Or they wish aloud that they had someone else to play the role of "wife." Others talk about major bouts of anxiety or sadness connected with doing the marketing or cleaning up, all tasks with intense emotional connections to their previous caretaking responsibilities.

And then there is what many believe to be the main peril of living alone: loneliness.

LONELINESS: HOW GREAT A HAZARD?

The fear of being terribly lonely haunts many women newly on their own. And there's no question that many people who live alone suffer from it. Author Barbara Holland writes:

> Loneliness may be a sort of national disease here, and certainly it's a shameful one, more embarrassing to admit than any of the seven deadly sins. Happy-ever-after has rejected us. The fairy story spit us out as unworthy, and sometimes we suppose we are.

Holland warns that you should only live alone if it is either voluntary or has a specific ending point.[13]

Loneliness could prove hazardous for women because of their tendency, when they feel bad, to "ruminate"—to analyze the cause of their sadness and dwell on it. Psychologists speculate that women's brooding about their troubles, instead of distracting themselves as men tend to do, may be a major reason why women become depressed twice as often as men.[14] One could speculate that women who live alone with too much time on their hands may do what comes naturally to them and, by focusing on their feelings of loneliness, begin the slide down a slippery slope to clinical depression.

I didn't see much evidence of this, however, and two recent studies show that **a great many unmarried women living on their own are doing very well. Their worries about being terribly lonely are rarely realized, and intense feelings of loneliness usually recede as a woman becomes accustomed to her new status.**

One survey, by Christopher Hayes and his colleagues at the National Center for Women and Retirement Research, of 352 divorced women over the age of forty concluded that most women get over their fears and feelings of loneliness within a year or two of their divorce.[15] Another study at the University of Pittsburgh of ninety single midlife women concluded that the belief that being single is synonymous with being lonely is a myth. Like the women I talked to, the women in the Pittsburgh study rarely mentioned loneliness as a predicament, instead expressing satisfaction with the freedom that living alone gave them.[16]

So it's likely that single women don't view loneliness as hazardous to their health because they understand that despite any hardships, only by living alone can they have the autonomy they come to cherish. To keep these periods of loneliness tolerable, they invent ways to stay connected with life, securing both the solitude and the fellowship needed to nourish body and soul.

When gerontologist Ruth Harriet Jacobs was first divorced over twenty years ago, she had trouble adjusting to living alone. So she made a list of places she could go to be with people at any time of day or night "if I just couldn't stand being alone." The list includes twenty-four-hour stores, hospital waiting rooms, hotel lobbies, and, for empty weekends, public libraries where you can take your work and reading.[17] Jacobs includes this list and others for women who live alone (like thirty-four ways to make new friends), in her book *Be an Outrageous Older Woman.*[18]

LIVING ALONE AS ONE ALTERNATIVE OVER TIME

Given the stages you go through in making the emotional leap from an identity as a married woman to an identity as single, and your evolution with age, you will likely choose different housing over time. Consider Yvonne, sixty-one and divorced from her husband for over sixteen years. She has had ten addresses since her divorce.

Yvonne now lives in a cozy suburban house that she shares with a man and a woman who are about the same ages as her own children. Wanting to live in a house again but unable to afford it, she chose compatible people to share one with, all moving in at the same time so no one had any "proprietary" interests. The three of them have had to work through some "situations," but she thinks that is just part of living with a group of people.

Watching her sip tea on the patio on a perfect autumn day, you recognize that Yvonne seems more than content with her home. Here she feels able to make a living at writing and to act as a guru to a group that meets with her regularly. But she is also considering living on her own again—something she has done periodically in the past. When she first tried it, she says, living alone made her feel "basically deep down lonely." That ceased when she moved back to the town where she was born:

> I remember standing in the middle of my living room on a sunny afternoon in the spring and all of a sudden realizing "I'm not lonely anymore." It was like when a toothache is gone and you don't know where it went. I just looked down inside and I thought, "What happened? It's gone!" The loneliness that had been in my gut probably all my life was gone.

Yvonne speculates that her feelings have to do with moving back to the area where she grew up, reconnecting with relatives, reconciling with her father before he died, and basically just no longer being an itinerant. "I look around this city and say, 'I own this place. This is my home. I grew up here. My father died in the house that I'd moved into when I was a year old.'" Though Yvonne admits that she still feels lonely sometimes, it's not "that deep aching loneliness."

Just a few years ago when she was living by herself in an

apartment, a course she was taking on "ageless wisdom" prompted Yvonne to seek out more solitude:

> I basically said, "I'm going to spend a lot of time alone. That's what I need to do. I need to go inside and pray and meditate. I need to listen to good music. I need to read. I need to study. I need to do all these things for myself."
>
> And that's what I did. I spent most of my evenings and my weekends home alone for about a year. It was a complete shock to the system. I'd never done that before. In the beginning I was real nervous about it. I thought, "I'm either going to get bored to death or lonely." I'm pretty much an extrovert. . . . But it didn't happen.

When she started to get lonely, she says,

> I decided to just stay with it. Just be lonely. It won't hurt anything. And after a while I just cherished it. I just loved it. I'd spend hours lying on my couch listening to music. Or writing in a journal. Or reading—there are so many wonderful books in the world to read.

The key to Yvonne's ability to tolerate and even benefit from loneliness may be that she freely chooses it. For her, living alone is just one alternative, one that she indulges in when she feels the need for solitude and leaves behind when she wants to feel more connected. Her living arrangements complement the work she is doing, illustrating her philosophy that "we call to ourselves whatever we need at whatever stage of growth we're in."

Communal Living: Wave of the Future?

THE GOLDEN GIRLS FANTASY

When the TV show "The Golden Girls" first began its long run on television, it was a breakthrough of sorts. This comedy series portrayed four mature single women (two were a mother and daughter) as active, attractive widows sharing a fairly luxurious home in Florida. The characters were quite a contrast to the preoccupation on TV with youth and traditional families.[19]

But even though the show was produced by a woman, it wasn't really all that positive about aging. While the "golden girls" presumably weren't stupid, they were generally portrayed doing stupid things—and then feeling humiliated when caught in the act. Apparently we were all supposed to share the notion that mature widows living together would be airheads in need of constant supervision.

Although men are twice as likely to live in shared housing, AARP's Women's Initiative estimates that there are now 193,000 "Golden Girl" households, made up of women roommates over forty-five. (The vast majority are for women under sixty-five.) But AARP also points out that people who want to start or join these "nontraditional households" may face a number of problems, such as discrimination in zoning, in rental housing, and, where shared ownership is desired, in home purchases.[20]

Not all that many real-life models exist for mature women who want to live in some type of shared housing. I knew two women, however, who invented their own alternative: Tish Sommers and Laurie Shields. Their accomplishments as single-agains—founding both the National Displaced Homemakers Network and the Older Women's League—are described in chapter 12, "Pursue Your Passion." One reason for their success, I believe, was the special community they created which served them both for living and for working.

In the eleven years these women collaborated—from the time they met until Tish died of cancer at age seventy-one in 1985— they generated all their work out of a funky stucco bungalow in a run-down section of Oakland, California. There the two women lived and slept on the second floor, descending the stairs every day to join one paid secretary and a throng of volunteers who wanted to help them change the world so others wouldn't have to face the same kind of discrimination they had.

Theirs was obviously not a conventional living arrangement. And although it would not suit many of us, it provided a rich life for those two women and for those they toiled beside and influenced. The bonds formed in that small community were easily as strong and rewarding as the bonds in any nuclear family.

TACKLING RETIREMENT HOUSING: EDITH

In a certain sense, retirement housing is modified communal housing. Although residents usually live in separate units, the complexes offer all kinds of opportunities for interaction with one's neighbors, from communal meals to sports to social activities. That might seem the best of both worlds, offering both autonomy and support. But until I met Edith, the last thing I ever wanted to do was to live in retirement housing. I tended to agree with Maggie Kuhn, founder of the Gray Panthers, who referred to them as "padded playpens for wrinkled babies."[21] Like all prejudices, this one dies hard, but Edith certainly made me rethink mine.

Edith is in her seventies, widowed ten years ago after a long, fascinating marriage lived mostly outside the United States with her Foreign Service husband and two daughters. Tiny and grandmotherly-looking, she is an African American who would seem to fit in wherever she goes because of her attitude that "people are people."

Edith's decision to move to the retirement community was precipitated by a series of heart attacks that began in 1989. They made obvious what she already knew: the urban home where she and her husband had lived was too big and hard to keep up. "I didn't want to feel a slave to a house, taking care of it, wondering whether someone would break in and steal my things. . . . I wanted to concentrate on other things"—like her love of art, literature, and the textiles she studies, collects, and makes by hand. Besides, she missed being around other people all the time and felt scared and lonely a lot.

Edith spent a lot of time researching all the apartments in the metropolitan area. She chose a huge retirement complex of homes, townhouses, and apartments for older persons living independently. Even though the complex was attractive and well maintained, her friends complained that it was too far away (almost an hour's drive), and the residents were mostly white and old. Why would she want to isolate herself out there, segregated from the real world? But Edith saw it another way—as an opportunity to be in a community where she could be close to people she could identify with.

I found Edith happily ensconced in her apartment, full of artifacts and textiles she had collected during the twenty years her family had lived in Africa. But she hadn't exactly felt love at first sight for her new home. Isolated and blue at first, she actively intervened to make herself feel better, using her lifelong technique of talking herself out of a funk: "You just make up your mind and do it." She began to reach out in a lot of different directions to make new friends, especially ones who share her interests.

Edith is now the self-appointed liaison between the textile museum in town, where she is a volunteer docent, and residents of the complex who share her passion. She also joined a Great Books group that discusses issues and philosophy.

Edith has also begun informally to counsel a few newly widowed women. One piece of advice she gives is to set a goal you can easily meet for each day, scheduling just one piece of a larger project for any time period. When the goal is met, you feel a sense of accomplishment, an important step toward beginning to take back control over your life.

※※※※※

Getting the Mix Right

One common feature of living arrangements that seem to work for single women is that they provide both independence and support. Independence is a given when you live alone, but it can also be created in other kinds of living arrangements. Support most often comes from easy access to a community in which to anchor yourself—whether it's a small town, a large apartment complex, a friendly neighborhood, or just a loyal group of friends. For nearly all of us, such a community is an absolute prerequisite to life on our own. As one widow put it, "I think a single woman needs community more. The community has to be your family."

Such balanced living arrangements are not readily available, however, to the one woman out of every seven who lives alone.[22] In a society increasingly fragmented and lacking in community, many single women are much more isolated than they would like. They echo the complaint of author Ray Oldenburg about the vanishing of comfortable, accessible loitering places where you are known and can safely hook up with others. His book's title says it all: *The Great Good Place: Cafes, Coffee Shops, Community Centers, Beauty Parlors, General Stores, Bars, Hangouts, and How They Get You Through the Day.*[23]

Finding just the right mix of voluntary seclusion and fellowship may be the most important challenge you face when choosing where to live. Through trial and error, the women in this book mainly achieved a mix of privacy and companionship that served them well. They settled for a short time or permanently into environments that fit their images of who they are and what they want. And for the most part, they succeeded in finding sheltered spots where a rich soil of solitude and a temperate climate of friends provided everything they needed to blossom forth.

11

Step by Step
to a Career

Dreams don't just come true. Being what we want to be and doing what we want to do with our lives don't just happen. Dreams are made real one step at a time, over the proverbial long haul. Dreams take long-term commitment. From first to last, we need focus, discipline, persistence, and the ability to keep in sight the vision of what we are slowly creating.

—Rebecca Maddox
Inc. Your Dreams[1]

⌘⌘⌘⌘⌘

Use What You Know and Love

In a recent cartoon in *The New Yorker,* a bespectacled man in suit and vest is introducing the older woman beside him to three attentive briefcase-carrying business types. The woman being introduced is dumpy-looking—wearing a flowered dress, flat shoes, an open overcoat, a decorated hat. From one hand, she dangles a large handbag. Behind her, in her other hand, is a wire shopping cart. The caption reads: "This is Mrs. McBride from marketing."[2]

It's funny because it's so ludicrous. Presumably no one would believe that the kind of marketing that a dowdy older woman does is at all connected with the complex world of business marketing. But is it really all that far-fetched? Long-time housewives know it's not. As prime targets of all that selling, they know a lot about what's convincing and what isn't. They could, if they *happened* to be given a job in marketing—just like the boy in a man's body in the movie *Big* who was such a hit developing new toys—dress themselves up and do just fine.

The countless widows who take on their dead husband's work without missing a beat have always shown that to be true. The working world isn't all that complicated after all, as most women who enter it after years at home usually discover. **Women have gotten a wealth of experience from their lives that they can apply to a career.**

Pearl, who took her first paid job at the age of fifty-three when her husband went into treatment for his alcoholism, put it this way:

> People of my era were so brainwashed because we stayed home with the children. We were constantly reminded, subtly or not so subtly, that our jobs were not worth anything really. Later on I discovered, not to my surprise, that our jobs were far harder. And the men didn't work

nearly as hard as they led us to believe. The only thing I didn't have when I got a job was a wife.

As you'll see later, even though she got such a late start, Pearl was able to make a career out of her job, one she continues today at the age of sixty-eight. And she is certainly not unique. Out of the eighty-eight women I interviewed for this book—none of them rich or famous—twenty-eight had been able to make a career *after* they became single, seventeen of them, like Pearl, creating one from scratch since they had no recent work history. The other eleven transformed an existing job into a career. Another eight had a career but changed it after they became single, a feat that Martin Sicker, director of AARP's workforce program, says is difficult to pull off.[3]

When these women tell me they have a "career," not just a job, what exactly do they mean? In general, they are speaking about fields they stay in over a period of years, which can refer either to the subject matter they are pursuing, like health care, or to the skills they are using, like management. (One widow who was reluctant to refer to her progressively responsible administrative jobs as a career referred to it as a "mini-career.")

None of my career women claimed it was easy, and they were all justifiably proud of making it against the odds. They are testimony that **making a new career at midlife is not just a pipe dream for a widow or divorcée. Being single may make it *more* feasible, because you no longer suffer from the role conflicts and guilt brought on by obligations to your husband.**

Sometimes, a woman who sets out to pursue a career when she's single-again goes in a dramatically new direction.[4] But for most, having a career is about the process of using existing talents and interests, either active or dormant ones, in new income-generating ways. As a recent article in *Fortune* put it: "Shifting to a new career rarely turns out to be the sort of apocalyptic, burn-the-bridges, run-off-to-Seattle-with-your-mistress experience that some might expect."[5]

This chapter shows how women can parlay a job into a career, pursuing greater responsibilities and rewards either by moving up the ladder in one organization or by changing jobs and employers a number of times. And it shows how women who believe in themselves and are willing to take risks can transform what they already do for little or no pay into a career, achieving that transition either by taking one well-orchestrated leap to a professional job or by setting out on their own as entrepreneurs.

Convert a Job into a Profession

KNOWING WHAT SHE'S GOOD AT: PEARL

Let's turn now to Pearl, who was "brainwashed" to think that her volunteer work wasn't worth much. When I talked to her, Pearl was sixty-eight and had made a lot of progress, both career- and ego-wise. Still youthful-looking, with a plumpish blond beauty (like a Rubens painting), she speaks with the soft twang and the forthright language she learned growing up in a small town in the Ozarks. She is full of a wry, self-deprecating humor, which has served her well through hard times. (In her Christmas letter, she emotes, "I am still hale and hearty for an old broad.")

Loaded with artistic talents and social skills, Pearl had flourished as a housewife, mother of two sons, and volunteer *par excellence*. Because women of her era—she came of age in the late 1940s—were responsible for everything that "living" entails, she always waited until after everyone was in bed to begin work on all the creative projects she loved. Sometimes she stayed at them until dawn.

Pearl had tried not to notice as her husband succumbed to the pressures of a demanding job and immersed himself deeper and deeper in drinking. Her denial phase ended when he entered residential treatment. During the nine years that he was in and out of treatment until they divorced, she never really trusted him again, quickly separating their finances to protect herself from his growing debts.

At first, Pearl says, "I was scared to death. Here I was fifty-three years old hanging out on my own. I remember keeping the temperature of the house at sixty degrees and turning off all the lights." To make ends meet, she took shorthand and typing classes and became a temporary, "doing the most scummy jobs in the world."

Eventually she found a job in a new health management company of just six employees. She took the job because it was close to home, they didn't discriminate because of age, and there were other single women employees. She was one of two secretaries. "I was the very bad one," she recalls.

During her job interview, Pearl told them she was open to doing anything and wanted to increase her skills. So when they called on a Friday to say they had bought new software to process medical claims and could she go to Wausau, Wisconsin, on Monday for training in how to operate it, Pearl said, "Sure!"

Taking that opportunity put her in on the ground floor of a company that was developing the concept of managed care. Because the company was growing by leaps and bounds, she had a lot of room to maneuver. She maneuvered her way out of secretarial work by volunteering to handle an orientation for new employees, something they were going to hire a consultant to do. As she told her bosses, "I know how to do it. I used to do this all the time in my other life. I just didn't get paid for it."

With some trepidation, they gave her permission and were amazed to watch the orientation go off without a hitch. Pearl even acted as the master of ceremonies. After that, her career took off. She moved from handling claim payments, where she developed training manuals, to training and development, putting together a four-day continuing education course for all the nurses, followed by a client conference (where she initiated the company's first survey of client interests). When they were going to hire a firm to make a marketing video, Pearl made it instead, writing the script, directing it, and hiring a photographer. It cost $4,000, not the $300,000 they had budgeted. They made her head of marketing.

More recently, she was in charge of wellness services, but the company got into financial trouble. To avoid being laid off, she maneuvered once again, creating a niche for herself as the only older employee in their new HMO for senior citizens. Now, in addition to her wellness program, she writes a newsletter, makes presentations, and generally tends to their Medicare-age clients.

Pearl thinks she has been successful in staying with and moving up in the same company because she can do *anything* nonclinical and is "low maintenance." But she knows that she would not have gotten any of her promotions if she hadn't taken the initiative. That took a lot of courage, something she developed along the way:

> It took me a long time in my job to actually believe I was as good at something as I now know I am. Because my mother always made me think I was a disappointment to her, and in an alcoholic marriage your self-esteem is knocked down, you become a people pleaser, and you don't know how to say no. You can't ever accept that anything you do is good enough. It was a long slow process for me but I'm finally there. I know what I'm good at and I also know what I'm not good at, and I'm very comfortable with that.

How to Climb the Ladder

Pearl has a good sense of what qualities have made her successful at moving up in the same company. She is competent, works hard, takes risks; is creative, flexible, and a self-starter; and believes in herself. And, I would guess, she must be easy to work with.

There are no real surprises there. She displays many of the same characteristics and behavior that were found in a study of fifty-five successful women executives:[6]

- Early in their careers, *successful career women draw attention to themselves by being open and frank.*

- They *learn how to be more diplomatic* as they move up the ladder.

- They *become team-oriented managers* using personal approaches to influence people they manage.

- A number *take risks* by involving themselves in company innovations.

- And they *work extremely hard, producing first-rate products.* In fact, work and tending to their colleagues take up most of their waking and sleeping hours.

For want of a better comparison, these successful women are married to their jobs. Those who also have husbands are aware of all the personal compromises they made to get to the top. Of those who are single, some regret not having taken time to have a family. But other singles are delighted with their lives. That last group is like the single-again career women I interviewed, who knew they couldn't go home and curl up in bed with their paychecks, but who viewed their careers as nothing short of blessings.

Another characteristic these successful professional women cultivate is a particular type of assertiveness: although they are frank and open about their views, they also listen well and have good insights into others.[7] That kind of assertiveness appears to be especially important for women who want to move ahead to more responsible jobs. If they hide their views, they are just overlooked when it comes time for raises or promotions. But if they lack practice at being assertive and overdo it a bit, they can come across as shrill, or out-of-line, or (worst case) hysterical.

That's why many displaced homemaker programs still offer some training in assertiveness. And it's why manuals like the one developed for divorced women by the National Center for Women and Retirement Research offer a checklist to explain what it means to be assertive about getting promoted.[8] The center proposes that you

- *determine if you have all the information you need* about any possible career ladders, where you are on any of those ladders, and how high it is possible to go;

- make sure to *let everyone concerned—your boss and people in personnel—know* that you want a challenge and a promotion;

- find out about and *apply for any job openings or training opportunities*;

- *understand the process for promotions*—who decides and on what basis;

- look for possibilities to *transfer to another job* at your same level that would have better promotion potential;

- once your job has become easy or routine, *ask for more difficult tasks*, and then try to get your position upgraded;

- *only take a promotion if it leads in the right direction* or will ultimately benefit you;

- figure out what course you'll follow to be promoted and *develop a schedule and plan of action*;

- and, last but not least, *enlist the support of your co-workers, friends, and family*.[9]

That's really all there is to the mystique of being assertive instead of aggressive in getting promoted. It amounts to being logical rather than irrational, methodical rather than impulsive.

Make a plan, carry it out, and be calmly persistent in pursuing all options. You already know how to do it in other parts of your life. You just have to apply it to getting ahead with your career.

Even if you determine that you aren't going to get a promotion (at least not right now), you shouldn't abandon trying to get a better salary in the job you have. Chances are you're woefully underpaid. (Remember that women over fifty-five only earn 54 percent of what similarly educated men do.)[10] And chances are your boss may not even think you deserve a raise unless you ask for one. Most men seem to understand this fact of life, while a lot of women are raised to believe, as career coach Carol Olmstead puts it, "Good girls don't talk about money."[11]

Just as in seeking a promotion, to ask for a raise, you have to be composed and systematic:

- First *figure out what you should be paid*, which you can do by asking around and checking publications like *National Business Employment Weekly* and *Working Woman* magazine.

- Then *come up with reasons why you deserve that higher salary*. For example, author Debra Benton suggests thinking of ways your job has contributed to producing revenue for the company.[12]

- Once you've developed your case, *approach your boss and try to persuade him or her*. Again, don't push so hard that you antagonize anyone, and don't threaten to leave.

- *Don't give up, either, after just one try. Sound reasoning and persistence and something Benton calls "professional presence" are key*. The title of Benton's book gives the right image: *Lions Don't Need to Roar: Using the Leadership Power of Professional Presence to Stand Out, Fit In, and Move Ahead*.[13]

- And don't seek just a salary increase, especially if that looks unlikely. *Pursue other options, like a bonus, or tuition reimbursement, or flexible hours.* Whatever you get will enhance not only your standing in the eyes of your boss and co-workers but also your own confidence in yourself.[14]

PARLAYING VOLUNTEER WORK INTO A PROFESSION: SUGAR

Sugar didn't need any help convincing herself she was qualified for a career in management. She knew that she was—from seventeen years of community volunteering. That was work she says she did because "I'm not one of these people who has to be paid to be validated. I'm interested in power." Even though she hadn't had a paycheck in all that time, her volunteer experience gave her the skills and self-confidence she needed to get direct entrée into a career.

Sugar is not a particularly dignified nickname for a mature woman, but then dignity has not been the key to Sugar's success in life. Tiny and still slim at the age of sixty-three, she is full of intelligence and humor, telling stories of her life nonstop in a deep, throaty voice. When I talked to her, she had been divorced for almost thirteen years from a husband who married her when she was twenty-three, and who left her and their two teenage sons when she was fifty.

She describes her husband as "a great guy, somebody I liked a lot"—a successful lawyer who had a fantastic job. He also had an eighteen-room house on the ocean, a forty-foot boat, two great kids, a dog, and "an attractive and interesting wife." Then one day he asked her, out of the blue, if that was all there was to life. Shortly afterward, he ran off in his sports car with a woman twenty years younger, leaving her, she says, "holding the bag."

Her main motivator became fear. "When he left, I got quite frightened. I decided this was something quite serious. I wanted to be in a position where I could earn a living," Sugar recalls. So although her main priority initially was to get her husband back,

Sugar also began to search for work. She contacted everyone she knew through her husband and through her positions on the boards of the Girl Scouts, a halfway house, an alcohol center, a drug rehabilitation center, a music school, and her college. As a result, one of her husband's colleagues alerted her to a national job search for a new executive director for the local arts council. She applied, filling a four page resumé with her accomplishments as a volunteer.

Sugar got the job in a head-to-head competition with arts administrators from around the country. She won out, she thinks, because they wanted someone with broad community contacts. But perhaps the main reason was their unusual interview process, one aimed at picking the candidate with the best "people skills."

Interviewed all together by the hiring committee, the finalists were given a hypothetical problem to solve: how should the council be funded? The other candidates were put off by the situation, assuming they were being asked for free consulting advice. But for Sugar, the interview was a real turn-on. She treated it like a real-life problem full of conflicts and disparity, the kind of challenging situation that she calls her "life blood." Her superb performance during the interview gained her what she calls "a very perfect job," one she still holds some fifteen years later.

Sugar was able to demonstrate her people skills because she had honed them as a community volunteer. She is like millions of other women of her generation in that respect—she has devoted enormous energy to unpaid work. In her interviews with midlife women, Lillian Rubin found such women more able to express confidence in their abilities than their peers who had paid jobs. Rubin writes:

> Interestingly enough, the women who most often describe themselves as competent and capable are those who spend much of their time in volunteer activities in the community—women who call themselves home-

makers but who, in fact, spend many hours each week as unpaid administrators in community and civic organizations.[15]

Another source of her confidence, Sugar says, was a fascination with Juliette Low, who served as a role model for years, "long before I knew I would become single." As Sugar tells it, Low founded the Girl Scouts at the age of fifty-two, after a disastrous nineteen-year marriage to an English lord. When her husband died, Low felt liberated. Sugar explains:

> I was fascinated by the fact that this woman's life began at 52. And for the next 15 years she lived her whole life. She did this incredible thing of starting a worldwide movement in 1912, seeing it grow to a huge national organization so that by the time she died in 1927 the Girl Scouts was enormously successful.[16]

Because of Low's example, Sugar says that when she reached her late forties, "my sense was that, although I had no idea that my husband was going to leave, I was on the verge of something tremendously exciting." And indeed she was. Summing up her experience in a letter to a male friend who had just lost his job, she says she wrote him: "Look at what happened to me. Two weeks before I turned fifty, I was summarily fired by my husband of twenty-seven years. Look at how I managed. You must look at this as though it is one of the greatest opportunities that ever happened."

The only real hitch with using your experience as a volunteer when you look for a professional job is that employers may tend to either discount it or think it's less valuable than paid experience. (Pearl used to scold her boss when he expressed amazement at some unknown skill she displayed by saying, "Just because we didn't get a paycheck, you'd be surprised what some of us old gals did.") Keep in mind, however, that you have the law on your side. To discount volunteer work is one clear sign of illegal discrimination against older women. (See chapter 5.)[17]

⛋⛋⛋⛋⛋

Ferret Out What You Need to Succeed

GET MAINSTREAM CREDENTIALS

The women in this book followed different routes to developing a career. But their initial step was always the same: proving that they were qualified for the career they wanted.

One way to prove you're qualified, of course, is to get mainstream credentials that everyone recognizes. For some careers, in technical fields, for example, that is the only way. The number of mature women who take the credentialed route to a career is growing as fields become more complex and as more schools are admitting qualified applicants without regard to age or gender. An AARP survey, for example, reported extensive activity among its members in pursuing nursing as a new career at midlife. But taking up a career like that one, they point out, involves "a willingness to invest sizable amounts of time and money, endure and overcome hardship and . . . some luck."[18]

Despite these difficulties, many women follow this path, both to prove to the world that they are qualified and to prove it to themselves. When Pearl went back to earn a Master's degree to move her career along, she realized about two-thirds of the way through that a degree wasn't going to help much. She decided to finish anyway—for her own sense of satisfaction. When she graduated at the age of sixty-five, her two grown sons were perhaps the most impressed.

Therapist Alice Umbach tries to convince unhappily married women to stay in their marriages long enough to get the credentials they need to begin a career. She offers them a supportive ear, she says, "but I also lean on them to get out and get skills before they walk out the door—unless they are being abused—because

I don't recommend walking off into quicksand." She suggests a book, *Learning to Leave,* for women in long-term marriages who want out.[19]

Even without help from your husband, you shouldn't give up if school is a necessity to get where you're headed. There are a variety of other ways to get the financing you need with higher education and vocational education:

- If you have one, *your current employer might help.* Pearl's paid most of her tuition costs for her Master's degree, which made the feat possible.

- *Displaced homemaker programs are another source,* as explained in chapter 5, "Get a Job (Or Keep the One You Have)."

- *Financial aid money is available from government and private sources for mature women.* AARP's *The Back to School Money Book* provides sources of some $38 billion in assistance. The book also provides suggestions for ways to reduce your educational expenses.[20]

Repackage Yourself

For careers where credentials aren't an absolute requirement, sometimes it's a question of repackaging yourself to prove you're qualified for a particular job—and then making yourself believe what you've done. Maureen Shiells, who counsels career changers in Palo Alto, California, is quoted by *Fortune* magazine as saying, "People often assume that everything is wrong, that they'll have to throw everything away, start all over again, go back to school, go into debt, learn a whole set of new skills." The *Fortune* article goes on: "But changing careers is not really about dramatic change. It's about continuity, about translating your experience and your expertise into transferable, marketable skills."[21]

Helping you with that repackaging has become a major U.S. industry. By one count, there were some thirty-one hundred nonfiction books for career seekers published between 1990 and 1995. And at least 165,000 individuals call themselves job counselors, consultants, or advisors. Their advice is not always worth the fees they charge, however, so approach these experts with the same kind of caution you use in picking out a therapist, lawyer, or financial planner.[22]

But convincing a potential employer about your qualifications for your career is perhaps not as important as convincing yourself. That task can be particularly difficult for women, according to psychiatrist Jean Baker Miller, who writes, "Although real weaknesses are a problem for every human being, women's major difficulty lies more in admitting the strengths they already have and in allowing themselves to use their resources."[23]

So what exactly are your strengths and resources? Often a woman will take them for granted, not really considering the possibility of exploiting them to create a career, until someone *else* points out their value. But recognizing and cataloguing them, according to career consultant Richard Bolles, is the key to finding a satisfying new career.

To uncover your strengths—things you do well and enjoy doing—conduct an inventory of what Bolles calls "the gifts that God gave you."[24] These skills include:

- *What you do with people, information, and things.* These skills are transferable to any field you choose. You can improve them, but you won't lose them. They can be as undistinguished on the surface as secretarial skills, which entrepreneurial women have been able to parlay, like Pearl did, into progressively responsible administrative positions.

- *Any special knowledge you have.* You could have learned such knowledge in school, but also could have just picked it up through daily living or activities like a hobby. One woman, for example, turned her hobby of writing freelance travel articles into a writing career by getting her travel paid for by the countries she visits.

- *The style with which you interact with people or do something.* Qualities such as persistence or kindness are important. Bolles calls them self-management skills or traits.

Your inventory consists of the things you love to do and how you do them. One asset that many women have (although they tend to discount it) is especially important in the modern world: people skills. According to author Caroline Bird, "Much of what comes naturally to [women] is managing human relationships: counseling, mentoring, nurturing, networking, matchmaking, mediating, getting people to work together. . . . This person-to-person work is becoming vital now that organizations are being restructured."[25] And people skills can also be used in entrepreneurial ways, as they were by several women I interviewed. They had turned their natural gifts for understanding themselves and others into careers helping other women heal themselves and build their self-esteem.

The next step in repackaging yourself is to decide *where* you want to do these things, choosing a field in which you will be able to surround yourself with whatever subject matter or topic attracts you most. Once you do that, you will be ready to create a resumé that reflects all your skills and is tailored toward exciting employment.

One widow who successfully followed this process summed it up as "First, know yourself." Debra had been happily married, employed in what she calls "a not-having-to-support-myself job." Suddenly on her own and very much in need of a stable career, her self-analysis led to her conclusion that she is "a person who likes to find things out and tell other people about them."

Debra says that it took her six months to take that idea and translate it into language to use on the top six lines of her resumé: three lines for her job objective (the three things that she wanted from a job); and three for her professional strengths (why she was qualified). When it was finished, she worked on acquiring anything she needed to be able to demonstrate those qualifications. She says the resumé was so focused that it was an immediate success, leading to a great new job that turned into an impressive career.

Like Debra, you should be sure that your repackaging is complete and that *you* believe in it, before you **proceed to tap into all of your resources. Those resources are primarily other people— all of your personal ties, weak ones as well as strong.** In fact, Bolles believes that weak ties work especially well because people outside your usual circle of acquaintances often know other people you don't know and can connect you with them. Given that 70 percent of jobs are filled by networking,[26] it's difficult to argue that the best path to a new career is through mailing out resumés and reading want ads, rather than through personal contacts.

WHAT MENTORING CAN OFFER

Another kind of assistance that someone developing a career or starting a business may find useful is mentoring. Typically, mentoring is a kind of one-on-one personal relationship in which a person who has more of a particular type of knowledge connects with someone lacking that knowledge and passes it on to him, in an attempt to advance his success in the world. Author Carolyn Heilbrun describes a mentor as something more than this—"more than a mere teacher, in fact, a guide or exemplar in dealing with the central concerns of one's life."[27]

With respect to careers, mentoring has traditionally taken place among white males—one reason often cited for why women and minorities still come up against a "glass ceiling" in their careers, despite thirty years of antidiscrimination laws.[28] And as Heilbrun points out, even when accomplished women have had mentors, they have mainly been males.[29]

Psychologist Hillary Lapsley, who is writing a book on mentoring for women, believes that's so because often even successful women don't think of themselves as qualified to be mentors and therefore don't seek out that role. Plus, younger women in need of advice don't understand that they might need to take the initiative to make the relationship happen.

Studies show that finding a mentor is similar to the courtship one goes through when seeking a mate. The person seeking a mentor finds someone she wants to hook up with, then gives out a variety of signals and waits to see if the desired party responds. If either or both parties don't know that these relationships happen this way, it's unlikely a match will occur—a likely reason for why there has been such a dearth of woman-on-woman mentoring relationships.[30]

Mentoring involves not just passing on information but providing support in matters of personal concern to the person being mentored. It involves mutual admiration, but unlike friendships or support groups, the parties involved are not equals (at least in the arena where the mentoring is occurring). For the mentors, the rewards are having someone who admires them and takes their advice seriously. And men have often used mentoring as a means to build a power base.

Women who attribute their career accomplishments to a mentor or mentors along the way speak of a number of ways mentoring helps:

- Being singled out for attention by someone you admire professionally *validates you and helps you believe in your own potential.*

- Having someone who will listen to your concerns who has already faced and surmounted the hazards you confront is *an emotional lifeline during the rough spots in your career.*

- In addition to support, *a mentor provides direction, gives advice about career paths, and shows how to avoid serious mistakes* along the way.

- A mentor provides you with *the chance to network, formally and informally, with other successful people in your field.*

Finding someone to mentor you should be less difficult than it was when there were fewer women in the workforce. First, you need to identify someone you admire and would like to have a relationship with; then, begin the courtship process. As a woman, you've had a bit of practice both at asking for support and at giving it, so you won't have to develop any new skills here. Psychologist and corporate consultant Kathleen Shea points out, "Gender-wise, women are open to more support than men are. And as a group, we are able to stop and ask directions."[31]

Recognizing the value of mentors, formal programs are springing up where you can turn for practical career advice. One woman I interviewed who attributed much of her success to a male mentor, for example, helped set up a mentoring program at her community college, where she counsels other women making career transitions.

Senior women in a number of big corporations are also beginning workplace networks so women can connect with each other. The Small Business Administration (SBA) pairs up women starting small businesses with more experienced women through its Women's Network for Ownership Entrepreneurial Training. And you can find mentors in professional societies and other places where women gather. The Women's Center in Vienna, Virginia, for example, keeps a computerized listing of hundreds of women who are willing to mentor other women in their same field. Women seem to love the conferences the center sponsors, where women like Betty Friedan and Cokie Roberts talk about how they built their careers.[32] In time, the supply of mentors may gradually catch up with the demand.

✂✂✂✂

Become an Entrepreneur

MAKE WHAT YOU ALREADY DO YOUR CAREER

Another way to build a career, when you're stymied in finding a good job or in upgrading the one you have, is to go to work for yourself. Because at first glance it can appear to be the path of least resistance, this is the route many widows and divorcées take. They set up a home-based business, such as one dealing with a former hobby, for example. But this option is not without its hazards. Take the following, for example:

- Most home businesses do little or nothing to decrease the *isolation* newly single women usually face.

- Most home businesses make *so little money initially* (and even for years) that they can only supplement other income. Others, of course, make nothing or even cost more than they bring in.

- With no start or stop time to a work day, and defeat always looming at the horizon, a home-based business can cause *enormous stress*.

- And *if a home business fails*, as many do, *it can be a real ego blow*.

For all these reasons, many advisors like Rebecca Maddox caution that the dream of starting one's own business is not something most people can or should take on.[33] On the other hand, a lot of newly single women don't have that much to lose. The authors of a recent review of entrepreneurship by women put it more delicately: "[T]he difficulties encountered in the workplace and the opportunities offered by the marketplace lower the perceived career risk and make business ownership a viable career alternative for many women."[34]

So, if you're considering going into business by yourself, first do some soul-searching to determine whether deep down you are an entrepreneur. If you feel energetic and healthy enough to do whatever it will take to launch your business, and brave enough to risk your own and other's money, that's great. If not, don't go ahead. Being a one-woman band is exhausting.

Here are some steps to take, if you decide to explore further:[35]

1. *Decide what your business will be and who your target market is.* You'll know if you should move ahead if you have a passion for your choice and know precisely who your customers or clients will be.

2. *Define your objectives.* Make them specific and write them down, including how much money you need to earn and what you'll need to borrow.

3. *Try out your idea on friends and relatives, as well as other entrepreneurs who wouldn't be competing with you.* Listen carefully to what they say and factor it into your planning.

4. *Turn to a variety of resources and how-to books on the topic of starting a small business.* Local offices of the SBA offer courses and hand-holding through the Senior Corps of Retired Executives (SCORE). They also sponsor a telephone information line and a woman-on-woman mentoring program. Plus, you can turn to the SBA's Small Business Development Centers that exist in every state. (The Resources section for chapter 11 gives contact information.) And a recent survey found a "virtual explosion" of all kinds of courses about entrepreneurship offered by undergraduate and graduate schools, community colleges and high schools.[36]

5. *Make a list of the actions required and the target dates for their completion.* They should include consulting with a lawyer and an accountant.

6. Even if you're not going to seek a commercial source for funding, *make a business plan and work out some financial projections*. Doing these things will force you to think through your goals and expenses and can head off a lot of difficulties down the road. Among the organizations that provide technical assistance with such planning are the American Women's Economic Development Corporation; the Women's Business Development Center; and the National Association of Women Business Owners (NAWBO).[37]

7. *Obtain the seed money you need to get going.* (See the following section, below.)

8. Set up your office, your books, and *go to it*.

GET BACKING FOR YOUR BUSINESS

A recent *Business Week* article concludes:

Raising money for small businesses is daunting for any entrepreneur, but . . . it's particularly vexing for women. Although they now own 40% of U.S. businesses and start them twice as often as men, women have not been welcomed by traditional sources of financing such as banks and venture capitalists.[38]

Naturally, banks claim that they aren't biased against making loans to women. They say their track records are poor because the small loans most women require don't provide enough profit and because most female-headed businesses are in the service sector and therefore lack collateral. Happily, new sources of funding for women entrepreneurs are emerging. (*Business Week* calls them "a 'new-girl' network.")[39] And there are signs, apparently, that banks are starting to move into this "niche" market.

But most experts advise you to approach commercial sources of financing only after you exhaust your own resources. Begin by selling any luxury items, remortgaging your home, borrowing on your life insurance, and getting an advance on your credit cards—something that 52 percent of women do to finance their businesses.[40]

The next potential source, experts say, is friends and family. Because most financing for a business results not from how good the idea or plan is, but from how trustworthy and capable the person in charge is, your friends and family should be the people most willing to back you. The problem is, however, that you risk losing those friendships in the event that the business doesn't work out and you cannot repay the loans. You'll have to decide whether that's a risk you're willing to take.

If you need just a small amount of money (anything under twenty-five thousand dollars the SBA terms a "microloan"), you might approach organizations like the SBA (which offers two types of direct loans), Accion International, and Women's World Banking (listed in the Resources section for chapter 11). The SBA also offers a new program targeted at women entrepreneurs. It uses a simplified precertification process that guarantees a loan from a local bank.[41] But even without this guarantee, you should try a local bank or two. If they say no, ask the loan officer to explain what's wrong with your application and to give you advice about other organizations that might lend to you or help you with your application.[42]

✄✄✄✄✄

Common Themes

A number of common themes emerged among women who built careers after they became single-again:

- While luck plays a role, you must get out in the world and *be prepared to grab any chance that comes your way.*

- Although you have to retain control of your life, *don't be afraid to ask for help.* While many of us might do this when we need emotional help, it's equally as important to ask for help in making a career or finding a way to support yourself.

- *Flexibility and creativity are especially important character-istics.* Certainly those are cherished skills in any business or profession. But grasping new ideas and making them work for you is also essential in the transition from being married to being single. When a single-again woman demonstrates that she can do this by building a career, her psychic and fiscal rewards are considerable.

- *Don't be afraid to charge well for what you already do well.* Because people assume that they have to pay for quality, no one else will value what you do until you price it in accordance with its worth.

- To ensure that you're not overwhelmed by the enormity of your objective, *break your tasks into small pieces,* each of which is achievable within a short time frame.

- *You may have to step backward temporarily to move ahead.* There's nothing wrong with doing this, just as long as you know where you're headed and are reasonably certain going backward will eventually get you there. But have an alternative plan just in case your original one doesn't work out.

- *Take it one step at a time.* Just as when you start a career when you're young, you can't count on being an overnight success, because that almost never happens. As hard as it is to have the patience for the tiny steps needed to move ahead, there's usually no other way.

Building a career is just one way to reap the benefits of a new life. Some single-again women's dreams and talents lie in other directions. Pursuing other options is the subject of the next chapter.

12

Pursue
Your Passion

༄༅༅༅༅༅༅༅༅༅༅༅༅༅༅༅༅༅༅༅༅༅

There is only one solution if old age is not to be an absurd parody of our former life, and that is to go on pursuing ends that give our existence a meaning—devotion to individuals, to groups or to causes, social, political, intellectual or creative work. In spite of the moralists' opinion to the contrary, in old age we should wish still to have passions strong enough to prevent us turning in upon ourselves.

—Simone de Beauvoir
Old Age[1]

"Turning in upon ourselves," as French philosopher Simone de Beauvoir terms it, doesn't only happen when you get old. It can happen at any age if you become disillusioned with life because it hasn't lived up to your expectations. De Beauvoir was generally unhappy with her life as she grew older, producing the venomous *Second Sex* when she was forty and the pessimistic *Old Age* when she was sixty.[2] All the more surprising, then, that de Beauvoir would conclude at the end of *Old Age* that there *is* a way to avoid feeling a victim of life as you grow older.[3]

De Beauvoir's answer—pursuing a passion for something or somebody—is a path to happiness that the most impressive women I interviewed discovered on their own. These women did not settle for the status quo. They made what they cared most about into the centerpiece of their lives and channeled prodigious energy into it. Intent on finding meaning in their existences, they pursued lives as artists, or devoted themselves to helping others, or became advocates for changes to the status quo.

Become an Artist

A Solo Flight through Poetry: Jean Kalmanoff

In 1990, thirteen years after being widowed, Jean Kalmanoff's poem titled "Painting Session" won second place in the senior division of a national contest.[4] Only then did she finally dare to call herself a poet and to publish her first book of poems.

Kalmanoff's evolution into a poet was slow and often painful. Married at nineteen, Kalmanoff says she and her husband were together for so long that "we forged a wedge of steel." When he died at the age of fifty-nine, she remembers being "overwhelmed at not having my husband to share my thoughts, reactions, worries, joys, touch."[5]

Kalmanoff had been a daydreamer and a writer as a girl but had stopped. As an adult in mourning, she turned to writing as a way to express the emotions that besieged her. Her first poem, "Lament," just poured out of her three months after her husband's death. Revised years later, after a writing workshop at Bennington College, it begins:

> When we were young
> you used to say, "Hello my friend, my little friend."
> and I, impatient with waiting all day for your kisses,
> would whisper of passion.

> I was your friend, your lover, your strong-willed wife
> who waited for your tender, tracing touch.
> How sweet was your breath! I wanted to inhale it all.
> I never understood how mortal breath could be so sweet

> And now you are dead. . . .

The poem ends:

> Come back, my love. Don't be dead.[6]

Kalmanoff says that her writing, by providing a meaningful outlet for her feelings, became the most important element in her eventually getting back on her feet. Some of the poems she wrote about her grief and anger that her husband died so young are grouped together in her book *Solo Flight,* in a section titled "In Memoriam."

The next section of her book, however, shifts decidedly toward escape from her grief, toward seeing the positive side of being single. Her lifestyle also expresses that growing appreciation. She lives by herself and says she likes it because creative people need to be alone to respond to their inner selves. She prefers traveling by herself too, because without the distractions of others, she can "experience things more intensely."

Now in her seventies, Kalmanoff teaches a workshop on creative writing or poetry appreciation every fall, leaving the spring and summer open for her writing and travel. She encourages students to write for the sheer joy of it, not just to get published. She counsels widows to write down their feelings every day, so that they can see their progress over time.

Recently Kalmanoff titled a new poem, appropriately enough, "In Praise of Solitude":

> Too many wasted years
> before I learned
> that filling empty spaces
> is a solitary job.
> I packed all those spaces
> with defective insulation . . .
> porous sex and ersatz love.
> Finally turning inward
> unbinding all the ties,
> my mind . . . churning, surging . . .
> solid fill supplied.
> I survived.

No longer lamenting her single status, Jean Kalmanoff has achieved a new identity by tapping into and nurturing the creativity that allows her to derive joy from her solo flight.

YOU, AN ARTIST?

It took Jean Kalmanoff years of immersion in her craft before she would claim to be a poet. Neither she nor other women I talked to, however—women who had seriously taken up writing, painting, music, and acting—used the word "artist" to describe themselves. But in the primary sense of the word, of course, they are. Although we usually think of artists as people who are especially good at what they do, an artist is actually just a person who practices the creative arts.

Given the time, space, and urge, we all have the potential to be artists. Still, very few of us claim to be creative, even though as children we all have a creative, playful streak. Most of it is trained out of us as we grow up and enter the serious worlds of learning and work.

And then, not everyone has a temperament suited for a creative life, even one that is just part-time. There are certain characteristics that most creative people share that lead them to the arts; psychotherapist Eric Maisel calls these common characteristics their "shared identity":[7]

- They are in a constant *search for the truth* about themselves and their lives.

- Their curiosity leads them to be *self-reliant* thinkers and dreamers.

- They cultivate a certain *wildness*, but one held in check.

- They have a burning *desire to create* in one form or another.

- They have the *courage* to take the first uncertain steps toward creating.

- They are able to tolerate and *manage the anxiety* that accompanies the creative process.

- They *commit themselves* enthusiastically to an ongoing struggle with inevitable frustrations and failures.[8]

If you find you share many of these characteristics, and harbor a dormant longing to express yourself through the arts, it's not too late to experiment with letting your creative side loose.

HOW TO FIND YOUR CREATIVE SELF

Psychologist Robert Epstein believes, based on years of studies of novel behavior in animals and people, that **creativity "is not something mystical; it's an extension of what you already know. . . . [N]ew behaviors (or 'ideas') emerge as old behaviors interact, and the process by which behaviors interact is orderly."**[9] You don't need a lot of help in the creative process. Epstein asserts that "creativity is always an individual process, and social disapproval is the major deterrent to creativity our entire lives."[10]

Epstein recommends using four techniques to stimulate creativity:

- *Capturing.* Pay attention to and write down new ideas wherever they occur to you—in bed, in the bath, or on the bus (what he calls the three B's of creativity). The scores of women who wrote daily journals were using this technique to good effect.

- *Challenging.* Consciously put yourself in situations where you are likely to feel frustrated and confused, might even fail, thereby forcing yourself to devise new behaviors and ideas. It goes without saying that widows and divorcées already have this technique built into their lives!

- *Broadening.* Creativity involves making original connections among wide-ranging subject areas, so you need to have basic knowledge in a variety of fields. Epstein advises you to learn about subjects you know absolutely nothing about.[11] Doing this worked for Melinda, who found that acting on her passion for courses on all kinds of new topics was like "the domino effect. The more I accomplish, the more I'm willing to try, even though I've had my share of flops."

- *Surrounding.* Activate new behaviors and ideas by surrounding yourself with a variety of stimuli and changing them often. Among the most creative women I talked to were Sue Ellen and Darleen, who spent considerable time with people of all ages and types who regaled them with novel, engaging ideas.

Analysts like Eric Maisel believe that **one important deterrent to realizing your creative potential in the arts is anxiety**. In his book *Fearless Creating,* Maisel names six different stages in the creative process and the various types of anxiety that accompany each stage. Maisel's notion is *not* to do away with these anxieties but to live and deal with them. He writes:

In large measure, these are anxieties that you *should* experience because, while anxiety is the greatest impediment to aliveness, in order to create you must invite anxieties into your life and live anxiously.... *If you are to create, you must invite anxiety in.* But then you must manage it. [12]

Maisel lists a variety of techniques you can use to become creative while managing your anxieties.

- *Consciously quiet your mind by "hushing,"* entering into a kind of trancelike state where you have few or no thoughts, and stay there. In this quiet place, you are likely to find an idea or vision that can be the kernel of your future creative work. As discussed in chapter 2, there are many approaches to relaxation and meditation that will enable you to "hush" your mind effectively.

- *Care for your emerging idea by "holding it:* giving it space, giving it a container, offering it life."[13] You can accomplish this as you go about your everyday life, letting your idea gestate until it becomes an image that demands to be expressed.

- *Begin your creative act by just taking a baby step,* like picturing a scene in your screenplay, or writing one line of your poem. Other baby steps will follow. As artist Julia Cameron says, "Set small and gentle goals and meet them."[14]

- *Nurture your wildness,* by being as sensitive, self-indulgent, passionate, nonconforming, inquisitive, rebellious, original, and spontaneous as you feel like being. Stop worrying for a while about what others think, follow your instincts, take risks, and be your own person.

- At the same time, *manage your wildness* by maintaining enough "healthy tameness" to be able to function in the world. "Wildness is the heat, tameness the thermostat," Maisel writes.[15]

Artist Julia Cameron advocates another useful approach in courses she offers on discovering your creative self. The primary tool you should use, according to Cameron, is **a daily technique called "the morning pages"**—three pages of stream-of-consciousness writing—done longhand, to be read *only* by you but not until some weeks later. The purpose of these pages is simple: "By spilling out of bed and straight onto the page every morning you learn to avoid the Censor."

For Cameron, the Censor is that negative part of you that is never satisfied, that denigrates everything you do, your "internalized perfectionist, a nasty internal and eternal critic." The obligatory daily act of unburdening yourself of your Censor's (and other) thoughts in the morning pages works this way:

> All that angry, whiny, petty stuff that you write down in the morning stands between you and your creativity. Worrying about the job, the laundry, the funny knock in the car, the weird look in your lover's eye—this stuff eddies through our subconscious and muddies our days. Get it on the page.[16]

Women who have tried this technique swear by its effectiveness. You can learn more about Cameron's approach in her book *The Artist's Way: A Spiritual Path to Higher Creativity.*

Help Yourself by Helping Others

FIND MEANING THROUGH VOLUNTEERING

Another way that women of all ages, races, and classes express themselves and find meaning is through volunteering for a cause they believe in. In doing so, they put into action the concerns that showed up in a recent national survey of voters that concluded that, more so than men, women are concerned about the economic circumstances of others, especially children and old people. These concerns ranked even higher than the women's concerns about *their own* economic situations. In particular, they worried about the increasing gap between the wealthy and poor in the United States.[17] Such humanitarian concerns, which motivate many women to become volunteers for causes close to their hearts, are part of a long tradition, as described by writer Caroline Bird:

> From the very beginning of America, women have banded together to improve their communities and help one another as well as people who can't help themselves. For generations, doing good was the only role a decent woman was allowed to play outside her home.[18]

This tradition springs from our society's notion that women *should* serve the needs of others. Psychiatrist Jean Baker Miller warns that this notion can lead to "the martyr syndrome or the smothering wife and mother"—if the woman puts her own needs second to those of others.[19] But, Miller advises, women are adept at serving others' needs, and doing so can be beneficial to them if their service is done willingly and simultaneously allows for their own self-development.

For women coping with the loss of a husband, doing good for others often serves this other purpose: doing good for themselves. That's what Tilly told me about her recovery after she was widowed in her forties. Overwhelmed by having to take a clerical job in order to support five children on her own, she still felt the need to do more to come to terms with her loss. "You can accept it with a grudge against the world or you can accept it by going out and helping other people. . . . My therapy was doing what I'm still doing—getting out there and being involved."

Tilly began by working for meaningful causes connected with her church and the senior center in her neighborhood. When that center began to sponsor a Widowed Persons Service, she jumped in and became one of the program's mainstays. Not only did she take a lead in its administration, but she began to counsel other widows one-on-one in their homes (although Tilly says she doesn't do counseling per se—she is just a good listener, asking questions and letting the other person talk). In that work, Tilly says, she found herself:

> If you can possibly help another person to heal, that heals you. Whatever I did in volunteer work probably did me more good than whatever good I was doing . . . There's a feeling of self-satisfaction in listening to someone and being able to say, "I know how you feel because I've been there myself." And that person knows, "I'm not alone in this."

Like Tilly, many women find enormous satisfaction as volunteers after they become single-again. Eva and Nadine experienced significant personal growth during stints with the Peace Corps. One Chinese American woman felt she was called to serve God after her husband of twenty years died. After studying in India with Mother Theresa, she was a missionary for a while in China and now, even though she is ill, continues her missionary work in Mexico.

Others like Fanny, who was widowed twice, first after a twenty-eight-year marriage and again after a five-year marriage, become full-time volunteers in their communities. When Fanny was first widowed, teaching school and raising their eight children took all her time and energy. But when her second husband left her well-off financially, she made a conscious decision to take charge of her life. "I have filled my life with activities where you don't need a partner," Fanny says. At one point, she believes she must have been on every board in the city. She does it, she says, because "I'd like to make the world a better place."

Locate Your Niche

Volunteering can be rewarding and exciting, but only if you find the right spot in the right organization. In selecting an organization to hook up with, take your time and shop around care-fully, asking and finding out the answers to these questions:

- *What are the group's goals, who belongs to it, and why?* You're looking for a match in terms of the cause you're interested in and compatible people to associate with.

- *What have they accomplished?* Find out what they actually *do* as well as what they take credit for.

- *Who does the work?* In a mixed-gender group, note espe-cially the role of women.

- *How much time is spent on "housekeeping" tasks* like financing and maintenance? Avoid organizations where these chores seem to be the main focus.

- *What would your role be?* What kind of roles do volunteers play, and are you interested in any of them?

- *What would the organization do for you?* Would it stimulate you and move you in a general direction you'd like to go in?

- *Would volunteering at the organization fill some of your social needs?* Whether you will want to stay with a group over the long term depends on whether you feel comfortable with other members of the group.

- *What could you contribute?* Is there something special or distinct about you that the group could profit from?[20]

Become an Activist

"I Can Change the World"

During the last half of this century, the concept of volun-teering has broadened considerably to include the increasing number of women interested less in ameliorating bad and unfair conditions than in changing the policies and institutions that cause them. Using as models the early feminists and the civil rights movement, these women pick issues that have particular resonance in their lives and team up to convince others that basic changes are needed. Their actions reflect the words of one woman to whom I talked: "I do believe that I can change the world. I am absolutely convinced that I can make a difference."

This woman, May, had been an active volunteer in all kinds of good causes during her twenty-six years of marriage. Her husband's death when she was fifty made her painfully aware of the problems faced by mature single women. As a result, May gradually became more and more involved in the Older Women's League (OWL), founding the local chapter where she lives and eventually serving on its national board of directors. Now retired, she organizes other women to lobby the state legislature to correct inequities that affect mature women.

May's evolution as a volunteer resembles that of OWL's founder, Tish Sommers, who discovered after her midlife divorce that she couldn't purchase health insurance at any price because of a history of breast cancer. Sommers decided to become an activist on issues like health care and jobs, which present special problems for older women. Looking for help, Sommers met newly widowed Laurie Shields, who was furious because, still in her fifties and with good credentials in advertising, she couldn't get a job. Sommers immediately recruited Shields.

Together, they started what was to become the National Displaced Homemakers Network—a grass-roots organization working on behalf of women who, like themselves, had lost their primary occupation—unpaid service to their families—when their husbands divorced them or died. That accomplished, they moved on to found OWL, one of the first national organizations to advocate for the needs of older women, including access to health care as "a right, not a privilege."[21] Both women are now deceased, but the organizations continue to carry out their platforms for reform.[22]

Although Sommers had always been an activist before turning to older women's issues, Shields had led a more conventional existence before her husband died. Radicalized by her encounters with life inequities *after* she became single-again, Shields became as committed to her goals and as adept at motivating and organizing others as any veteran change agent.

To Sommers, this was perfectly understandable: "No amount of study can substitute for the emotion engendered by direct experience," she wrote in an early organizing manual.[23] As sociologist Ruth Harriet Jacobs points out, that emotion is in great part rage.[24] **But instead of turning your rage inward and becoming bitter and depressed, you can turn it outward and become a missionary for a cause of crucial importance to you.**

A number of women I interviewed had become full-fledged activists after becoming single:

- Sue Ellen's lifelong activism and job experience in Congress emerged as critical assets when her divorcing husband vowed she'd never get a penny of his government pension. To prove otherwise, she formed a group of some ten women who called themselves "Civil Service Spouses for Equity." They drew up a bill authorizing survivorship benefits for ex-wives, organized State Department ex-wives to lobby for it, and saw it made into law.

- Anna found her mission in life after she divorced and then transformed a volunteer job with a Polish American organization into a job running it. Born in Poland before World War II of a Jewish father and a Catholic mother, she had survived her teen years in a Nazi detention camp. Now Anna works to build bridges between Jews and Catholics in Poland and the United States.

- After her beloved husband died, Tamara became a serious

advocate on behalf of bringing other deaf people like herself into the mainstream. A firm believer that all deaf people should know how to speech read (lip read) in order to function adequately in the hearing world, she travels all over the world to give papers and argue her views.

- Margie's recovery from a painful divorce led her to pursue a teaching and counseling career helping other "women in transition" move beyond their problems. Ready to retire, she discovered to her horror that she was ineligible for any Social Security and would get nothing from her husband's two pensions. Margie now uses what she learned from those experiences to help motivate other women to demand reforms to pension and Social Security laws.

SEEK TEAMMATES TO START FROM SCRATCH

Women like these did not go searching for a cause they cared about. It found *them*. If that has already happened to you, there are a number of ways you can work on behalf of that cause. You can, of course, operate on your own—filing a complaint or lawsuit to correct some inequity, for example, or speaking out in public or through the media. You can also take up the cause of someone else less fortunate or educated.[25]

But if you are serious about advocacy for social change on an ongoing basis, you need to locate like-minded people. That means either joining an existing organization or constructing your own. This step is essential because only by banding together with others can one person have any power. Tish Sommers explained what power should mean for women:

> To women, power is a frightening word, but it need not be. Power should be: having a say in things that affect our lives; representing truly or being truly represented; influencing decisions; being listened to and respected; becoming a full person with others who are likewise full people.[26]

To find an organization that does what you want to do, ask the same questions of a group that you would ask if you were going to volunteer as a service-provider. (See "Locate Your Niche," above.) Only this time ask them while wearing your activist hat. But because far fewer voluntary organizations do advocacy work than provide services, don't be surprised if no groups exist that fit your requirements.

If you do come up empty-handed in your search for a compatible organization, you may be faced with forming your own group. Although it's not an impossible task, you shouldn't take it lightly. One way to tackle it is by initially creating a study group or support group. Often such groups help members realize that others share their personal problems, which are caused in part by wrongheaded policies and attitudes. That recognition can lead the group to become active on behalf of needed changes.

That happened to A J Brand when she began to meet regularly with an informal support group of four other middle-aged women who found each other by participating in a YWCA divorce group. She soon realized that they were all being "steamrolled" in the divorce courts. "It was so outrageous to spend so much on lawyers to get so little. I thought, 'I simply must do something about this,'" A J recalls.

When these women began to make their complaints public, a reporter for their suburban Chicago paper wrote an article about them. That spawned responses from over fifty women with similar tales of woe. Out of that group, A J founded (and now directs) the National Organization for Financially Abused Women (NOFAW). She has written *A Common-Sense Guide to Divorce*[27] and is working to have the legislature change state law so that divorces in long-term marriages with children, where the inequities between the spouses are greatest, are no longer no-fault.[28]

A J sets an excellent example of how one woman can start from scratch to address a problem that affects her deeply. Here are some basic steps you can follow to do the same:

1. *Start with a core group of energetic teammates.*

2. *Learn as much as you can about the problems you have in common*—what Tish Sommers called the "bad scene"—in NOFAW's case, the women's unfair treatment in the divorce courts.

3. Out of that bad scene, *define an issue*—an aspect of the problem that shows the basic inequities involved and that your group has a good chance of doing something about in a short amount of time.

4. Do your homework so that you can *refine the issue* to make it clear-cut and easily comprehensible.

5. *Pick a target, freeze it* (don't get diverted to another), *personalize it* (give it a human face), and *polarize it* (point out the bad guys).[29]

6. *Find a theme or slogan that expresses the principle at stake*, what Sommers called "the peg that crystallizes all the wrongs into a 'right.'"[30]

7. *Seek other individuals to support your cause.* The best collaborators will be people with personal experiences with the injustice. But if they haven't been involved in the other steps, you'll need to be patient until they've caught up and are on board.

8. *Find other groups to act as allies.* At the same time, figure out who will oppose you and how to counter their arguments and criticisms.

9. *Get your message aired widely* though the media, public meetings, and debates.

10. *Be persistent until your message is heard and heeded.*[31]

Once you've won your first victory, you can use it as a stepping stone to other wins and to building a permanent organization. But remember that if you want to make an impact on more than just state and local laws and practices, you should hook up with a national organization by, for example, turning your group into a chapter or affiliate.[32]

❊❊❊❊❊

What These Women Have in Common

These women—artists, volunteers, and activists—share an obvious trait: devotion to what they care most about. But they also share other traits that mark them as women who have made a successful transition to a single life full of challenges and satisfactions:

- *They reject being marginalized and stereotyped as widows and divorcées.* Rather than feeling ashamed of their single status, they feel on the cutting edge of a new social trend.

- *They use their loss as an opportunity to dig deep into themselves to uncover what is most important to them.* They transform those values into a coherent belief system and a vision of the kind of person they want to become.

- *Mustering the courage to break taboos, they tell the truth as they see it,* risking accusations that they are eccentric, or too selfish, or aggressive, or unfeminine. They follow Ruth Harriet Jacobs's admonition: "Don't Rage. Be Outrageous."[33]

- *They seek personal fulfillment by pursuing their own passions* even when doing so is difficult—because although they recognize that the costs can be great, so can the rewards.

In many ways, they are like the pinecones that writer Kay Stoner unearthed in a California redwood forest. A park ranger told her that in order to get the cones to open and release their seeds, they had intentionally set fire to the woods. But Stoner says none of the cones showed any signs of fire, only "hopeful cracks in its shell, testifying to its success in scattering its seeds."[34]

None of the passionate women in this chapter showed any signs of the fire they had encountered when they lost their husbands either. But they had indeed been burned, even cracked open, allowing them to take on new missions, challenge conventional thinking, and become healers and agents of change. Their own private fires had galvanized them to scatter seeds that might ultimately change the world for the better.

13

To Be or Not to Be (Married)

The social change that has occurred in the last quarter of a century doesn't support the old model of marriage. Today's midlife women are having to discover new forms of intimacy, and often to rewrite the rules of marriage. Their new self-sufficiency (and the self-sufficiency of their children) allows them to say, "I can pull the wool off my eyes here. I don't have to pretend. I can decide what I need. I can choose what I want."

—Colette Dowling
Red Hot Mamas[1]

✂✂✂✂✂✂

Marriage as a Besieged Fortress

MAYBE I WILL; MAYBE I WON'T

Martha Stewart, a 90s icon, has been dubbed the "high priestess of style at home." After her husband left her in 1990, Stewart turned a catering business into a multimillion-dollar empire that includes books, her magazine, and a TV series.[2] Asked in an interview in *Fortune* magazine what she sacrificed for success, Stewart answers:

> I sacrificed family, husband. Not my choice. His choice. Now, I'm so happy that it happened. It took a long time for me to realize that it freed me to do more things. I don't think I would have accomplished what I have if I had stayed married. No way. And it allowed me to make friends that I know I never would have made.

When the interviewer says, "You make a great argument for never marrying," Stewart immediately responds, "Oh, I'd love to be married! To the right person."[3]

Does Stewart's answer surprise you? It should—if you've been reading the latest research about how divorced and widowed women feel about remarrying. One article in the *New York Times* states unequivocally that more and more middle-aged divorced women are indifferent to the prospect of remarrying. It says that they view "marriage as a vise, solitary life as an unexpected pleasure and relationships with men as better in small doses."[4]

An increasing number of widows over forty-five feel the same way, according to another article in the *Times* titled "'What? Me Marry?' Widows Say No." The author quotes sociologist Gordon Clanton as saying that more widows are choosing to stay unmarried. That's not only because of increased status and career opportunities but also because they understand that "marriage is not always a fair deal for women and it is possible to be a full person without being married."[5]

I don't entirely agree with this idea that there is a transformation in attitudes about marriage among single-again women. **Most of the women I interviewed appreciated the benefits they got from being single, but they hadn't given up on marriage.** Like Martha Stewart, given the right man and the right situation, no one told me that she would refuse to remarry.

What is more, many harbored buried (but still recognizable) pieces of the fantasy of a perfect marriage, expressed as a kind of longing for that certain someone. He would be the perfect companion—at home or traveling or going out socially. Someone who would nurture them and whom they could nurture in return. Someone who would provide warm, relaxed sex.

These confusing, contradictory attitudes about remarrying are exceedingly common. Writer Elsie Bliss quotes Montaigne as saying that "marriage is like a besieged fortress; those who are inside want to get out and those who are outside want to get in." But that doesn't mean that either being single or being married is a superior state. Bliss writes: "I readily admit I frequently miss what married people have when a marriage is going well, just as they miss the freedom I have to decide my own goals and priorities."[6]

Both the married and the single women I talked to agree with Bliss's analysis of the state of being single: it is not necessarily better or worse, just different. One woman who had remarried put it this way: "I've come to feel from myself and other women juggling all this that there are two sets of problems. One is all the things you have when you're married. And the other is all the things you have when you're single. There are advantages to both."

But even for women who are sure they want to, remarrying may be unlikely, for a whole lot of reasons.

WHY WOMEN DON'T REMARRY

One reason true love the second time around is so unattainable is that the deck is stacked against women past a certain age.

We all know the reasons: the best men are all married; men begin to die off just as women are hitting their stride; and when the few decent single men who manage to survive decide to marry, they usually pick a younger bride. So it's a strong possibility that the main reason more women are staying single is simply the dearth of single, attractive, compatible men their age (or younger) willing to marry *and* let them keep much of their newly won autonomy.

Somehow, though, when you become single, it takes a while to grasp that the demographics apply to you. **After a certain age, finding someone great to marry is a little like winning the office pool.** An informal estimate given me by demographer Martha Farnsworth Riche put "the gap between the number of women who would want a marriage and the number of men they might want to marry at as much as ten, or even twenty, to one."[7]

Things get even more discouraging if you perform an analysis of the costs of getting married when you are no longer young. Here they are:

- Even though you may want to set up an alliance in which you and your husband are fairly equal, *you may find that men your age or older have traditional expectations about your role as a wife.* Psychiatrist Jean Baker Miller points out that once you buy into the role of helpmate to and housekeeper for your husband, the possible ways you could make his life better are infinite.[8]

- *The need to mold yourself to your new partner's interests and hobbies can be less appealing once your own tastes and interests are set.* And when your new partner's interests include a whole slew of friends and a family that must be blended with your own, it presents a formidable challenge.

- Once you've become accustomed to the peace and quiet of living on your own, *you may be hesitant to plunge into the kinds of conflicts inevitable in an intimate relationship.* As one divorcée put it, "To me, marriage means learning to relate better, learning to deal with conflict, with differences. And I'm busy enough as it is without wanting to deal with differences."

⚅⚅⚅⚅⚅

The Search for Single Bliss

"THE CAPTAIN OF YOUR SHIP"

It's often easier to list the *dis*advantages of remarrying than it is to list the advantages of being single. One woman who makes a specialty of the latter, however, is Elsie Bliss, who has been on her own for many years after being divorced. In her articles and in courses with names like "Single Bliss" and "Advice for the Loveworn," Bliss is a humorous advocate for singlehood. She writes, "Being single is quite respectable. It is a valid way of life. It is not a tragedy or a handicap. It is being the boss; the captain of your ship."[9]

Bliss has put in a nutshell the main benefit of being single—you're in charge. Here's what other women said about their single lives:

- *About being in charge:* "I can finally run my own life," one woman told me. "I don't have to answer to my children. I don't have to answer to my friends. They don't even ask," said another.

- *About having to support themselves:* Very few women, even some of the poorest, said that living without a husband's financial support was all that onerous. Their pride in being able to support themselves seemed to compensate for any anxiety about not having enough money or a desire to live more opulently.

- *About living by themselves:* This from a widow: "I like my space and I like to be able to do things. If I don't want to come home from work, I don't have to come home from work. If I want to go for a weekend, I just do it." And this from a divorcée who had raised six biological and two step-children: "I'm living by myself for the first time in my whole life. And I think I'm going to like it. It's really cool to have your own space."

- *About the time they spend alone:* "I'm really enjoying my own company. I like to read. I like to listen to music. I'm kind of jealous of time I spend by myself." And this: "I like my solitude . . . I treasure it . . . It's delicious."

- *About feeling lonely:* Women explain that the payoffs for any loneliness are peace of mind, freedom from caregiving duties, and an ability to indulge in selfish pleasures, with little accompanying guilt.

These single-again women are alone, yes, but they are certainly not hermits. Lacking emotional sustenance from a husband, they form strong emotional bonds with others. Some transcend old resentments against their parents or siblings and breathe new life into those bonds. Others approach their grown children as adults and form deep friendships there. Still others build profound connections with their grandchildren. Outside their families, they reach back to revive meaningful friendships from the past. They turn to new friends from work and make them part of a network. They seek out other single women whose lifestyles and interests match their own to serve as soulmates and playmates.

SHEDDING YOUR LOVE ADDICTION

Finding peace of mind as a single-again doesn't happen overnight. Indeed, once a woman decides she will probably not remarry, she can become quite anxious, even depressed. That's because many women are afraid that they won't be able to find adequate substitutes for love or won't be safe or feel satisfied on their own.[10]

Women who meet those fears head-on, however, often discover that they are much more mature and self-contained than they had realized. One widow, for example, told me what a revelation it was when, several years after her husband died, she realized that she didn't have to have a relationship with a man to survive. A divorcée described a similar kind of turning point:

> About five years after my divorce, it finally occurred to me that I was responsible for myself. Down deep I had this feeling that of course there was a man out there somewhere who was going to marry me and take care of me. . . . Somewhere in my late forties, early fifties, it really began to sink in and take hold that I'm responsible for myself and I'm always going to have to provide for myself. And that's okay. That's not a terrible thing to have happen to you. That's not a tragedy. It's being an adult.

Not everyone can make the transition to feeling good about being alone without some help, however. David Burns, author of the classic *Feeling Good: The New Mood Therapy,* believes that many of us have a kind of love addiction that is hard to break because it is based on a "silent assumption": "I cannot be a truly happy and fulfilled human being unless I am loved by a member of the opposite sex. True love is necessary for ultimate happiness."[11] Clinging to that attitude is unhealthy because it incapacitates you, leading to more isolation, not less. It's great to *want* and enjoy a love relationship, but not okay to *need* one in order to feel whole.

Burns suggests a series of "pleasure predicting" exercises to help challenge your belief that "being alone is a curse."[12] First, write down a number of activities that you enjoy or that give you a feeling of accomplishment and the name of the person with whom you do them. (Write "self" if you do them alone.) Then, before doing them, predict how much pleasure you will get from each activity on a scale of 0 to 100 percent. Next, do each activity, recording afterward how much pleasure you actually got, using the same scale.

What you are likely to find is that you overestimate how much pleasure you will get from doing things with other people and underestimate the enjoyment of doing things on your own. The exercise helps because it makes clear how unnecessary it is to be with someone else to feel good about what you're doing or who you are. It shows, as many single-again women learn simply by trial and error, that life can be satisfying once you begin to have a good relationship with yourself—once you begin, as Burns describes it, "to treat yourself like a beloved friend."[13]

SOMETIMES IT TAKES TWO TRIES: FANNY

Most widows or divorced women move only gradually from pleasing others to focusing on their own unique interests and strengths, a transition that Gail Sheehy describes in her book *New Passages*. Sheehy documents how women in their forties move "from pleasing to mastery" as they enter "second adulthood." Both married and unmarried women can reach that state of maturity, Sheehy writes, but it frequently happens to women after a loss such as divorce or widowhood.[14]

For Fanny, it took two losses before she decided to move from pleasing others to pleasing herself. Her first marriage, to her high school sweetheart, lasted twenty-eight years. She worked to support him until he became a college teacher, finally going to college herself at the age of thirty-six, after they had had eight children.

When he died, she was left with just her salary as a grade-school teacher, three teenage children, and a thirteen-room house. "So just taking care of the house and taking care of the kids, going to school every day, getting their food, and getting their clothes, I didn't have time to worry about anything else," Fanny remembers. She had loved socializing with their married friends and kept it up for a while, only to be treated at social events as "that loose woman." Feeling more and more out of place, she gradually withdrew to more acceptable activities like needlepointing with her teacher friends.

That all changed when she started dating a widower she had known for over thirty years, who just happened to be head of a big union and a multimillionaire. After less than three years as a widow, she married him and took full advantage of what he had to offer her and her children.

When he died five years later, she was in her late fifties. She immediately knew that, after two husbands and eight children, she never wanted to take care of anyone else—"not even a pet or a plant." So she incorporated what she cared about most—friends and family—into a new, more carefree, unmarried life.

Fanny lives alone now in an unpretentious suburban rambler. She fills her life with loads of friends, volunteer work, and activities for which she doesn't need a partner. Her friends stuck by her during a four-year bout with cancer, one friend told me, because her positive attitude about life makes everyone want to be with her. During my few hours with Fanny, the telephone rang incessantly and a male bridge partner, intent on repairing her dining room table, kept coming and going from the house.

Fanny seems to thrive on the turmoil, especially when it involves her children and grandchildren. She has charted a course, by herself, to a place in the eye of the storm. "This is the calmest my life has ever been," she declares.

<hr />

Sex in the Nineties

GOING AGAINST STEREOTYPE

Sometimes single-again women find that they have little or no desire to have sex with a man, especially when they're still too angry or sad about losing the man they had. But as they get a handle on their grief, they may find their sexual desire returning—sometimes with a vengeance. Women who had a satisfying sex life when they were married seek out new sexual partners. And even those who had repressed their sexuality when they were married can experience a kind of awakening.

Sue Ellen was one of these, finding her first sexually satisfying relationship in her fifties. Although she had had five children, she characterizes her status before her divorce as "akin to the Virgin Mary"—absolutely no sexual experiences before she married and perhaps one orgasm during their thirty-five-year marriage.

That all changed after her divorce. Reading an underground paper one of her children brought home, Sue Ellen learned what a clitoris is and what it does, opening up a whole new arena of how her own body could respond sexually. She decided to take a risk when she began to date a man named Vic, showing him what he needed to do to get her excited. He was, she says, more intrigued than shocked.

Together they began to explore different kinds of lovemaking. Now in her sixties, she and Vic are still happily at it. And because her approach worked so well for her, Sue Ellen advises other women who don't get anything out of sex "to learn to speak up, for God's sake. . . . I think this sex thing is very very important. I realized I was on the verge of lunacy because I really needed it."

If you think Sue Ellen's attitude is a bit kinky, think again. Among women in their sixties who responded to a survey by *New Woman* magazine, some 24 percent said they were more interested in sex now than ever before.[15] These women hadn't bought into the stereotype about no-longer-young females: that their sexual desire is somehow inappropriate, even perverse, and should be repressed.

It's an idea that plagues even the most liberated of women,

claims Colette Dowling who wrote the classic feminist book *The Cinderella Complex.*[16] As Dowling, single and in her fifties, began to contemplate the idea of a new sexual relationship, she had a dream about chin hairs:

> Well, not chin hairs exactly, more like quills—long yellow-white quills that covered my chin. . . . The worst part was that I was trying to seduce someone in the next room and was worried that he might already have seen the quills and that it was too late. I had no tool for removing them, no tweezers or Klipette, only my fingers. Peering in the mirror, I pulled on one of the longer ones, determined to get it out, and miraculously I did. But then I saw how many more there were, dozens lying flat and thick and long against my chin. I was filled with a kind of frantic fear that I would never be able to keep up with them and that *he*, waiting in the next room, would find me hideous.[17]

Alarmed that her sexual yearning was leading to such anxiety about her aging (chin hairs are one manifestation she loathes), Dowling began to research the topic of midlife sexuality. Not only did she find authorities decrying the "heightened sexuality" of older women, but "the media were making middle-aged women seem pathetic: loveless, shapeless, with nothing to offer, yet fatally attracted to their boy toys." Out of that research, Dowling produced *Red Hot Mamas,* a book that urges women over fifty to fight the negative stereotypes and make the most of the last half of their lives, including keeping sexually active.[18]

WHY AND WITH WHOM?

Women cite a number of reasons for why they opt for sexual relations:[19]

- *For comfort and consolation.* Especially in the early stages of being single, sex with a caring partner can provide a temporary balm for your feelings of loss.

- *To affirm their desirability.* When you're uncertain about whether you're still attractive, sex with someone who admires you can boost your feelings of femininity and self-worth.

- *For the thrills it provides.* Freed up from the constraints of marriage, you can act out fantasies and seek unconventional sex.

- *As a stepping-stone to emotional intimacy.* When you think a relationship has potential, you need to know whether you are compatible sexually.

Once you've decided to be sexually active, you'll need to decide what kind of partner you're looking for and go after him. **Although you may have always let a potential partner take the initiative in the past, that isn't as likely to happen now.** And with as few men as there are who are (a) near your age, (b) unmarried, (c) heterosexual, and (d) sexually adequate, you may have to expand your notions about whom you might seek as a lover.

Some single-again women do that by choosing a sexual relationship with another woman. That choice often brings intimacy, fun, and companionship—from the relationship as well as the links it affords to a community of other homosexual and bisexual women. The down side, of course, is that it can subject a woman to criticism, possibly intense, from friends and family.

Whether your choice is male or female, no arrangement will satisfy all of your reasons for wanting a sexual partner. The following table lists some pros and cons of possible different arrangements:

Option	Advantages	Disadvantages
Sleep around with whoever is willing and available	Ultimate in freedom of choice and thrills	Ultimate in uncertainty and risk of sexually transmitted disease (including AIDS)
Sleep with a friend or former lover occasionally	Comfortable and comforting, while keeping lust at bay	Friendship and sex aren't always compatible; difficult to define "occasionally"
Seduce a married person	Thrills of forbidden sex	Lack of companionship; danger of becoming emotionally involved; possibility of spouse finding out
Link up with a single younger person	An ego booster; likely to be fun	Emotional committment uncertain; little in common
Have one lover and live in separate quarters	More privacy and freedom	No real home; emotional committment uncertain
Have one lover only and live together	Companionship, committment	Many of the same problems that married couples have

If none of these options appeals to you, you may decide, like many single people, to become celibate. Although the word "celibate" implies a monastic existence, celibacy does not have to be that way. Feminist Germaine Greer is a firm supporter of freedom of sexual expression for everyone, including the right *not* to have sex in order to have a deep bond. She writes, "Human love does not depend upon the need to mate or the need for orgasm; the greatest love can survive distance and even death."[20]

Single-again women who are celibate find all kinds of ways to treat and nurture themselves and to meet their needs for physical love, including

- masturbation;

- hugging their children and grandchildren and friends a lot;

- buying a dog or cat (or maybe more than one); and

- getting a massage or self-massage.

The problem, of course, is that substitutes for an intimate sexual relationship with another man or woman are just that—substitutes. As such, they're only very pale imitations of the real thing. But in the end, a lot of women choose to accept the loss of their former physical relationship. They seek out these and other substitutes, as well as a more cerebral lifestyle, something that can be hard at first, but becomes easier over time.

GETTING UP THE NERVE TO PRACTICE "SAFER SEX"

Women who became single in the 1980s and 1990s can look back with some envy at their sisters who were single-agains in the decades before the scourge of AIDS. Then, regardless of whether their sexual experiences had been good while they were married, women of all ages could experiment with different kinds of sexual relationships. With luck, they might find someone with whom sexual intimacy—and even marriage—was possible.

But that was then and this is now. Today, a disease that was once confined mainly to homosexual males and intravenous drug users has become a major threat to women of all ages and classes, increasing at a faster rate among women than among men.

One-fourth of new AIDS cases among women are in those over forty. (These women may be at increased risk because menopause can result in thin or dry vaginal tissues that are more likely to tear during intercourse.)[21] A book by Gena Corea reveals that women are ten times more likely to get AIDS from a man during sex than the other way around. The book's title, aptly, is *The Invisible Epidemic: The Story of Women and AIDS.*[22]

The first step, then, is to make women more aware of the threat. But even when sexually active single women are aware of AIDS, they often don't follow through with safer-sex practices. In one survey, 71 percent said they did not even use a condom.[23] Women are reluctant to insist on condoms for fear of seeming pushy, or because a potential partner appears healthy or claims to be celibate, or because it might put a damper on their partner's pleasure.[24] And yet *not* insisting is to engage in a version of Russian roulette, where, if you lose, the outcome is just as lethal as if you had been shot in the head.

It may be difficult initially, but it's vital to work up the nerve to discuss your potential partner's sex history, even when having sex is just a remote possibility. A *Lear's* magazine survey found that one in four of the respondents were making these kinds of queries *ahead of time*, while 13 percent said they ask a potential partner to have an AIDS test.[25]

Because of the looming threat to women, the Boston Women's Health Book Collective added new sections on AIDS and HIV, which causes AIDS, when they came out with revised editions of both *Our Bodies, Ourselves* and *Ourselves, Growing Older.* Here's what *The New Ourselves, Growing Older* recommends you do to prepare yourself for being sexually active:

- Explore with your friends how to say "yes" to sex you want and "no" to sex you don't want. . . .

- Think and talk about HIV prevention *long before* engaging in sexual activity. You could practice a safe-sex "script" with a friend.

- Avoid drugs and alcohol and any situation that might impair your judgment and ability to practice safer sex.

- Be responsible and realistic. Keep your safer sex kit(s)—latex gloves, latex condoms, water-based lubricant, etc.—well stocked and close at hand by your bed and in your bag.

The most important aspect to staying safe is understanding the way you can get infected. HIV is a virus that is in all body fluids, but only in strong concentrations in blood, semen, and vaginal secretions. Engaging in unsafe sexual activity (activity that allows fluid with a strong concentration of HIV to enter your bloodstream) puts you at risk.[26]

If you don't have sufficient information about how HIV is transmitted and what you need to do to protect yourself, you can get it from the National Women's Health Network, which publishes an information packet on the topic.[27] It should be obligatory reading for anyone venturing into the dating world today. (See the Resources section for chapter 13.)

The Search for Happily-Ever-After

WHAT WOMEN MISS ABOUT MARRIAGE

There are three different aspects of being married that women who are single-again miss: the lifestyle; the intimacy; and the financial and physical support.

Missing a Married Lifestyle

For many women, anything other than a married lifestyle just misses the mark. As one woman put it, "In spite of everything, it's still a world that is set up by the Noah's Ark principle." The principle plays itself out like this:

- *Single women are left out of all kinds of social activities among couples.* They're often not invited, but even when they are, some women won't go out in mixed company if they don't have a male partner. As for going alone or in the company of another woman, they'd rather stay at home.

- *Without the power and visibility that a husband offers, a mature single woman can feel invisible, especially sexually.* Asked how it is to be single at her age (fifty), a widow replies, "I hate it. . . . I hate the loss of power that women experience."

- *Many women genuinely enjoy nurturing a man and respond- ing to what he wants and likes.* When someone isn't making demands on this kind of woman, as Germaine Greer puts it, "She becomes a moon without an earth. What she wants is to be wanted, and nobody wants her."[28]

Missing Intimacy

For many women, being married is vital because of the emo- tional and sexual intimacy it can bring. One study comparing women aged thirty-five with women twenty years older found that the older women generally demonstrated renewed vigor and feel- ings of confidence. But one problem often haunted those who were neither married nor mothers: they lacked intimacy in their lives.[29]

One woman wrote to tell me why she had decided to remar- ry after her husband of thirty-three years died:

> I missed no longer being primary in someone's life and having that person primary in mine. . . . When my beloved [husband] left me, there was no longer any one person who needed me, to whom I was number ONE. When I married [my second husband], I regained that position—with him.

Another reason for my wanting to marry again was that I missed the emotional and sexual intimacy of a satisfying relationship. I was fifty-five when [my first husband] died and I had other relationships but they were only palliative, not enduring or what a conventional mother-grandmother like me desired.

Lacking emotional and sexual intimacy leads some single-again women to feelings of "deadness" or "pointlessness," which propels them toward remarrying. "I lost an enormous amount of my joie de vivre and my sensuality," one widow said, feelings that she has not been able to replace. Others spoke of **something that often hits with particular force: the lack of touching someone and being touched in return.** That was especially hard for Tilly:

I miss having someone to dress up for. I miss hearing compliments that make my cheeks rosy. I miss having someone touch me or hug me or kiss me. I miss being loved by a man. There's an expression, "My husband died but my libido didn't."

What single-again women can do to express that libido is covered in the previous section, "Sex in the Nineties."

Missing Financial and Physical Support

Financial guru Frances Leonard sums up the research on what happens financially when married women become single:

Marital status determines wealth. At all ages, but especially in later years, if you draw a line between the American haves and have-nots, the single most reliable predictor of wealth is not race or gender, but marital status. If you put the marrieds on one side of the line and the unmarrieds on the other, you will divide the poor from the rich.[30]

Most of the women I interviewed were not really poor

(although several were), but they were all obviously less well off than when married. Although lowered economic status had been a source of great anxiety in the beginning, they said their fears had gradually diminished as they took charge of their finances and found ways to support themselves.

Still, not having to worry so much about finances, especially about their retirement, was an enticement to marry. One widow joked about tracking down a rich man with a heart condition and no relatives. A divorcée, venting her frustration about losing her former lifestyle, told me, "I would like to be back in my great big house on Long Island Sound with a rich husband and a boat and I would like to be traveling. I would like to have money."

Another common complaint was the lack of having someone in the kind of physical role a husband traditionally plays—fixing things in the house, taking care of the car, handling tasks that take upper-body strength. Even in the more traditional marriages where the wives had left money management to their husbands, these women often complained more about how difficult it was to assemble purchases that came unassembled than about how difficult it was to handle the finances on their own.

Connected to that physical role, but usually unstated, was the wish to have someone they felt could protect them from harm. Although violent crime is down in the United States, fear of crime is not, and women suffer disproportionately from that fear. For many, it is an important factor in where they choose to live and in where and when they are willing to go out, especially at night.[31] It may be unrealistic for women to assume that a husband will be able to protect them from someone intent on harming them, but many women harbor that notion.

WHAT'S MOST IMPORTANT?

Out of this list of physical and emotional needs that a marriage can fill, are there any that tip the balance, that would make even women who are quite happy being single consider remarrying? One study of divorced women over forty, most contented with their lot, asked them why they might want to remarry. While less than 40 percent of the women said it would be for financial reasons, over half said they would remarry for sexual intimacy or to have someone to grow old with.[32]

This would not come as much of a surprise to psychiatrist Peter Kramer, whose explorations of intimacy and autonomy have led him to conclude, "Certainly attachment is an essential drive, as basic as sex or hunger."[33] A woman can find this intimacy with another woman as well as with a man, of course, either in a sexual or in a close platonic relationship. **What is important in achieving intimacy is not whether a woman remarries but whether she can create a relationship in which there is mutual caring, respect, and commitment — one where both parties are comfortable being themselves and letting each other grow.**

Revising the Rites of Courtship

Apparently, finding a man today requires a lot of ingenuity. It's like being back in school, where the pretty girls get all the boys, even if you *are* smarter and have a better personality. Only in this case, the pool of pretty girls is huge because it includes everyone your own age, plus all of them from every decade behind you.

Also, the tried and true method for meeting someone to date—having a friend introduce you—seems to be less and less in practice now, most women said. As a result, the techniques for finding a prospect have changed considerably. Here are some tips that women gave me about courtship in the nineties:

- *Join a group or activity for singles, often sponsored by a church or temple, or try Parents Without Partners.* Such groups allow you to socialize with members of the opposite sex without having to worry constantly about pairing up.

- *Take the initiative instead of the other way around.* Melinda says she discovered that fact of life at her first singles' event: "I saw that all the women approached the men. Not one man approached a woman. So I said, 'Okay, this is what it is later in life.'"

- *At a singles' event, sit by the door* so you can assess each man who comes in and select in advance which ones to approach.

- *Try a personal ad, but place the ad, don't just respond to one, and pick a local magazine or newspaper that targets readers who are like you.* By placing the ad, you retain some control and can ask for whatever you think is important—like a photo, or a sense of his values. Jean, who met her fiancé through an ad she placed, advises single friends to do the same because other ways of meeting men are so limited.

- *Meet a blind date for lunch or a drink in a public place.* Then, if it obviously isn't going to work out, you won't be stuck with him all evening and you can escape more gracefully.

- *Try to get a widower's attention during that small window of opportunity when he is no longer overwhelmed by grief and before someone else snatches him.* But be aware that you'll be competing with the legions of "casserole ladies"—single women who show up at a newly widowed man's door with his dinner—even when they barely knew him when he was still married.

- *Try a dating service.* There are even some that target mature people; their services can cost anywhere from $70 to $4,000, according to *Modern Maturity* magazine. (The article doesn't say how well the services work—just that you should be careful not to get ripped off.)[34]

- *Link up via cyberspace.* When I was monitoring conversations on SeniorNet, two couples said that they had met online and eventually married. One widow told me she had found a few prospects on Romance Connection (on America Online), but they had all fizzled out once she proceeded past the initial get-acquainted stage.

- *Stir up the embers of an old romance, or just add new embers to an old friendship.* Merna, who married a man she had dated in college, commented, "People I know who have remarried late in life often have known the person they marry for a long time. And I think that helps you get up the nerve to do this—that the person knew you not just when you were older, but knows more of your life. There's another connection with you." What she doesn't mention is that the connection might be enhanced because each of you has memories of a more youthful physical version of the other.

How Will You Know?

What if, after trying single-again life for a while, you are still intent on getting remarried? What exactly are you looking for in a permanent partner, and how will you know if you've found him (or her)?

Psychologists who specialize in the analysis of personality types speculate that people of both genders may be attracted initially to individuals who are quite different in how they perceive and relate to the world—introverts to extroverts, for example, or emotional people to rational ones. Because one person has what the other person lacks, those differences make the other person exciting. But the man or woman who makes a good date or a satisfying lover does not necessarily make a good permanent partner. In fact, he or she may be totally unsuitable for the long haul. As time goes by, the very differences that were attractive begin to grate and conflicts arise.[35]

When it comes to living happily ever after, or even to keeping a close friend, it is easier if two people are more similar than they are different, especially in the way they view life.[36] That's probably also true when it comes to how mature we are, something psychiatrist Peter Kramer says includes an "amalgam of traits like maturity, autonomy, and integrity." Taken together, these traits compose one's level of development of self.[37]

So if you're thinking about getting married, it's important to watch out for whether someone you are dating measures up in two respects—similar worldview and level of maturity. But watching out is no real guarantee that you'll know for certain. During courtship, people often try to emphasize their opposite side to make an impression.[38] And Kramer describes how limited we are in identifying a good partner:

> Humans give off ambiguous signals and engage in deception, so that skill at detection competes with skill at concealment. To these intricacies are added the variety of our appetites and the discontinuity of our character. Personality is in part a function of fluctuating mood. Judgement is clouded by our inertia once we have bonded and by our fear of loneliness, which causes us selectively to ignore unpleasant truths.[39]

If you've only known someone for a short time, it's likely you'll only find out whether he's who he seems to be *after* you've tied the knot and the honeymoon is over. Even living together for a time is no guarantee, but obviously the longer you delay marrying, the better. Still, that assumes that *he* is not in a hurry to marry. Putting off marriage to a potentially suitable mate in order to be absolutely sure has cost many single-again women their only chance to remarry, when another woman more willing to take a risk moves in and snatches him. Whether they should have let that happen is something these women ponder for years afterward.

FORGING A PARTNERSHIP

Once you think you've found the partner of your dreams, what can you do to create a marriage in which you have the kind of intimacy you want but still retain your sense of yourself as an autonomous individual? **One important step is to make sure that you and your husband-to-be have the same *kind* of marriage in mind.** To that end, talk through what each of you expects from a partner and try to work out any differences before you marry.

What you want to achieve is an understanding about the nature of your marriage, which you can use as a reference point down the line. For example, *if your goal is a marriage of equals,* you might decide that you both will

- handle differences by negotiating them, making an effort to give and take rather than to win;

- take on a fair share of your joint responsibilities;

- refrain from viewing each other's personality traits as strengths and weaknesses, but instead see them as differences to be respected;

- be available to help and support each other whenever you can, at the same time granting each other independence and space.

The second step is to decide whether the benefits of taking on a new permanent partner outweigh the costs. Psychiatrist Kramer believes that second marriages are often not a whole lot better than first marriages. But when they are, "It is often because the second marriage benefits from efforts or compromises that might as readily have been applied to the first."[40]

Forging a new partnership means being willing to make those efforts and compromises. Those are the costs. For the benefits to outweigh them, your new partner must be someone who meets your needs for caring, intimacy, and autonomy. Although finding that person is rare, it does happen. And if it does, *you*, better than anyone, will be able to recognize, and grab hold of, the miracle it represents.

* * *

In a variety of ways, the women in this book transformed their former identities as wives into new identities as women living exciting, satisfying lives. Choosing to remain single-again or to remarry, they found the rewards that come from taking charge of the rest of their lives.

You can follow the courses they charted. Or using your own resources, intuition, and judgment, you can chart your own course. Either way, with patience, persistence, and courage, you can make it through rough waters to a life you can truly call your own.

Resources

General

Ahrons, Constance. *The Good Divorce*. New York: HarperCollins, 1995.

American Association of Retired Persons (AARP)
601 E Street, N.W.
Washington, D.C. 20049
(800) 424-2277
online: http://www.aarp.org
Single copies of AARP publications can be ordered free from AARP Fulfillment (EEØ8Ø8) at this address. Include the publication number with your order.

American Association of Retired Persons. *Divorce After Fifty—Challenges and Choices*. Washington, D.C.: author, 1987.

Anderson, Carol, and Susan Stewart, with Sona Dimidjian. *Flying Solo: Single Women in Midlife*. New York: W. W. Norton & Company, 1994.

Apter, Terri. *Secret Paths: Women in the New Midlife*. New York: W. W. Norton & Company, 1995.

Bird, Caroline. *Lives of Our Own: Secrets of Salty Old Women*. Boston: Houghton Mifflin, 1995.

Brothers, Joyce. *Widowed.* New York: Ballantine, 1991.

Caine, Lynne. *Being a Widow.* New York: Viking/Penguin, 1988.

Doress-Worters, Paula, and Diana Laskin Siegal, eds. *The New Ourselves, Growing Older: Women Aging with Knowledge and Power.* New York: Simon & Schuster/Touchstone, 1994.

Engel, Margorie, and Diana Gould. *The Divorce Decisions Workbook: A Planning and Action Guide with FORMulas to Help You in Four Key Decision Areas—Financial, Legal, Practical and Emotional.* New York: McGraw-Hill, 1992.

Hayes, Christopher, Deborah Anderson, and Melinda Blau. *Our Turn: The Good News about Women and Divorce.* New York: Pocket Books, 1993.

Jacobs, Ruth Harriet. *Be an Outrageous Older Woman.* Rev. ed. New York: HarperPerennial, 1997.

Kaganoff, Penny, ed. *Women on Divorce: A Bedside Companion.* San Diego: Harcourt Brace, 1997.

Lerner, Harriet. *Life Preservers: Staying Afloat in the High Seas of Love and Life.* New York: HarperCollins, 1996.

National Center for Women and Retirement Research. *Women and Divorce: Turning Your Life Around.* Southampton, N.Y.: author, Long Island University, 1993.

Penn, Shana. *The Women's Guide to the Wired World: A User-Friendly Handbook and Resource Directory.* New York: Feminist Press at the City University of New York, 1997.

Porcino, Jane. *Growing Older, Getting Better: A Handbook for Women in the Second Half of Life.* New York: Continuum, 1991.

Sheehy, Gail. *New Passages: Mapping Your Life Across Time.* New York: Random House, 1995.

Trafford, Abigail. *Crazy Time: Surviving Divorce and Building a New Life.* Rev. ed. New York: HarperPerennial, 1992.

Triere, Lynette, and Richard Peacock. *Learning to Leave.* Rev. ed. New York: Warner Books, 1993.

1. Facing the Chasm

Caine, Lynn. *Widow.* New York: Morrow, 1974.

James, John, and Frank Cherry. *The Grief Recovery Handbook: A*

Clearly Defined Program for Moving Beyond Loss. New York: HarperPerennial, 1989.

Kingma, Daphne Rose. *Coming Apart.* New York: Fine Communications, 1997.

Koman, Aleta. *How to Mend a Broken Heart: Letting Go and Moving On.* Lincolnwood, IL: NTC/Contempory Publishers, 1997.

Kübler-Ross, Elisabeth. *On Death and Dying.* New York: Macmillan, 1969.

Lieberman, Morton. *Doors Open, Doors Close: Widows Grieving and Growing.* New York: Grosset/Putnam, 1996.

Lightner, Candy, and Nancy Hathaway. *Giving Sorrow Words: How to Cope with Grief and Get On with Your Life.* New York: Warner, 1990.

Manning, Douglass. *Don't Take My Grief Away: What to Do When You Lose a Loved One.* San Francisco: HarperCollins West, 1984.

Parkes, Colin Murray, and Robert Weiss. *Recovery from Bereavement.* New York: Aaronson, 1995.

Pennebaker, James. *Opening Up: The Healing Power of Expressing Emotions.* New York: Guildford Press, 1997.

Rapoport, Nessa. *Woman's Book of Grieving.* New York: Morrow, 1994.

Stearns, Ann Kaiser. *Coming Back: Rebuilding Lives After Crisis and Loss.* New York: Ballantine, 1988

2. Coping with the Stress That Accompanies Change

Abramson, Edward. *Emotional Eating: A Practical Guide to Taking Control.* New York: Simon & Schuster/Jossey-Bass, 1993.

Benson, Herbert, and Eileen Stuart. *The Wellness Book: The Comprehensive Guide to Maintaining Health and Treating Stress-Related Illness.* Reprint ed. New York: Simon & Schuster/Fireside, 1993.

Borysenko, Joan. *Minding the Body, Mending the Mind.* New York: Bantam Books, 1988.

Boston Women's Health Book Collective
240A Elm Street

Somerville, MA 02144
(617) 625-0271
Publishes Our Bodies, Ourselves *and* Ourselves, Growing Older. *Requests to their Women's Health Information Center are answered for a nominal fee.*

Domar, Alice, and Henry Dreher. *Healing Mind, Healthy Woman: Using the Mind-Body Connection to Manage Stress and Take Control of Your Life.* New York: Dell, 1997.

Goleman, Daniel. *The Meditative Mind.* Los Angeles: J. P. Tarcher, 1988.

Jahnke, Roger. *The Healer Within: The Four Essential Self-Care Techniques for Creating Optimal Health.* San Francisco: HarperSanFrancisco, 1997.

Kabat-Zinn, Jon. *Full Catastrophe Living: Using the Wisdom of Your Body and Mind to Face Stress, Pain, and Illness.* New York: Delacorte Press, 1990.

Lasater, Judith. *Relax & Renew: Restful Yoga for Stressful Times.* Berkeley, CA: Rodmell Press, 1995.

Louden, Jennifer. *The Woman's Comfort Book: A Self-Nurturing Book for Restoring Balance in Your Life.* San Francisco: Harper, 1992.

Norden, Michael. *Beyond Prozac.* New York: HarperCollins, 1995.

Solo Dining Savvy (The Newsletter Devoted to "Taking the Bite Out of Eating Alone")
P.O. Box 1025
South Pasadena, CA 91031
(800) 299-1079
e-mail: solodining@aol.com

Voight, Karen. *Precision Training for Body and Mind.* New York: Hyperion, 1996.

3. A Tiger by the Tail: Dealing with Lawyers

Academy of Family Mediators
(617) 674-2663
Request a list of local practitioners who are members.

American College of Trust and Estate Counsel
3415 South Sepulveda Blvd., Suite 460
Los Angeles, CA 90034

Widows can write for a listing of trust and estate lawyers who are members of the college and who practice in their state.

Brand, A J. *A Common Sense Guide to Divorce*. Divorce Reform Publishing, 1996.
For a copy, send $12.95 plus $3 shipping to P.O. Box 823, Northfield, IL 60093.

Leonard, Frances. Divorce and Older Women. Washington, D.C.: Older Women's League, 1987.
Contact OWL at 666 11th Street, N.W., Suite 700, Washington, D.C. 20001 (202) 783-6686.

Nolo Press *(newsletter, books, and self-help legal materials)*
950 Parker Street
Berkeley, CA 94710
(510) 549-1976
online: http://www.nolo.com

Pistotnik, Bradley. *Divorce War!: Fifty Strategies Every Woman Needs to Know to Win*. Holbrook, MA: Adams Media Corp., 1996.

Wilson, Carol. *The Survival Manual for Women in Divorce*. Dubuque, IA: Kendall/Hunt Publishing, 1995.

Winner, Karen. *Divorced from Justice: The Abuse of Women by Divorce Lawyers and Judges*. New York: Regan Books, 1996.

4. Gain Financial Expertise: Your Own and Others'

American Association of Retired Persons. *Facts About Financial Planners*. Rev. ed. Washington, D.C.: author, 1994. *Request publication No. D14050.*

Armstrong, Alexandra, and Mary Donahue. *On Your Own: A Widow's Passage to Emotional and Financial Well-Being*. Chicago: Dearborne Financial Publishing, 1993.

Beardstown Ladies Investment Club, with Leslie Whitaker. *The Beardstown Ladies' Common Sense Investment Guide*. New York: Hyperion, 1994.

Campbell, Gillie, and Caroline Chauncey. "Money Matters: The Economics of Aging for Women." In *The New Ourselves, Growing Older: Women Aging with Knowledge and Power*. Ed. Paula Doress-Worters and Diana Laskin Siegal. New York: Simon & Schuster/Touchstone, 1994. 187–203.

Crockett, Marilyn. *The Money Club: The Park Avenue Women's Guide to Personal Finance.* New York: Simon & Schuster, 1997.

Dowling, Colette. *Maxing Out: Why Women Sabotage Their Financial Security.* New York: Little Brown, 1998.

Hayes, Christopher, and Kate Kelly. *Money Makeovers: How Women Can Control Their Financial Destiny.* New York: Doubleday, 1997.

Lee, Barbara. *The Financially Independent Woman: A Step-by-Step Guide to Successful Investing.* Secaucus, N.J.: Carol Publishing Group, 1996.

Leonard, Frances. *Money and the Mature Woman: How to Hold On to Your Income, Keep Your Home, Plan Your Estate.* Reading, MA: Addison-Wesley, 1993.

Lieberman, Annette, and Vicki Lindner. *Unbalanced Accounts: Why Women Are Still Afraid of Money.* New York: Viking/Penguin, 1988.

The National Association of Investors Corporation affiliates:
The National Association of Individual Investors (NAII) and
The National Association of Investment Clubs (NAIC)
P.O. Box 220
Royal Oak, MI 48068
248-583-NAIC (6242)
Members of NAII receive their monthly magazine Better Investing. *NAIC clubs pay $35 a year, plus $14 for each club member. Club members receive NAIC's official guide, "Starting and Running a Profitable Investment Club."*

Orman, Suze. *The Nine Steps to Financial Freedom.* New York: Crown, 1997.

Quinn, Jane Bryant. *Making the Most of Your Money.* Rev. and updated ed. New York: Simon & Schuster, 1997.

Unger, Alan. *Financial Self-Confidence for the Suddenly Single: A Woman's Guide.* Los Angeles: Lowell House, 1997.

Women's Financial Information Program
American Association of Retired Persons-Dept MM
601 E Street, N.W.
Washington, D.C. 20049
(800) 424-2277
Request information on one of the thousand sites near you that offer courses on money management for women.

5. Get a Job (or Keep the One You Have)
See also the resources for Chapter 11, "Step by Step to a Career"

AARP Work Force Program
c/o American Association of Retired Persons
601 E Street, N.W.
Washington, D.C. 20049
(800) 424-2277
Request information on the ninety sites that teach job search skills.

American Association of Retired Persons. *Returning to the Job Market: A Woman's Guide to Employment Planning.* Washington, D.C.: author, 1992.
Request publication No. D14952.

America's Job Bank
online: http://www.ajb.dni.us

Bloomburg, Gerri, and Margaret Holden. *The Women's Job Search Handbook.* Charlotte, VA: Williamson Publishing Company, 1991.

Bolles, Richard. The 1998 *What Color Is Your Parachute?* Berkeley, CA: Ten Speed Press, 1997.

Dodson, Diane, and Deborah Chalfie. *The Contingent Workforce: Implications for Today's and Tomorrow's Midlife and Older Women.* Washington, D.C.: AARP, 1996.
Request publication No. D14561.

King, Julie Adair, and Betsy Sheldon. *The Smart Woman's Guide to Resumés and Job Hunting.* Hawthorne, N. J.: Career Press, 1991.

National Employment Lawyers Association (NELA)
600 Harrison Street, Suite 535
San Francisco, CA 94107
Send a self-addressed stamped business-size envelope to request a listing of the lawyers in your state who represent employees.

Peace Corps
1990 K Street, N.W.
Washington, D.C. 20526
(800) 424-8580

Riley, Margaret, Frances Roehm, and Steve Oserman. *The Guide to Internet Job Searching.* Lincolnwood, IL: NTC Publishing Group, 1996.

Schlachter, Gail. *The Back-to-School Money Book: A Financial Aid Guide for Midlife and Older Women Seeking Education and Training.* Washington, D.C.: American Association of Retired Persons, 1994. *Request publication No. D15400.*

The Senior Community Service Employment Program (SCSEP)
c/o American Association of Retired Persons
601 E Street, N.W.
Washington, D.C. 20049
(800) 424-2277
AARP publishes an "SCSEP Fact Sheet." Request English version publication No. D14038 or Spanish version publication No. D162570.

In addition to AARP, the national sponsors of the Senior Community Service Employment Program are The National Council on the Aging, The National Urban League, Green Thumb, The National Council of Senior Citizens, The National Caucus and Center on Black Aged, The U.S. Forest Service, the Asociacion Nacional Pro Personas Mayores, The National Indian Council on Aging, and the National Pacific Asian Resource Center. Other funds are administered by state agencies on aging.

Shuman, Nancy, and William Lewis. *Back to Work: How to Re-enter the Working World.* New York: Barron's, 1985.

Smith, Maggie. *Changing Course: A Positive Approach to a New Job or Lifestyle.* San Diego: Pfeiffer & Company, 1993.

Thrailkill, Diane. *Temp by Choice.* Hawthorne, N.J.: Career Press, 1994.
Order from Career Press, 800-CAREER-1

Toropov, Brandon. *303 Off-the-Wall Ways to Get a Job.* Franklin Lakes, N.J.: Career Press, 1996.

Women Work! The National Network for Women's Employment
(formerly the National Displaced Homemakers Network)
1625 K Street, N.W., Suite 300
Washington D.C. 20006
(202) 467-6346
Request their most recent directory of some thirteen hundred employment programs.

6. Turn to Wise Friends—Where You Can Find Them

Hochman, Andee. *Everyday Acts and Small Subversions: Women Reinventing Family, Community and Home.* Portland, OR: Eighth Mountain Press, 1993.

Johnson, Barbara. *Brothers and Sisters: Getting Back Together with Your Adult Siblings.* Buffalo, N.Y.: Prometheus Books, 1991.

Jonas, Susan, and Marilyn Nissenson. *Friends for Life: Enriching the Bond Between Mothers and Their Adult Daughters.* New York: Morrow, 1997.

Lerner, Harriet. *The Dance of Intimacy: A Woman's Guide to Courageous Acts of Change in Key Relationships.* Reprint ed. New York: Harper & Row, 1990.

McGoldrick, Monica. *You Can Go Home Again: Reconnecting with Your Family.* New York: W. W. Norton & Company, 1997.

Miller, Jean Baker, and Irene Pierce Stiver. *The Healing Connection: How Women Form Relationships in Therapy and in Life.* Boston: Beacon Press, 1997.

Moore, Thomas. *Soul Mates: Honoring the Mysteries of Love and Relationship.* New York: HarperPerennial, 1994.

Pogrebin, Letty Cottin. *Among Friends: Who We Like, Why We Like Them, and What We Do with Them.* New York: McGraw-Hill, 1986.

Rubin, Lillian. *Just Friends: The Role of Friendship in Our Lives.* New York: Harper & Row, 1985.

Traeder, Tamara, and Carmen Renee Berry. *Girlfriends: Invisible Bonds, Enduring Ties.* Berkeley, CA: Ten Speed Press, 1997.

Weinstock, Jacqueline, and Esther Rothblum, eds. *Lesbian Friendships: For Ourselves and Each Other.* New York: New York University Press, 1996.

7. Tap Into Religion

Bender, Sue. *Everyday Sacred: A Woman's Journey Home.* San Francisco: HarperSanFrancisco, 1996.

Benson, Herbert, and Margaret Stark. *Timeless Healing: The Power and Biology of Belief.* New York: Scribner's, 1996.

Bolen, Jean. *Goddesses in Everywoman: A New Psychology of Women.* New York: HarperCollins, 1993.

Borysenko, Joan. *A Woman's Book of Life: The Biology, Psychology, and Spirituality of the Feminine Life Cycle.* New York: Riverhead Books, 1997.

Boucher, Sandy. *Opening the Lotus: A Woman's Guide to Buddhism.* Boston: Beacon Press, 1997.

Carnes, Robin Deen, and Sally Craig. *Sacred Circle: A Guide to Creating Your Own Women's Spirituality Group.* San Francisco: HarperSanFrancisco, 1998.

Epstein, Mark. *Going to Pieces without Falling Apart: A Buddhist Perspective on Wholeness.* New York: Broadway Books, 1998.

Imber-Black, Evan, and Janine Roberts. *Rituals for Our Times: Celebrating, Healing, and Changing Our Lives and Our Relationships.* Reprint ed. New York: HarperCollins, 1993.

Moore, Thomas. *Care of the Soul: A Guide for Cultivating Depth and Sacredness in Everyday Life.* New York: HarperPerennial, 1994.

Ochs, Carol. *Women and Spirituality.* 2nd ed. Lanham, MD: Rowman and Littlefield, 1997.

Ochshorn, Judith, and Ellen Cole, eds. *Women's Spirituality, Women's Lives.* Binghamton, N.Y.: Harrington Park Press, 1996.

Puttick, Elizabeth. *Women in New Religions: In Search of Community, Sexuality and Spiritual Power.* New York: St. Martin's Press, 1997.

8. Discharge Your Emotional Overload

Self-Help and Support Groups:

Alcoholics Anonymous: see your local telephone book

Al-Anon: see your local telephone book

American Self-Help Clearinghouse
St. Clares-Riverside Medical Center
25 Pocono Road
Denville, N.J. 07834
(601) 625-7101
Order their Self-Help Sourcebook: Finding and Forming Mutual Aid Self-Help Groups, *4th ed., Ed. Barbara White and Edward Madras, 1992.*

Burns, David. *Feeling Good: The New Mood Therapy.* New York: Avon Books, 1992.

Institute for Recovery. *Women in AA: Personal Stories of Recovery.* Lake Forest, IL: Whales' Tale Press, 1996.

Jacobs, Ruth Harriet. *Older Women: Surviving and Thriving (A Manual for Group Leaders). Order from Families International, Inc., 11700*

W. *Lake Park Drive, Milwaukee, WI 53224 (800) 852-1944.*

McGuire, Kathleen. *Building Supportive Community—Mutual Self-Help Through Peer Counseling. Order from 3440 Onyx Street, Eugene OR 97405 (503) 342-1033.*

National Mental Health Assocation
(800) 969-6642
Request referral to local support groups and community health centers.

National Self-Help Clearinghouse
c/o CUNY
25 W. 42nd Street, Suite 620
New York, NY 10036
Write for information about self-help groups.

Parents Without Partners: *see your local telephone book or contact PWP at*
401 N. Michigan Avenue
Chicago, IL 60611-4267
(800) 637-7974

Silverman, Phyllis. *Widow-to-Widow.* New York: Springer, 1985.

Widowed Persons Service
c/o AARP
601 E Street, N.W.
Washington, D.C. 20049
(800) 424-2260
Request their publications list and information on local groups for newly widowed persons near you.

Wuthnow, Robert. *Sharing the Journey: Support Groups and America's New Quest for Community.* New York: Free Press, 1996.

Professional Counseling

American Psychiatric Assocation
Public Affairs Dept. 498
1400 K Street, N.W.
Washington, D.C. 20005
(202) 336-5800
online: http://www.psych.org
Order their pamphlet on "Let's Talk Facts about Psychotherapy."

American Psychological Association
750 First Street, N.E.

Washington, D.C. 20002
(202) 336-5705
online: http://www.helping.apa.org
Order their pamphlet on "Finding Help: How to Choose a Psycho-therapist" or "How Therapy Helps People Recover from Depression."

Anxiety Disorders Association of America
11900 Parklawn Drive, Suite 100
Rockville, MD 20852
(301) 231-9350
online: http://www.adaa.org
Send $3.00 with request for information about treatments and specialists.

Connexions—National Depressive and Manic Depressive Association
(888) 222-1213
Recorded information for individuals who are depressed.

Depression & Related Affective Disorders Association
(410) 955-4647
Request information and referrals.

Dowling, Colette. *You Mean I Don't Have to Feel This Way? New Help for Depression, Anxiety, and Addiction.* New York: Bantam, 1993.

Gorman, Jack. *The New Psychiatry.* New York: St. Martin's Press, 1996.

"Mental Health: Does Therapy Help?" Part 1 and Part 2. *Consumer Reports,* November 1995.

National Alliance for the Mentally Ill
(800) 950-6264
online: http://www.nami.org
Offers information on research and treatment and referrals to local groups.

National Institute of Mental Health:
Anxiety Disorder Education Program
(888)-8-ANXIETY
Clearinghouse on Depression Awareness, Recognition, and Treatment
(800) 421-4211

Papolos, Demitri, and Janice Papolos. *Overcoming Depression: The Definitive Resource for Patients and Families Who Live with Depression and Manic-Depression.* New York: HarperPerennial, 1997.

Pittman, Frank III. "A Buyer's Guide to Psychotherapy." *Psychology Today,* January/February 1994.

Ross, Jerilyn. *Triumph over Fear: A Book of Help and Hope for People with Anxiety.* New York: Bantam, 1994.

Seligman, Martin. *Learned Optimism.* New York: Knopf, 1991.

————. *What You Can Change and What You Can't: The Complete Guide to Successful Self-Improvement.* New York: Fawcett Columbine, 1993.

Yapko, Michael. *Breaking the Patterns of Depression.* New York: Doubleday, 1997.

9. What Kind of Life Do You Want?

Ben-Lesser, Jay. *A Foxy Old Woman's Guide to Traveling Alone Around Town and Around the World.* Freedom, CA: The Crossing Press, 1995.

Birren, James, and Linda Feldman. *Where to Go from Here: Discovering Your Own Life's Wisdom in Your Second Fifty.* New York: Simon & Schuster, 1997.

Earthwatch
P.O. Box 9104
Watertown, MA 02272
(800) 776-0188
Write for a catalog of their scientific expeditions to more than fifty countries.

Elderhostel
75 Federal Street
Boston, MA 02110
(617) 426-7788
online: http://www.elderhostel.org
Request a catalog of their classes and field trips for people over fifty-five, held on nineteen hundred campuses in the United States and forty-five foreign countries.

Estes, Clarissa Pinkola. *Women Who Run with the Wolves.* New York: Ballantine, 1992.

Gaines, Patrice. *Moments of Grace: Meeting the Challenge to Change.* New York: Crown Publishers, 1997.

Greer, Germaine. *The Change: Women, Aging and the Menopause.* New York: Fawcett Columbine, 1991.

Hancock, Emily. *The Girl Within: Recapturing the Childhood Self, the Key to Female Identity.* New York: Fawcett, 1990.

Heilbrun, Carolyn. *Reinventing Womanhood*. New York: W. W. Norton & Company, 1979.

———. *Writing a Woman's Life*. New York: Ballantine, 1988.

Hudson, Pat. *The Solution-Oriented Woman: Creating the Life You Want*. New York: W. W. Norton & Company, 1996.

International Women's Writing Guild

Caller Box 810 Gracie Station

New York, NY 10028

(212) 737-7536

Johnson, Alexandra. *The Hidden Writer: Diaries and the Creative Life*. New York: Doubleday, 1997.

Ledoux, Denis. *Turning Memories into Memoirs: A Handbook for Writing Lifestories*. Lisbon Falls, ME: Soleil Press, 1993.

Lerner, Harriet. *The Dance of Deception: Pretending and Truth-Telling in Women's Lives*. New York: HarperPerennial, 1994.

Maddox, Rebecca. *Inc. Your Dreams*. New York: Viking, 1995.

Rainier, Tristine. *Writing the New Autobiography*. New York: Putnam, 1997.

Roseman, Janet Lynn. *The Way of the Woman Writer*. Binghamton, N.Y.: Haworth Press, 1994.

Rubin, Lillian. *Women of a Certain Age: The Midlife Search for Self*. New York: Harper Colophon, 1979.

Schiwy, Marlene. *A Voice of Her Own: Women and the Journal Writing Journey*. New York: Simon & Schuster/Fireside, 1996.

Scott, Lucy, Kerstin Joslyn Schremp, Betty Soldz, and Barbara Weiss. *Wise Choices Beyond Midlife: Women Mapping the Journey Ahead*. Watsonville, CA: Papier-Mache Press, 1997.

Viorst, Judith. *Necessary Losses: The Loves, Illusions, Dependencies and Impossible Expectations That All of Us Have to Give Up in Order to Grow*. New York: Fawcett Gold Medal, 1987.

10. A Nest of Your Own

Chalfie, Deborah. *The Real Golden Girls: The Prevalence and Policy Treatment of Midlife and Older People Living in Nontraditional*

Households. Washington, D.C.: AARP, 1995.
Request publication No. D15572.

The CoHousing Company
1250 Addison Street, #113
Berkeley, CA 94702
(510) 549-9980
online: www.cohousingco.com
Publishes a book on cohousing, a brochure, and a resource list. Can refer you to cohousing communities near you.

Friedman, Mickey Troub. "Housing Alternatives and Living Arrangements." In *The New Ourselves, Growing Older: Women Aging with Knowledge and Power.* Ed. Paula Doress-Worters and Diana Laskin Siegal. New York: Simon & Schuster/Touchstone, 1994. 151–68.

Holland, Barbara. *One's Company: Reflections on Living Alone.* Reprint ed. Pleasantville, N.Y.: Akadine Press, 1996.

Hyde, Joan, and Susan Lanspery, eds. *Staying Put: Adapting the Places Instead of the People.* Amityville, N.Y.: Baywood Publishing, 1994.

Marklein, Mary Beth. "Living Together: Innovations Abound as Americans Experiment with Shared Housing." *AARP Bulletin* 38.8 (Sept. 1994): 10–.

National Center for Home Equity Conversion (*comparison shopping for reverse mortgages*)
online: http://www.reverse.org

Porcino, Jane. *Living Longer, Living Better: Adventures in Community Housing for Those in the Second Half of Life.* New York: Crossroad Continuum, 1991.

Scholen, Ken. *Consumer's Guide to Home Equity Conversion: Man-Made Money.* Rev. ed. Washington, D.C.: American Association of Retired Persons, 1991.
Request publication No. D12894.

Tone, Teona, and Deanna Sclar. *Housemates: A Practical Guide to Living with Other People.* New York: Ballantine, 1985.

11. Step by Step to a Career

Refer also to the resources for Chapter 5, "Get a Job."

Accion, International
120 Beacon Street

Somerville, MA 02143
(617) 492-4930
online: http://www.accion.org

Antoniak, Mike. *How to Start a Home-Based Business.* New York: Avon, 1996.

Benton, Debra. *Lions Don't Need to Roar: Using the Leadership Power of Professional Presence to Stand Out, Fit In and Move Ahead.* New York: Warner Books, 1993.

Bird, Caroline. *Second Careers: New Ways to Work after Fifty.* New York: Little Brown, 1992.

BizWomen: online address: www.bizwomen.com

Black, Pam. "Buoying Women Investors." *BusinessWeek,* Feb. 27, 1995.

———. "A 'New-Girl' Network Starts to Take Root." *BusinessWeek,* Oct. 2, 1995.

Boe, Anne. *Winning the Networking Game: How to Enhance Your Career and Stay Ahead in Business.* New York: John Wiley & Sons, 1994.

Bolles, Richard. *What Color Is Your Parachute?* Berkeley, CA: Ten Speed Press, 1997.

The Career Planning and Adult Development Network
4965 Sierra Road
San Jose, CA 95132
(408) 559-4946
Request names of career counselors and coaches in your area.

CareerTrack:
(800) 334-6780
Request a list of their publications and training for career development.

Entrepreneur Magazine
(800) 274-6229

Fallek, Max. *Finding Money for Your Small Business: The One-Stop Guide to Raising All the Money You Will Need.* Chicago: Dearborne Financial Press, 1994.

Florence, Mari. *The Enterprising Woman.* New York: Warner Books, 1997.

Huff, Priscilla. *101 Best Home-Based Businesses for Women.* Rocklin, CA: Prima Publishing, 1995.

Lowstuter, Clyde, and David Robertson. *Networking Your Way to Your Next Job—Fast.* New York: McGraw-Hill, 1995.

Maddox, Rebecca. *Inc. Your Dreams.* New York: Viking/Penguin, 1995.

Milano, Carol. *Hers: The Wise Woman's Guide to Starting a Business on 2,000 Dollars or Less.* 2nd rev. ed. New York: Allworth Press, 1997.

Murphy, Kate. "Closing the Gender Gap—With Capital." *Business-Week,* Apr. 18, 1994.

National Association of Women Business Owners (NAWBO)
1100 Wayne Avenue, Suite 830
Silver Spring, MD 20910
(800) 55-NAWBO
online: http://www.nawbo.org

Wells Fargo/NAWBO Loan Program:
(800) 359-3557, ext. 120

National Board for Certified Counselors
3 Terrace Way
Greensboro, N.C. 27403
(910) 547-0607
Request a listing of academically accredited job counselors.

National Association of Home-Based Business
10451 Mill Run Circle, Suite 400
Owings Mills, MD 21117
(410) 363-3698
online: http://www:usahomebusiness.com
Members include two hundred types of home-based businesses.

Northcutt, Cecilia. *Successful Career Women: Their Professional and Personal Characteristics.* Westport, CT: Greenwood Press, 1991.

Pedersen, Laura. *Street-Smart Career Guide: A Step-by-Step Guide to Your Career Development.* New York: Crown, 1993.

Pollan, Stephen, and Mark Levine. *Starting Over: How to Change Careers or Start Your Own Business.* New York: Warner Books, 1997.

Scollard, Jeannette. *The Self-Employed Woman: How to Start Your Own Business and Gain Control of Your Life.* New York: Simon & Schuster, 1989.

Service Corps of Retired Executives (SCORE—the SBA mentor program)

Call (800) 634-0245 for the office nearest you.

Sheldon, Betsy, and Joyce Hadley. *The Smart Woman's Guide to Networking.* Philadelphia, PA: Chelsea House, 1996.

Small Business Administration (SBA):
Small Business Answer Desk: (800) 872-5722

SBA Office of Financial Assistance
409 Third Street, S.W.
Washington, D.C. 20416
(202) 205-6490

SBA Office of Women's Business Ownership
1441 L Street, N.W., Suite 414
Washington, D.C. 20416
(202) 653-8000

SBA On-Line: http://www.sbaonline.sba.gov

SBA Small Business Development Centers
Call (402) 595-2387 for one near you.

smallbizNet: online: http://www.lowe.org

Women in Franchising
53 W. Jackson Blvd., Suite 205
Chicago, IL 60604
(312) 431-1467
(800) 222-4WIF
online: http://infonews.com/franchise/wif

Women's Business Center
online: http://www.onlinewbc.org

Women's Business Development Center
230 N. Michigan Avenue, Suite 1800
Chicago, IL 60601
(312) 853-3477
Request information packet on small business development.

Women's Wire online: http://www.womenswire.com

Women's World Banking affiliates in North America
(for small business loans):

Montana Women's Capital Fund
302 N. Last Chance Gulch, Suite 402
Helena, MT 59624

Women's Business Development Corporation
P.O. Box 658
Bangor, ME 04402

Women's Entrepreneurial Growth Organization
c/o The Akron Industrial Incubator
526 S. Main Street, Suite 235
Akron, OH 44311

Women's Opportunities Resource Center
1930 Chestnut Street, Suite 1600
Philadelphia, PA 19103

Women's World Finance Cape Breton Association
54 Prince Street
Sidney, NS B1P6J7

Working Woman Magazine
(800) 234-9675

Zuckerman, Laurie. *On Your Own: A Woman's Guide to Building a Business.* 2nd ed. Dover, N.H.: Upstart Publisher, 1993.

12. Pursue Your Passion

Adams, James. *Conceptual Blockbusting: A Guide to Better Ideas.* Reading, MA: Addison-Wesley, 1990.

Banner, Lois. *In Full Flower: Aging Women, Power, and Sexuality.* New York: Vintage Books, 1993.

Cameron, Jean. *The Artist's Way: A Spiritual Path to Higher Creativity.* New York: J. P. Tarcher/Perigee Books, 1992.

Csikszentmihalyi, Mihaly. *Creativity: Flow and the Psychology of Discovery and Invention.* New York: HarperCollins, 1997.

Elderhostel Service Program
75 Federal Street
Boston, MA 02110
(617) 426-7788
online: http://www.elderhostel.org

Gray Panthers
2025 Pennsylvania Avenue, N.W.

Washington, D.C. 20005
(202) 466-3132

Gullette, Margaret Morganroth. *Declining to Decline: Cultural Combat and the Politics of Midlife.* Charlottesville: University of Virginia Press, 1997.

Hot Flash: A Newsletter for Midlife and Older Women
c/o National Action Forum for Midlife and Older Women
Box 816
Stony Brook, N.Y. 11790-0609

Houston, Jean. *A Course in Enhancing Your Physical, Mental, and Creative Abilities.* Los Angeles: J. P. Tarcher, 1982.

Huckle, Patricia. *Tish Sommers, Activist, and the Founding of the Older Women's League.* Knoxville: University of Tennessee Press, 1991.

Kuhn, Maggie. *No Stone Unturned: The Life and Times of Maggie Kuhn.* New York: Ballantine, 1991.

League of Women Voters
1730 M Street, N.W.
Washington, D.C. 20036
(202) 429-1965

Maisel, Eric. *Fearless Creating: A Step-by-Step Guide to Starting and Completing Your Work of Art.* New York: J. P. Tarcher/Putnam, 1995.

National Organization for Women (NOW)
1000 16th Street, N.W., Suite 700
Washington, D.C. 20036
(202) 331-0066

Older Women's League (OWL)
666 11th Street, N.W., Suite 700
Washington, D.C. 20001
(800) TAKE OWL; (202) 783-6686

Phillips, Jan. *Marry Your Muse: Making a Sacred Commitment to Your Creativity.* Wheaton, IL: Theosophical Publishing, 1997.

Sommers, Tish. "Changing Society and Ourselves." In *The New Ourselves, Growing Older: Women Aging with Knowledge and Power.* Eds. Paula Doress-Worters and Diana Laskin Siegal. New York: Simon & Schuster/Touchstone, 1994.

Gloria Steinem. *Moving Beyond Words.* New York: Simon & Schuster, 1994.

13. To Be or Not to Be (Married)

American Association of Retired Persons. "Are There Dating Services for Seniors?" *Modern Maturity,* Apr.–May 1993. 84.

Burke, Christie. "HIV and Safer Sex." In *The New Ourselves, Growing Older: Women Aging with Knowledge and Power.* Eds. Paula Doress-Worters and Diana Laskin Siegal. New York: Simon & Schuster/Touchstone, 1994. 96–97.

Clunis, D. Merilee, and G. Dorsey Green. *Lesbian Couples: Creating Healthy Relationships for the '90s.* Seattle: Seal Press, 1993.

Corea, Gena. *The Invisible Epidemic: The Story of Women and AIDS.* New York: HarperCollins, 1992.

Cowan, Connell, and Melvyn Kinder. *Smart Women, Foolish Choices: Finding the Right Men and Avoiding the Wrong Ones.* New York: New American Library-Dutton, 1986.

Cutler, Winnifred. *Searching for Courtship: The Smart Woman's Guide to Finding a Good Husband.* New York: Villard Books, 1993.

Dowling, Colette. *Red Hot Mamas: Coming into Our Own at Fifty.* New York: Bantam, 1996.

Ide, Mary, with Wendy Sanford and Amy Alpern, eds. "AIDS, HIV Infection and Women." In The Boston Women's Health Book Collective, *The New Our Bodies, Ourselves.* New York: Simon & Schuster/Touchstone, 1992. 327–42.

Kalish, Nancy. *Lost and Found Lovers: Facts and Fantasies of Rekindled Romances.* New York: Morrow, 1997.

Kramer, Peter. *Should You Leave?* New York: Scribner's, 1997.

National Women's Health Network. *AIDS: Women and HIV/AIDS,* 1998.
Order from NWHN, 514 10th Street, N.W., Suite 400, Washington, D.C. 20004 (202) 347-1140.

O'Hanlon, Bill. *Love Is a Verb: How to Stop Analyzing Your Relationship, Start Making It Great!* New York: W. W. Norton & Company, 1995.

Rubenstein, Carin. "The *Lear's* Report: How AIDS Has Changed Our Sex Lives." *Lear's,* Nov. 1992. 62–67.

Scarf, Maggie. *Intimate Partners: Patterns in Love and Marriage.* New York: Ballantine, 1988.

SeniorNet
399 Arguello Blvd
San Francisco, CA 94118
(415) 750-5030
An online bulletin board available by subscription or through America Online.

Sills, Judith. *Biting the Apple: Women Getting Wise about Love.* New York: Viking, 1996.

Simpson, Eileen. *Late Love: A Celebration of Marriage after Fifty.* Boston: Houghton Mifflin, 1994.

Notes

Preface

1. Betty Friedan, 1993, *The Fountain of Age*, p. 133.
2. Frances Leonard, 1993, *Money and the Mature Woman: How to Hold On to Your Income, Keep Your Home, Plan Your Estate*, p. 4.
3. Population Reference Bureau, 1993, *What the 1990 Census Tells Us About Women: A State Factbook*, p. 22. The PRB's analysis of the 1990 census produces these statistics about the marital status and age of women in the United States:

Age	Number Divorced Women	Number Widowed Women	Total Number Women in U.S.
35 to 44	2,787,942	290,594	18,954,886
45 to 54	2,025,923	655,723	12,984,859
55 to 64	1,225,830	1,764,548	11,138,433
65 to 74	706,402	3,606,163	10,202,029
75 to 84	268,488	3,863,907	6,279,286
85 & over	58,562	1,771,289	2,177,302
TOTAL	7,073,147	11,952,224	61,736,795

4. Unintentionally, my "sample" consists of more divorcées than widows—59 divorcees to 29 widows. That ratio would only be true in the real world for widows and divorcées under the age of 65. Between the ages of 35 and 54, divorcées outnumber widows by a ratio of five to one. But between the ages of 55 and 64, widows already outnumber divorced women. And between 65 and 74, the five-to-one ratio reverses itself in favor of widowed over divorced women

5. The ages of the 88 women interviewed break down as follows:

Age of Woman	Number Interviewed	Percent of Sample
40–49	20	23%
50–59	22	25%
60–69	26	30%
70–79	18	20%
80–89	2	2%

6. Following is the breakdown of how many years the 88 women had been without a permanent partner after being divorced or widowed:

Number of Years Alone	Number of Women	Percent of Sample
1–4	18	23%
5–9	22	28%
10–14	18	23%
15–19	9	10%
20–24	6	8%
25–29	4	5%
30–34	0	0%
35–39	0	0%
40–44	1	1%

7. Following is the breakdown of the number of years the women interviewed were married:

Number of Years Married	Number of Women Interviewed	Percent of Sample
10–14	8	9%
15–19	18	20%
20–24	21	24%
25–29	12	14%
30–34	17	19%
35–39	3	3%
40–44	8	9%
45–49	0	0%
50–54	1	1%

8. Personal communication with Washington, D.C., psychologist Dr. Sarah Ellis on May 6, 1996.

9. Colin Murray Parkes and Robert Weiss, 1995, *Recovery from Bereavement.*

10. Personal communication with Dr. Margaret Huyck, Illinois Institute of Technology Professor of Psychology, on March 26, 1996.

11. Wolfgang Stroebe and Margaret Stroebe, 1987, *Bereavement and Health: The Psychological and Physical Consequences of Partner Loss.*

Introduction: The Challenge of Being Unmarried

1. Population Reference Bureau, Mar. 1992, Proposal to the Ford Foundation on "Women: Still in Transition, A Policy Perspective for the 21st Century," p. 1.

2. Monica McGoldrick, 1989, "Women and the Family Life Cycle," in Betty Carter and Monica McGoldrick, eds., *The Changing Family Life Cycle: A Framework for Family Therapy,* 2nd ed., p. 53.

3. Kathleen Hall Jamieson, 1995, *Beyond the Double Bind: Women and Leadership.* Jamieson identifies a double standard that women face which holds that while men gain wisdom and power with age, older women become invisible, gaining only wrinkles and hot flashes.

4. Personal communication with Edie Irons, Ed.D., on May 29, 1996.

5. Jon Kabat-Zinn, 1990, *Full Catastrophe Living: Using the Wisdom of Your Body and Mind to Face Stress, Pain, and Illness.*

6. Carolyn Heilbrun, 1988, *Writing a Woman's Life*, p. 60.

7. Carolyn Heilbrun, 1988, *Writing a Woman's Life*, p. 118.

8. Quoted in Nancy Gazze, "Wake-Up Calls and Ambulance Promises," *The Washington Post,* Jan. 12, 1996, p. D5.

9. Personal communication with Dr. Margaret Huyck on Apr. 16, 1996. Huyck studied women's experiences over their life course, initially under Bernice Neugarten and then in collaboration with David Gutmann.

10. David Gutmann, 1994, *Reclaimed Powers: Men and Women in Later Life.*

11. Gisela Labouvie-Vief, 1994, "Women's Creativity and Images of Gender," in Barbara Turner and Lillian Troll, eds., *Women Growing Older: Psychological Perspectives.*

12. Gail Sheehy, 1995, *New Passages: Mapping Your Life Across Time*, p. 142.

1. Facing the Chasm

1. Jon Kabat-Zinn, 1990, *Full Catastrophe Living: Using the Wisdom of Your Body and Mind to Face Stress, Pain, and Illness,* p. 3.

2. Wolfgang Stroebe and Margaret Stroebe, 1987, *Bereavement and Health: The Psychological and Physical Consequences of Partner Loss*, pp. 10–12.

3. Wolfgang Stroebe and Margaret Stroebe, 1987, *Bereavement and Health*, p. 9.

4. Wolfgang Stroebe and Margaret Stroebe, 1987, *Bereavement and Health*, p. 5.

5. Wolfgang Stroebe and Margaret Stroebe, 1987, *Bereavement and Health*, p. 1.

6. Martin Seligman, 1993, *What You Can Change and What You Can't.*

7. Wolfgang Stroebe and Margaret Stroebe, 1987, *Bereavement and Health*, pp. 96–97.

8. Wolfgang Stroebe and Margaret Stroebe, 1987, *Bereavement and Health*, pp. 13–15.

9. Wolfgang Stroebe and Margaret Stroebe, 1987, *Bereavement and Health*, p. 16.

10 Eric Lindemann described the grief process in a 1944 article on "Symptomatology and Management of Acute Grief," in the *American Journal of Psychiatry* (101): 141–48. Cited in Wolfgang Stroebe and Margaret Stroebe, 1987, *Bereavement and Health*, p. 18.

11. S. E. Taylor, "Adjustment to Threatening Events: A Theory of Cognitive Adaptation," *American Psychologist* 38.1 (1983): 161–73.

12. Barbara Holland, 1992, *One's Company: Reflections on Living Alone*, pp. 166–67.

13. Barbara Holland, 1992, *One's Company.*

14. Jon Kabat-Zinn, 1990, *Full Catastrophe Living*, p. 3.

15. Jon Kabat-Zinn, 1990, *Full Catastrophe Living*, p. 320.

16. James Miller, 1995, *What Will Help Me? 12 Things to Remember When You Have Suffered a Loss.*

17. The key word on America Online is SeniorNet.

18. Evan Imber-Black, 1991, "Rituals of Stabilization and Change in Women's Lives," in Monica McGoldrick, Carol Anderson, and Froma Walsh, eds., *Women in Therapy: A Framework for Family Therapy*, p. 451.

19. Evan Imber-Black, 1991, "Rituals of Stabilization and Change in Women's Lives," p. 467.

20. Faye from Fargo, ND, as quoted on the Internet by James E. Miller: jmiller@willowgreen.com

21. Germaine Greer, 1991, *The Change: Women, Aging and the Menopause*, pp. 270–71.

22. Wolfgang Stroebe and Margaret Stroebe, 1987, *Bereavement and Health*, p. 97.

23. James Pennebaker and R. C. O'Heeron, "Confiding in Others and Illness Rate among Spouses of Suicide and Accidental Death Victims," *Journal of Abnormal Psychology* 93 (1984): 473–76.

24. Susan Nolen-Hoeksema, 1990, *Sex Differences in Depression*, pp. 160–72.

25. Martin Seligman, 1993, *What You Can Change and What You Can't*, pp. 217–18; and "Strategies for Smiles," *Psychology Today*, Jan./Feb. 1994, p. 22.

26. Eric Lindemann, 1979, *Beyond Grief: Studies in Crisis Intervention*, p. 234.

27. Martin Seligman, 1991, *Learned Optimism*, p. 217.

28. Martin Seligman, 1991, *Learned Optimism*, p. 217. This technique and others are also described in a classic book on how to control self-defeating attitudes and actions entitled *Feeling Good: The New Mood Therapy* by David Burns, 1992.

29. Emma Drake, 1902, *What Every Woman of Forty-five Ought to Know*, pp. 92–93. Cited in Germaine Greer, 1991, *The Change*, pp. 271–72.

30. Barbara Holland, 1992, *One's Company*, p. 184.

31. Brendan Gill, 1996, *Late Bloomers*, p. 42.

32. The forum for widows and widowers is part of SeniorNet Online, which can be accessed through a subscription to SeniorNet Online or to America Online (see note 17).

33. SeniorNet Online. These communications all took place at the end of Dec. 1995.

34. Wolfgang Stroebe and Margaret Stroebe, 1987, *Bereavement and Health*, p. 15.

2. *Coping with the Stress That Accompanies Change*

1. Barbara Holland, 1992, *One's Company: Reflections on Living Alone*, p. 237.

2. "How to Stop Living on the Edge," *Harvard Health Letter* 23.9 (July 1998): 1–3.

3. Barbara Holland, 1992, *One's Company*.

4. Eric Widmaier, "So You Think This Is the 'Age of Stress?'" *Psychology Today*, Jan./Feb. 1996, pp. 41–.

5. Eric Widmaier, "So You Think This Is the 'Age of Stress?'" p. 41.

6. John Carpi, "Stress: It's Worse Than You Think," *Psychology Today*, Jan./Feb 1996, pp. 34–.

7. Jon Kabat-Zinn, 1990, *Full Catastrophe Living: Using the*

Wisdom of Your Body and Mind to Face Stress, Pain, and Illness, pp. 248, 254.

8. "Can Stress Make You Sick?" *Harvard Health Letter* 23.6 (April 1998): 1–3.

9. Quoted in Jon Kabat-Zinn, 1990, *Full Catastrophe Living,* p. 35.

10. Research which shows this to be true is detailed in Martin Seligman, 1993, *What You Can Change and What You Can't.*

11. John Carpi, "Stress: It's Worse Than You Think."

12. Martin Seligman, 1993, *What You Can Change and What You Can't.*

13. Herbert Benson, 1992, *The Relaxation Response.*

14. Cited in John Carpi, "Stress: It's Worse Than You Think," p. 39.

15. Barbara Boughton, "The Healing Arts," *Modern Maturity,* Sept./Oct. 1996, p. 70.

16. Jon Kabat-Zinn, 1990, *Full Catastrophe Living.*

17. Cited in John Carpi, "Stress: It's Worse Than You Think," p. 39.

18. Martin Seligman, 1993, *What You Can Change and What You Can't,* p. 267.

19. Jon Kabat-Zinn, 1990, *Full Catastrophe Living,* p. 22.

20. Jon Kabat-Zinn, 1990, *Full Catastrophe Living,* p. 23.

21. Jon Kabat-Zinn, 1990, *Full Catastrophe Living,* p. 442.

22. Jon Kabat-Zinn, 1990, *Full Catastrophe Living,* p. 431.

23. Barbara Lazear Ascher, "How to Free Yourself from Anger," *Self,* Feb. 1995, p. 142.

24. Personal communication with psychologist Dr. Andrew Morral, Feb. 4, 1997.

25. Gail Sheehy, 1995, *New Passages: Mapping Your Life Across Time,* p. 174.

26. Barbara Lazear Ascher, "How to Free Yourself from Anger," *Self,* Feb. 1995, p. 171.

27. A. Byrne and D. G. Byrne, "The Effect of Exercise on Depression, Anxiety and Other Mood States: A Review," *Journal of Psychosomatic Research* 37 (Sept. 1993): 565–74.

28. Jon Kabat-Zinn, 1990, *Full Catastrophe Living,* p. 255.

29. Dinha Kaplan, "When Less Is More," *Psychology Today,* May/June 1997, p. 14.

30. "Can Stress Make You Sick?" *Harvard Health Letter.*

31. "Strength Training after Sixty," *Harvard Health Letter* 18.9 (July 1993): 6–8.

32. John Ratey and Catherine Johnson, 1997, *Shadow Syndromes.*

33. Laura Elliott, "Help for Your Head," *The Washingtonian Magazine,* Apr. 1998, p. 80.

34. Martin Seligman, 1993, *What You Can Change and What You Can't,* p. 103.

35. Jean Baker Miller, 1986, *Toward a New Psychology of Women,* 2nd ed., pp. 50–51.

36. Evelyn Vuko, "Overdoing: A No-No," *The Washington Post,* Aug. 23, 1996, p. D5.

37. Barbara Holland, 1992, *One's Company,* p. 237.

3. A Tiger by the Tail: Dealing with Lawyers

1. Alexandra Armstrong and Mary Donahue, 1993, *On Your Own: A Widow's Passage to Emotional and Financial Well-Being,* p. 76.

2. Roxanne Roberts, "The *Other* Big 'A' Word," *The Washington Post,* July 11, 1995, p. E5.

3. Frances Leonard, 1987, *Divorce and Older Women,* p. 9.

4. Frances Leonard, 1987, *Divorce and Older Women,* p. 7.

5. Frances Leonard, 1987, *Divorce and Older Women, p. 7.*

6. Frances Leonard, 1987, *Divorce and Older Women,* p. 9.

7. Olivia Goldsmith, 1992, *First Wives Club.*

8. Bradley Pistotnik, 1996, *Divorce War! Fifty Strategies Every Woman Needs to Know to Win,* p. 8.

9. Bradley Pistotnik, 1996, *Divorce War!,* pp. 7–12.

10. Bradley Pistotnik, 1996, *Divorce War!,* p. xv.

11. Bradley Pistotnik, 1996, *Divorce War!,* p. 101.

12. Bradley Pistotnik, 1996, *Divorce War!,* p. 11.

13. Deborah Tannen, "For Argument's Sake: Why Do We Feel Compelled to Fight about Everything?" *The Washington Post,* Mar. 15, 1998, p. C1–. Tannen's book on this topic (1997) is *The Argument Culture.*

14. Frances Leonard, 1987, *Divorce and Older Women*, pp. 8–9.

15. Frances Leonard writes that attorney-negotiated settlements "are almost always superior to court-ordered results after trial" (1987, *Divorce and Older Women*, p. 9). Contradicting that, however, is DePaul University law professor Jane Rutherford's research which shows that "women who take their divorces to court have alimony awards three times higher than those who settle out of court" (cited in Stacey Singer, "Divorce-Law Crusade Backfires," *Chicago Tribune*, Nov. 2, 1995). The problem is, however, that few people can afford the legal costs.

4. Gain Financial Expertise: Your Own and Others'

1. Beardstown Ladies Investment Club, with Leslie Whitaker, 1994, *The Beardstown Ladies' Common Sense Investment Guide*, pp. 61–62.

2. Mary Beth Franklin, "Group Learns to Play the Market, Garners 'Outstanding' Profits," *Washington Senior Beacon*, June 1994, p. 18.

3. Mary Beth Franklin, June 1994, "Group Learns to Play the Market, Garners 'Outstanding' Profits."

4. Initially, the women calculated that they had earned a 23.4 percent annual return from 1984 to 1993. But apparently they had erred in their calculations, and the real average rate was the more modest 9.1 percent, a good return compared to the rate of inflation but not compared to the 15.73 percent average annual return of the Dow Jones industrial average. See Cindy Skrzycki, "Stock Recipe Needs a Grain of Salt: Beardstown Ladies Miscalculated Investment Returns," *The Washington Post*, Mar. 18, 1998, p. 1.

5. Allen R. Myerson, "Wall Street Addresses Women's Distinct Needs," *The New York Times*, July 31, 1993, p. A33.

6. Ann Conover Heller, "How to Make Money by Risking It," *Lear's*, Sept. 1991, p. 77.

7. Ann Conover Heller, Sept. 1991, "How to Make Money by Risking It," p. 77.

8. Annette Lieberman and Vicki Lindner, 1988, *Unbalanced Accounts: Why Women Are Still Afraid of Money*, p. 130.

9. Annette Lieberman and Vicki Lindner, 1988, *Unbalanced Accounts*, p. 130.

10. Christopher Hayes, Deborah Anderson, and Melinda Blau, 1993, *Our Turn: The Good News about Women and Divorce*, pp. 102–3.

11. Christopher Hayes, Deborah Anderson, and Melinda Blau, 1993, *Our Turn*, pp. 95–96.

12. Gillie Campbell and Caroline Chauncey, 1994, "Money Matters: The Economics of Aging for Women," in Paula Doress-Worters and Diana Laskin Siegal, eds., *The New Ourselves, Growing Older: Women Aging with Knowledge and Power*, pp. 189–90.

13. James Glassman, "Her Case of Nerves Needs Stock Treatment," *The Washington Post,* Dec. 15, 1996, p. H1.

14. Older Women's League, 1995, *The Path to Poverty: An Analysis of Women's Retirement Income.*

15. U.S. Bureau of the Census, Dec. 1992, "Marital Status and Living Arrangements: March 1992," *Current Population Reports, Series p-20, No. 468.*

16. Older Women's League, 1995, *The Path to Poverty.*

17. Stockbrokers, however they market their services, are never totally disinterested parties in how you invest your money because they earn commissions on the sale of stocks. Financial planners may or may not be selling something they will earn a commission on as well. You need to find that out right away so you can take it into account. See Frances Leonard, 1993, *Money and the Mature Woman: How to Hold On to Your Income, Keep Your Home, Plan Your Estate*, p. 48.

    Alarmed that too many people are turning to financial planners when they don't really need one, or to planners who are unqualified or even con artists, AARP has published a guide, "Facts About Financial Planners" (D14050), about how to identify and choose a planner, what to expect from one, and how fees are determined.

18. Frances Leonard, 1993, *Money and the Mature Woman*, pp. 261–62.

19. The National Association of Individual Investors and the National Association of Investment Clubs are part of the National Association of Investors Corporation (see Resources).

20. For someone with limited funds to invest, mutual funds allow you to follow one important rule for individual investors: diversify.

That's because the portfolio of each large fund consists of hundreds to thousands of companies, all bought and sold by a manager hired to make the difficult decisions. You pay that manager through an administrative fee of about 1 percent charged each year. See Frances Leonard, 1993, *Money and the Mature Woman*, pp. 29–35.

21. Al Cole, "Right on the Money," *Modern Maturity,* Jan./Feb. 1997, p. 77.

22. Pam Black, "Buoying Women Investors," *BusinessWeek,* Feb. 27, 1995, pp. 126–27.

23. Pam Black, Feb. 27, 1995, "Buoying Women Investors."

24. Frances Leonard, 1993, *Money and the Mature Woman*, p. 49.

25. Janet Bennett, "Many Happy Returns," *The Washington Post,* Feb. 18, 1997, p. D5. See also note 17.

26. Cited in Reed Abelson, "Our Portfolios, Ourselves," *The New York Times,* Oct. 15, 1995, Sec. 3, p. 4.

5. Get a Job (or Keep the One You Have)

1. Christopher Hayes, Deborah Anderson, and Melinda Blau, 1993, *Our Turn: The Good News about Women and Divorce*, pp. 242–43.

2. Paula Rayman, Kimberly Allshouse, and Jessie Allen, 1993, "Resiliency Amidst Inequity: Older Women Workers in an Aging United States," in Jessie Allen and Alan Pifer, eds., *Women on the Front Lines: Meeting the Challenge of an Aging America.*

3. Caroline Bird, 1995, *Lives of Our Own: Secrets of Salty Old Women.*

4. The study, "American Business and Older Workers: A Road Map to the 21st Century," was conducted by DYG Inc. for the American Association of Retired Persons. The findings were reported in "Negative Stereotypes Still Plague Older Workers on the Job," *AARP Bulletin* 36.4 (Apr. 1995): p. 3.

5. L. M. Greenwood-Audant, 1984, "The Internalization of Powerlessness: A Case Study of the Misplaced Homemaker," in J. Freeman, ed., *Women: A Feminist Perspective.*

6. A 1989 Louis Harris poll of discouraged workers, cited in Paula Rayman et al., 1993, "Resiliency Amidst Inequity," p. 143.

7. A 1992 study by the Commonwealth Fund, cited in Caroline Bird, 1995, *Lives of Our Own*, p. 188.

8. Lynne Caine, 1988, *Being a Widow*, pp. 216–17.

9. Lillian Rubin, 1979, *Women of a Certain Age: The Midlife Search for Self*, p. 22.

10. Personal communication with Alice Umbach on June 17, 1996.

11. A description of the founding and fortunes of the National Displaced Homemakers Network is included in Ruth Harriet Jacobs, 1993, "Expanding Social Roles for Older Women," in Jessie Allen and Alan Pifer, eds., *Women on the Front Lines*, pp. 197–99; and in Laurie Shields, 1981, *Displaced Homemakers: Organizing for a New Life*.

12. Women Work! The National Network for Women's Employment, 1994, *Women Work, Poverty Persists: A Status Report on Displaced Homemakers and Single Mothers in the United States*.

13. Women Work! 1994, *Women Work, Poverty Persists*.

14. Lois Shaw and Rachel Shaw, 1987, "From Midlife to Retirement: The Middle-Aged Woman Worker," in Karen Shallcross Koziara, Michael Moskow, and Lucretia Dewey Tanner, eds., *Working Women: Past, Present, Future*, p. 304.

15. Lois Shaw and Rachel Shaw, 1987, "From Midlife to Retirement," p. 305; and Frances Leonard, 1993, *Money and the Mature Woman: How to Hold On to Your Income, Keep Your Home, Plan Your Estate*, p. 124. Leonard writes: "Part of this is explainable by the fact that far more mid-life women are beginning workers than men. And part is because 'women's' jobs pay less than 'men's'. And part of it is flat-out age and sex discrimination."

16. Lois Shaw and Rachel Shaw, 1987, "From Midlife to Retirement," p. 312. The authors cite Mary Corcoran, Greg Duncan, and Michael Ponza, "A Longitudinal Analysis of White Women's Wages," in *Journal of Human Resources* 18 (Fall 1983); and Myra Strober, 1979, "Comment," in Cynthia Lloyd, Emily Andrews, and Curtis Gilroy, eds., *Women in the Labor Market*.

17. American Association of Retired Persons, 1992, *Returning to the Job Market: A Woman's Guide to Employment Planning*.

18. Carol Sowell, "Starting Over," *Modern Maturity* 29.3 (June/July 1986).

19. Personal communication with Jill Miller, co-executive director of Women Work! on March 29, 1996. The federal funds for these programs have been cut a great deal, so their viability depends more and more on what other state and local resources have been brought to bear. And some are only available to women below a certain income level. Women advocates continue to lobby Congress to get new funds for these programs but they are no longer a high priority. A further discussion of the programs can be found in Ruth Harriet Jacobs, 1993, "Expanding Social Roles for Older Women."

20. Personal communication with Sheila Rogers, program manager at Women Employed in Chicago, on Apr. 16, 1996.

21. Personal communication with Sheila Rogers on Apr. 16, 1996.

22. Ruth Harriet Jacobs, 1993, "Expanding Social Roles for Older Women," p. 217.

23. Gladys Thacher, "Seize the Day: The Coming of Age and the Age of Becoming," in *LifePlan Center: Comprehensive Planning for Later-Life Transitions* (Apr./May/June 1995), p. 1. The LifePlan Center is located at 5 Third Street, Suite 324, San Francisco, CA 94103.

24. Vikki Gregory, 1992, *Making Ends Meet: Midlife and Older Women's Search for Economic Self-Sufficiency through Job Training and Employment*, p. 39.

25. Horace Deets, "Job Program That Helps Now Needs Help Itself," *AARP Bulletin* 36.3 (March 1995): 3.

26. The main points come from Terry Mullins, "How to Land a Job," *Psychology Today*, Sept./Oct. 1994, pp. 12–13.

27. Richard Bolles, 1996, *What Color Is Your Parachute?*

28. Talk by Richard Bolles on "How to Face the Future Unafraid" at the World Bank in Washington, D.C., on Apr. 1, 1996.

29. Talk by Richard Bolles on "How to Face the Future Unafraid."

30. Talk by Richard Bolles on "How to Face the Future Unafraid."

31. Personal communication with Washington, D.C., psychologist Dr. Mary Lou Randour on Feb. 23, 1996.

32. Interview by Charleen Hunter-Gault with Laura Tyson, chairman of the National Economic Council on the PBS-TV "News Hour with Jim Lehrer" on Aug. 27, 1996.

33. Findings from a Labor Department survey reported in Rajiv Chandrasekaran, "U.S. to Train Workers for Tech Jobs," *The Washington Post,* Jan. 12, 1998, p. A7.

34. Richard Bolles, 1996, *What Color Is Your Parachute?*

35. Patrick Folliard, "Working Out Your Network," *The Washington Post,* Nov. 1, 1995, p. D5.

36. Hudson Institute, 1987, *Workforce 2000: Work and Workers for the Twenty-first Century.*

37. Hudson Institute, 1987, *Workforce 2000,* p. 22.

38. Hudson Institute, 1987, *Workforce 2000,* p. xiii.

39. Frances Leonard, 1993, *Money and the Mature Woman,* p. 128. Leonard cites a 1991 ruling by the U.S. Court of Appeals (2nd Circuit) "that 'overqualified' could be a code word masking illegal age discrimination."

40. Frances Leonard, 1993, *Money and the Mature Woman;* and Francine Weiss, 1984, *Older Women and Job Discrimination: A Primer.*

41. Frances Leonard, 1993, *Money and the Mature Woman,* p. 127.

42. Caroline Bird, 1995, *Lives of Our Own,* p. 172.

43. Women's Legal Defense Fund, 1996, *Employment Discrimination Against Midlife and Older Women: Volume I: How Courts Treat Sex-and-Age Discrimination Cases,* p. 23.

44. Kirstin Downey Grimsley, "The Ax That Cuts Both Ways," *The Washington Post,* Nov. 5, 1995, p. H1.

45. Karen Judd and Sandy Morales Pope, "The New Job Squeeze," *Ms.,* May/June 1994, pp. 86–90.

46. Vikki Gregory, 1990, *Making Ends Meet.*

47. Quoted in Karen Judd and Sandy Morales Pope, 1994, "The New Job Squeeze," pp. 88–89.

48. Personal communication with Sheila Rogers on Apr. 16, 1996.

49. Frances Leonard, 1993, *Money and the Mature Woman,* p. 125.

50. The study was done by Nuala Beck, an economic consultant and author of *Shifting Gears: Thriving in the New Economy.* Cited in James Aley, "Where the Jobs Are," *Fortune,* Sept. 18, 1995, p. 53.

51. Diane Thrailkill, 1994, *Temp by Choice*, p. 10.

52. Robert Lewis, "Escaping from the Jobless Maze," *AARP Bulletin* 35.9 (Oct. 1994): 2.

53. Len Strazewski, "Jobs on Rise for Retirees," *The Chicago Tribune*, Dec. 31, 1995, Sec. 18, pp. 56–58.

54. Bob Bobala, "The Tempers," *The Washington Post,* Apr. 5, 1996, p. F5.

55. Diane Thrailkill, 1994, *Temp by Choice*.

56. Caroline Bird, 1995, *Lives of Our Own*, p. 57.

57. Colman McCarthy, "A Perfect Match-Up," *The Washington Post,* Aug. 10, 1995, p. C5.

58. Betty Friedan, 1993, *The Fountain of Age*, pp. 222–23.

59. Caroline Bird, 1995, *Lives of Our Own*, p. 182.

60. Ann Kaiser Stearns, 1988, *Coming Back: Rebuilding Lives after Crisis and Loss*, p. 315.

6. Turn to Wise Friends—Where You Can Find Them

1. Jean Baker Miller, 1986, *Toward a New Psychology of Women,* 2nd ed., p. 110.

2. Monica McGoldrick, 1989, "Women and the Family Life Cycle," in Betty Carter and Monica McGoldrick, eds., *The Changing Family Cycle: A Framework for Family Therapy,* 2nd ed., p. 60.

3. Jacquelyn Mattfeld, 1996, "Close Relationships, Meaning-in-Life, and Well-Being: A Qualitative Study of Urban Women in Late Life," Master's Thesis, Department of Psychology, Northeastern Illinois State University, p. 86.

4. Terri Apter, 1995, *Secret Paths: Women in the New Midlife*, p. 309.

5. Jacquelyn Mattfeld, 1996, "Close Relationships, Meaning-in-Life, and Well-Being," p. 74.

6. Terri Apter, 1995, *Secret Paths,* p. 302. Whereas young adult women Apter interviewed referred to friends and friendships only about half as often as did adolescent girls, women who were forty to fifty-three referred to them about as often as did the adolescents.

7. Judith Viorst, 1987, *Necessary Losses: The Loves, Illusions, Dependencies and Impossible Expectations That All of Us Have to Give Up in Order to Grow,* p. 196.

8. Marian Osterweis, Frederic Solomon, and Morris Green, eds., 1984, *Bereavement: Reactions, Consequences, and Care*, pp. 203–4.

9. Toni Antonucci, 1994, "A Life-Span View of Women's Social Relations," in Barbara Turner and Lillian Troll, eds., *Women Growing Older: Psychological Perspectives*, pp. 239–69.

10. Toni Antonucci, 1994, "A Life-Span View of Women's Social Relations," p. 263.

11. Douglass Manning, 1984, *Don't Take My Grief Away: What to Do When You Lose a Loved One*, pp. 64–65.

12. Judith Viorst, 1987, *Necessary Losses,* p. 202.

13. Barbara Holland, 1992, *One's Company: Reflections on Living Alone*, p. 51.

14. Jacquelyn Mattfeld, 1996, "Close Relationships, Meaning-in-Life, and Well Being," pp. 45–46.

15. Barbara Holland, 1992, *One's Company*, p. 54.

16. Evelyn Vuko, "What's a Little Cancer Among Friends? Part 2: A New Circle of Friends," *The Washington Post,* Aug. 9, 1996, p. B5.

17. Audrey McCollum, *The Trauma of Moving: Psychological Issues for Women,* p. 125.

18. Audrey McCollum, *The Trauma of Moving*, pp. 126–29.

19. Jean Baker Miller, 1986, "What Do We Mean by Relationships?" Work in Progress #22, The Stone Center, Wellesley College, p. 1.

20. Jean Baker Miller, 1986, "What Do We Mean by Relationships?" p. 3.

21. Donna Damico Mayer, "Segment #15: Rolling Stones Tune Helps Woman Turn Life's Corner," *All Things Considered,* National Public Radio, Jan. 18, 1996.

22. Donna Damico Mayer, Jan. 18, 1996, "Segment #15: Rolling Stones Tune Helps Woman Turn Life's Corner."

23. Donna Damico Mayer, Jan. 18, 1996, "Segment #15: Rolling Stones Tune Helps Woman Turn Life's Corner."

24. Audrey McCollum, 1990, *The Trauma of Moving*, p. 134.

25. Betty Friedan, 1993, *The Fountain of Age*, pp. 290–91.

26. Audrey McCollum, 1990, *The Trauma of Moving*, p. 154.

27. Lynn Caine, 1988, *Being a Widow,* pp. 156–57.

28. Betty Friedan, 1993, *The Fountain of Age*, p. 291.

29. Carol Anderson and Susan Stewart with Sona Dimidjian, 1994, *Flying Solo: Single Women in Midlife*, p. 185.

30. Michael Yapko, "The Art of Avoiding Depression," *Psychology Today,* May/June 1997, p. 75.

31. Jean Baker Miller, 1986, *Toward a New Psychology of Women*, 2nd ed., p. 51.

32. Audrey McCollum, 1990, *The Trauma of Moving*, p. 154.

7. Tap Into Religion

1. Richard Bolles, "How to Face the Future Unafraid," talk at the World Bank in Washington, D.C., on Apr. 1, 1996.

2. Mark Epstein, "Opening Up to Happiness," *Psychology Today,* July/Aug. 1995, pp. 42–.

3. Eugene Taylor, "Desperately Seeking Spirituality," *Psychology Today,* Nov./Dec. 1994, p. 66.

4. Iris Krasnow, "The Fellowship of Women," *The Washington Post,* Aug. 6, 1996, p. B5.

5. Eugene Taylor, Nov./Dec. 1994, "Desperately Seeking Spirituality."

6. Germaine Greer, 1991, *The Change: Women, Aging and the Menopause*, p. 379.

8. Discharge Your Emotional Overload

1. Colin Murray Parkes, 1983, *Bereavement: Studies of Grief in Adult Life*, p. 207.

2. In addition to the local affiliates of Parents Without Partners, AARP and the National Retired Teachers Association sponsor local groups for newly widowed persons through their Widowed Persons Service (see Resources).

AARP estimates that there are half a million self-help groups in the United States helping more than 15 million people deal with problems like death, divorce, mental illness, addiction, and health problems. See AARP, 1994,"Tapping into the Benefits of Self-Help/Mutual Aid Groups," *AARP-Online*. Religious scholar Robert Wuthnow puts the number of small support groups at over 3 million, with over 40 percent of Americans belonging to one. The title of his book reveals the role Wuthnow believes these groups play in our lives: 1996, *Sharing the Journey: Support Groups and America's New Quest for Community*.

3. Personal communication with Alice Umbach on June 17, 1996.

4. From a speech by Jean Ellzey, "Running on a Road Less Traveled," at the Women's Forum, Naperville, IL, Jan. 12, 1996.

5. See, for example, Stan Katz and Aimee Liu, 1991, *The Codependency Conspiracy*; and Andrew Delbanco and Thomas Delbanco, "A.A. at the Crossroads," *The New Yorker,* Mar. 20, 1995.

6. William Galston, "One Day at a Time," *Washington Post Book World,* Apr. 3, 1994, p. 4 (a review of Robert Wuthnow's 1996 book *Sharing the Journey: Support Groups and America's New Quest for Community*).

7. William Galston, "One Day at a Time."

8. These criticisms appear in Stan Katz and Aimee Liu, 1991, *The Codependency Conspiracy*; Susan Faludi, 1991, *Backlash: The Undeclared War Against American Women*, pp. 348–53; and Carolyn Heilbrun, 1979, *Reinventing Womanhood*, pp. 26–27.

9. Stan Katz and Aimee Liu, 1991, *The Codependency Conspiracy*, pp. 40–61.

10. Barbara White and Edward Madras, eds., 1995, *Self-Help Sourcebook: National Guide to Finding and Forming Mutual Aid Self-Help Groups,* 5th ed.

11. Personal communications with psychologists Dr. Andrew Morral and Dr. Lisa Jaycox, Feb. 11, 1997.

12. See Wolfgang Stroebe and Margaret Stroebe, 1987, *Bereavement and Health: The Psychological and Physical Consequences of Partner Loss*, pp. 13–15; and Marian Osterweis, Frederic Solomon, and Morris Green, eds., 1984, *Bereavement: Reactions, Consequences and Care*, pp. 47–53. There are different versions

of these stages, and they are sometimes broken into five rather than four.

13. Colin Murray Parkes, 1983, *Bereavement*, p. 21.

14. Barbara Holland, 1992, *One's Company: Reflections on Living Alone*, p. 198.

15. Stanley Jacobson, "Overselling Depression to the Old Folks," *The Atlantic Monthly*, Apr. 1995.

16. Personal communication with psychologist Dr. Mary Lou Randour on Feb. 23, 1996.

17. M. L. S. Vachon, A. R. Sheldon, W. J. Lancee, W. A. L. Lyall, J. Rogers, and S. J. J. Freeman, 1980, "A Controlled Study of Self-Help Intervention for Widows," *American Journal of Psychiatry* 137: 1380–84.

18. "Mental Health: Does Therapy Help?" *Consumer Reports*, Nov. 1995.

19. "Mental Health: Does Therapy Help?" *Consumer Reports*, Nov. 1995.

20. According to psychologist Martin Seligman in his 1993 book *What You Can Change and What You Can't: The Complete Guide to Successful Self-Improvement*, pp. 110–16, p. 241, two treatments show special promise with the kind of anxiety, anger, and depression that often follows the loss of a husband through death or divorce. The treatments are cognitive therapy and inter-personal therapy. Cognitive therapy works in the present to change a person's conscious thoughts about her situation and the way she views it. It often works well, especially for moderate depression, and usually in just a few months time. (It brought relief to 70 percent of depressed people in a recent study.) The classic book on cognitive therapy is the much reprinted *Feeling Good: The New Mood Therapy* by David Burns (1992). The other effective short-term treatment (roughly equal in effective-ness and the time it takes) is interpersonal therapy. IPT addresses current problems like grief and role transitions head-on, helping you complete your mourning and come up with the social strengths you need to move ahead. When depression is severe, studies show the most effective treatment is antidepressive med-ications, or when they don't work, electroconvulsive shock. Most effective of all is an antidepressive supplemented by professional counseling.

21. Martin Seligman, 1993, *What You Can Change and What You Can't*, p. 241.

22. "Mental Health: Does Therapy Help?" *Consumer Reports,* Nov. 1995.

23. "Mental Health: Does Therapy Help?" *Consumer Reports,* Nov. 1995.

24. Personal communication with psychologist Dr. Andrew Morral, Feb. 11, 1997.

25. Kevin Gray, "Getting Help (The Kind People Don't Want to Mention)," *The Washington Post,* Jan. 14, 1997, p. C5. The American Psychological Association's 1995 guide is "How to Choose a Psychologist" (see Resources).

26. Frank Pittman III, "A Buyer's Guide to Psychotherapy," *Psychology Today,* Jan./Feb. 1994, pp. 51–52.

27. Frank Pittman III, "A Buyer's Guide to Psychotherapy," p. 50.

28. Personal communication with psychologist Dr. Lisa Jaycox on Jan. 28, 1997.

29. Personal communication with Alice Umbach on June 17, 1996.

30. Personal communication with Edie Irons, Ed.D., on May 29, 1996.

31. "Mental Health: Does Therapy Help?" *Consumer Reports,* Nov. 1995.

32. "Mental Health: Does Therapy Help?" *Consumer Reports,* Nov. 1995.

33. Kevin Gray, Jan. 14, 1997, "Getting Help (The Kind People Don't Want to Mention)."

9. What Kind of Life Do You Want?

1. Jean Baker Miller, 1986, *Toward a New Psychology of Women,* 2nd ed., pp. 113–14.

2. Lillian Rubin, 1979, *Women of a Certain Age: The Midlife Search for Self*, p. 42.

3. Lillian Rubin, 1979, *Women of a Certain Age,* p. 121.

4. Lillian Rubin, 1979, *Women of a Certain Age,* pp. 66–67.

5. Personal communication with Alice Umbach on June 17, 1996.

6. Personal communication with Dr. Andrew Morral on Dec. 26, 1996.

7. Helene Deutsch, 1973, *Confrontations with Myself: An Epilogue.* Cited in Germaine Greer, 1991, *The Change: Women, Aging and the Menopause*, p. 54.

8. See, for example, Ravenna Helson and Laurel McCabe, "The Social Clock Project in Middle Age," in Barbara Turner and Lillian Troll, eds., *Women Growing Older: Psychological Perspectives.*, pp. 68–93. The study found that just over one-half of "traditional" (i.e., married) women successfully changed themselves at midlife, while 80 percent of divorced women did. The most important factor in being able to go in a completely new direction was whether a woman had either an "achieved" or a "moratorium" identity. Women with these identities were able to change themselves, while women with "diffuse" or "foreclosed" identities remained stuck in their current roles.

9. Cited in Linda Feldman, "Having the Time of Their Life Writing the Times of Their Lives," *Los Angeles Times,* Feb. 13, 1994, p. 142. See also James Birren and Linda Feldman, 1997, *Where to Go from Here: Discovering Your Own Life's Wisdom in Your Second Fifty.*

10. Linda Feldman, "Having the Time of Their Life Writing the Times of Their Lives."

11. Tee Corinne, "Telling the World," *The Women's Review of Books* 13.10–11 (July 1996): 23.

12. Janet Lynn Roseman, 1994, *The Way of the Woman Writer* (see Resources for other books that teach journal writing).

13. Telephone communication with Hannelore Hahn on Dec. 2, 1996. Contact the IWWG at Caller Box 810 Gracie Station, New York, NY 10028 (212) 737–7536.

14. Personal communication with IWWG executive director Hannelore Hahn on Dec. 2, 1996.

15. Personal communication with Hannelore Hahn on Dec. 2, 1996.

16. Described in Hannelore Hahn, 1993, "The Essence and History of the IWWG." Hahn's autobiography, published in 1982, is titled *On the Way to Feed the Swans.*

17. Hannelore Hahn, 1993, "The Essence and History of the IWWG."

18. Personal communication with Joan Kurianski on Mar. 20, 1996.

19. Rebecca Maddox, 1995, *Inc. Your Dreams.*

20. Rebecca Maddox, 1995, *Inc. Your Dreams,* p. xii.

21. Richard Bolles, 1996, *What Color Is Your Parachute?*

22. Richard Bolles, "How to Face the Future Unafraid," talk given at the World Bank, Washington, D.C., on Apr. 1, 1996.

23. Wendy Swallow Williams, "50 Things to Do Before I Die," *The Washington Post,* July 4, 1996, p. C5.

24. Carolyn Heilbrun, 1988, *Writing a Woman's Life,* p. 60.

25. Carolyn Heilbrun, 1988, *Writing a Woman's Life,* pp. 115, 117, 119.

26. Kate Mulligan, "Heilbrunian Adventures," *AARP Bulletin* 37.2 (Feb. 1996): 16.

27. Richard Stradling, "The Golden Girls," *The Washington Post,* Feb. 28, 1995, p. D5.

28. Marybeth Bond, ed., 1995, *Travelers' Tales: A Woman's World,* p. xiii.

29. Personal communication with Elsie Bliss on Aug. 16, 1994.

30. Paul Roberts, "Goofing Off," *Psychology Today,* July/Aug. 1995, p. 35.

31. Johan Huizinga, 1985, *Homo Ludens: A Study of the Play Element in Culture.* Huizinga wrote *Homo Ludens (Man the Player)* in 1938. His theories are described in Paul Roberts, "Goofing Off," pp. 36–37.

32. Elsie Bliss, "Single Bliss," *The Single Parent: Journal of Parents without Partners,* Dec. 1979.

33. Gail Sheehy, 1995, *New Passages: Mapping Your Life Across Time,* pp. 142–43.

10. A Nest of Your Own

1. Joyce Carol Oates, "American Gothic," *The New Yorker,* May 8, 1995, p. 36.

2. Audrey McCollum, 1990, *The Trauma of Moving: Psychological Issues for Women.*

3. Kenneth Lelen, "Four Walls, Memories—and Tough Choices:

Newly Widowed Wrestle with Whether to Sell," *The Washington Post*, May 13, 1995, p. E1.

4. Kenneth Lelen, "Four Walls, Memories—and Tough Choices." Lelen cites an interview with Ann Studner, director of the American Association of Retired Person's Widowed Persons Service.

5. Good resources for how to approach financial planning are Alexandra Armstrong and Mary Donahue, 1993, *On Your Own: A Widow's Passage to Emotional and Financial Well-Being*; and Frances Leonard, 1993, *Money and the Mature Woman: How to Hold On to Your Income, Keep Your Home, Plan Your Estate*.

6. See "Fannie Mae Offers Reverse Mortgages," *AARP Bulletin* 36.11 (Dec. 1995): 3. For a discussion of the pluses and minuses, see Frances Leonard, 1993, *Money and the Mature Woman*, pp. 114–16. In addition to Fannie Mae, the Federal Housing Administration and Transamerica are reverse mortgage lenders.

7. Audrey McCollum, 1990, *The Trauma of Moving*, p. 60, pp. 85–94.

8. Described in Helen Glazer, "I Wouldn't Want to Be Young Again," *The Washington Post*, Feb. 28, 1995, p. D5. See Doris Grumbach, 1995, *Extra Innings: A Memoir*; and Doris Grumbach, 1995, *Fifty Days of Solitude*.

9. Malcolm Boyd, "When Change Is a Must," *Modern Maturity*, Jan./Feb. 1995, p. 78.

10. Betty Friedan, 1993, *The Fountain of Age*, pp. 352–53.

11. Betty Friedan, 1993, *The Fountain of Age*, p. 380.

12. Barbara Holland, 1992, *One's Company: Reflections on Living Alone*, p. 12.

13. Barbara Holland, 1992, *One's Company*, p. 6.

14. See Martin Seligman, 1991, *Learned Optimism*, pp. 85–87; and Susan Nolen-Hoeksema, 1990, *Sex Differences in Depression*, pp. 160–77.

15. Christopher Hayes, Deborah Anderson, and Melinda Blau, 1993, *Our Turn: The Good News about Women and Divorce*, pp. 80, 130.

16. Carol Anderson, Susan Stewart, with Sona Dimidjian, 1994, *Flying Solo: Single Women in Midlife*, pp. 283–86.

17. Ruth Harriet Jacobs, "Living Alone Outrageously," talk at Wellesley College on Oct. 3, 1996.

18. Ruth Harriet Jacobs, 1997, *Be an Outrageous Older Woman*.

19. Susan Faludi, 1991, *Backlash: The Undeclared War Against American Women*, p. 148.

20. Deborah Chalfie, 1995, *The Real Golden Girls: The Prevalence and Policy Treatment of Midlife and Older People Living in Nontraditional Households*.

21. Quoted by Caroline Bird, 1995, *Lives of Our Own: Secrets of Salty Old Women*, p. 242.

22. Population Reference Bureau, 1993, *What the 1990 Census Tells Us About Women: A State Factbook*, p. 50.

23. Cited in Barbara Holland, 1992, *One's Company*, p. 216.

11. Step by Step to a Career

1. Rebecca Maddox, 1995, *Inc. Your Dreams,* pp. 258–59.

2. Robert Weber, "This Is Mrs. McBride from Marketing," *The New Yorker,* July 8, 1996, p. 52.

3. Robert Lewis, "Up and Away: Second Careers Taking Off," *AARP Bulletin* 37.5 (May 1996): 1.

4. Many of the over two thousand respondents to a 1996 survey by the AARP on career changing reported "embarking on strikingly different careers." About one in five reported they had failed. See Robert Lewis, "Up and Away: Second Careers Taking Off," and Robert Lewis, "Career Changers Find Road to Success Marked by Perils," *AARP Bulletin* 37.6 (June 1996): 1.

5. Ronald Henkoff, "So You Want to Change Your Job," *Fortune,* Jan. 15, 1996, p. 54.

6. Lisa Mainiero, "The Longest Climb," *Psychology Today,* Nov./Dec. 1994, pp. 40–.

7. Lisa Mainiero, "The Longest Climb." Another examination of this topic is found in Cecilia Northcutt, 1991, *Successful Career Women: Their Professional and Personal Characteristics*.

8. National Center for Women and Retirement Research, 1993, *Women and Divorce: Turning Your Life Around*, p. 15.

9. National Center for Women and Retirement Research, 1993, *Women and Divorce*.

10. Lois Shaw and Rachel Shaw, 1987, "From Midlife to Retirement: The Middle-Aged Woman Worker," in Karen Shallcross Koziara, Michael Moskow, and Lucretia Dewey Tanner, eds., *Working Women: Past, Present*, p. 305.

11. Quoted in Cynthia Hanson, "Want a Raise? You've Got to Ask for the Salary You Deserve," *The Chicago Tribune*, Feb. 11, 1996.

12. Debra Benton, 1993, *Lions Don't Need to Roar: Using the Leadership Power of Professional Presence to Stand Out, Fit In and Move Ahead*.

13. Debra Benton, 1993, *Lions Don't Need to Roar*.

14. Cynthia Hanson, Feb. 11, 1996, "Want a Raise? You've Got to Ask for the Salary You Deserve."

15. Lillian Rubin, 1981, *Women of a Certain Age: The Midlife Search for Self*, p. 63.

16. For information on Low, consult Fern Brown, 1996, *Daisy and the Girl Scouts: The Story of Juliette Gordon Low*.

17. Francine Weiss, 1984, *Older Women and Job Discrimination: A Primer*.

18. Robert Lewis, "Career Changers Find Road to Success Marked by Perils," p. 8.

19. Personal communication with Alice Umbach on June 17, 1997. The book she recommends is by Lynette Triere and Richard Peacock, 1993, *Learning to Leave*.

20. Gail Schlachter, 1994, *The Back-to-School Money Book: A Financial Aid Guide for Midlife and Older Women Seeking Education and Training*.

21. Ronald Henkoff, "So You Want to Change Your Job," p. 54.

22. Ronald Henkoff, "So You Want to Change Your Job," p. 55. The National Board for Certified Counselors keeps a list of academically qualified job counselors (see Resources).

23. Jean Baker Miller, 1986, *Toward a New Psychology of Women*, 2nd ed., p. 36.

24. Richard Bolles, "How to Face the Future Unafraid," talk at the World Bank, Washington, D.C., Apr. 1, 1996.

25. Caroline Bird, 1995, *Lives of Our Own: Secrets of Salty Old Women*, p. 265–66.

26. Stephen Pollan and Mark Levine, 1997, *Starting Over*, p. 66.

27. Carolyn Heilbrun, 1979, *Reinventing Womanhood*, p. 164.

28. Women Employed, "The Glass Ceiling: A Women-Employed Fact Sheet."

29. Carolyn Heilbrun, 1979, *Reinventing Womanhood*, p. 164.

30. Hillary Lapsley, "Mentoring in Women's Lives," talk given at the Center for Research on Women, Wellesley College, on Feb. 27, 1992.

31. Quoted in Don Oldenburg, "Women at the Top," *The Washington Post*, Aug. 1, 1995, p. E5.

32. Don Oldenburg, "Women at the Top."

33. Rebecca Maddox, 1995, *Inc. Your Dreams*.

34. Jennifer Starr and Marcia Yudkin, 1996, *Women Entrepreneurs: A Review of Current Research*, p. 11.

35. See Stephen Pollan and Mark Levine, 1997, *Starting Over: How to Change Careers or Start Your Own Business*; and Mari Florence, 1997, *The Enterprising Woman*.

36. Jennifer Starr and Marcia Yudkin, 1996, *Women Entrepreneurs: A Review of Current Research*, p. 2.

37. Pam Black, "A 'New-Girl' Network Starts to Take Root," *BusinessWeek Online*, Oct. 2, 1995.

38. Pam Black, "A 'New-Girl' Network Starts to Take Root" (see Resources for further information).

39. Pam Black, "A 'New-Girl' Network Starts to Take Root."

40. Pam Black, "A 'New-Girl' Network Starts to Take Root."

41. Susan Chandler, "Closing the Gender Gap—with Capital," *BusinessWeek*, Apr. 18, 1994.

42 Mari Florence, 1997, *The Enterprising Woman*, p. 30

12. Pursue Your Passion

1. Simone de Beauvoir, 1970, *Old Age*, p. 601.

2. Simone de Beauvoir, 1970, *Old Age*. (The title of the book in French, *La Vieillesse*, was given its literal English meaning, "old

age," in the British edition, but changed by American publishers to the more optimistic *Coming of Age.)* Simone de Beauvoir, 1993, *Second Sex.*

3. De Beauvoir eventually came to terms with her aging, thanks in part to a passionate friendship with another woman, and as historian Lois Banner tells it, "she found her later years not a time of despair but rather of contentment." See Lois Banner, 1993, *In Full Flower: Aging Women, Power, and Sexuality,* pp. 303–4; and Dierdre Bair, 1990, *Simone de Beauvoir: A Biography.*

4. The poem was chosen out of six hundred entries to be published in a 1997 University of New Hampshire anthology, *The Continuum.*

5. Personal communication with Jean Kalmanoff on Apr. 13, 1994.

6. Jean Kalmanoff, 1991, "Lament," *Solo Flight,* p. 13.

7. Eric Maisel, 1995, *Fearless Creating: A Step-by-Step Guide to Starting and Completing Your Work of Art.,* p. xxv.

8. Eric Maisel, 1995, *Fearless Creating;* and Julia Cameron, 1992, *The Artist's Way: A Spiritual Path to Higher Creativity.*

9. Robert Epstein, "Capturing Creativity," *Psychology Today,* July/Aug. 1996, p. 43.

10. Robert Epstein, "Capturing Creativity."

11. Robert Epstein, "Capturing Creativity," p. 78.

12. Eric Maisel, 1995, *Fearless Creating,* pp. xvi–xvii.

13. Eric Maisel, 1995, *Fearless Creating,* p. 6.

14. Julia Cameron, 1992, *The Artist's Way,* p. 55.

15. Eric Maisel, 1996, *Fearless Creating,* p. 22.

16. Julia Cameron, 1992, *The Artist's Way,* p. 11.

17. Cited in "The Backlash Begins," *Notes from Emily,* Mar. 1996, pp. 1–2. The survey was conducted by *The Washington Post,* the Kaiser Family Foundation, and Harvard University for the WOMEN VOTE! project of EMILY's List.

18. Caroline Bird, 1995, *Lives of Our Own: Secrets of Salty Old Women,* p. 69.

19. Jean Baker Miller, 1986, *Toward a New Psychology of Women,* 2nd ed., p. 62.

20. Tish Sommers, 1973, *The Not-So-Helpless Female,* pp. 70–72.

21. A description of the founding and fortunes of the National Displaced Homemakers Network and OWL is included in Ruth Harriet Jacobs, 1993, "Expanding Social Roles for Older Women," in Jessie Allen and Alan Pifer, eds., *Women on the Front Lines*, pp. 197–99.

22. Tish Sommers, 1994, "Changing Society and Ourselves," in Paula Doress-Worters and Diana Laskin Siegal, eds., *The New Ourselves, Growing Older: Women Aging with Knowledge and Power.*

23. Tish Sommers, 1973, *The Not-So-Helpless Female*, p. 116.

24. Ruth Harriet Jacobs, 1997, *Be an Outrageous Older Woman.*

25. Tish Sommers, 1994, "Changing Society and Ourselves."

26. Tish Sommers, 1973, *The Not-So-Helpless Female*, p. 71.

27. A J Brand, *A Common Sense Guide to Divorce.*

28. Personal communication with A J Brand on Apr. 17, 1996.

29. Tish Sommers, 1973, *The Not-So-Helpless Female*, p. 121.

30. Tish Sommers, 1973, *The Not-So-Helpless Female*, p. 111.

31. Tish Sommers, 1973, *The Not-So-Helpless Female.*

32. Tish Sommers, 1994, "Changing Society and Ourselves," pp. 436–39.

33. Ruth Harriet Jacobs, 1997, *Be an Outrageous Older Woman.*

34. Kay Stoner, "Cracking the Husk," *The Sage Within* 1.1 (Winter Solstice 1995): 2.

13. To Be or Not to Be (Married)

1. Colette Dowling, 1996, *Red Hot Mamas: Coming into Our Own at Fifty*, p. 103.

2. Nora FitzGerald, "Martha: Soup or Art?" *The Washington Post*, Mar. 17, 1996, p. C1.

3. Patricia Sellers, "Cocktails at Charlotte's with Martha and Darla," *Fortune*, Aug. 5, 1996, p. 57.

4. Jane Gross, "Divorced, Middle-Aged and Happy: Women, Especially, Adjust to the 90's," *The New York Times*, Dec. 7, 1992, p. A14.

5. Enid Nemy, "'What? Me Marry?' Widows Say No," *The New York Times*, June 18, 1992, p. C1.

6. Elsie Bliss, 1991, "Why Isn't a Nice Person Like You Married?" in Ann Mosley and Jeanette Harris, eds., *Interactions: A Thematic Reader.*

7. Personal communication with Martha Farnsworth Riche on Aug. 10, 1994.

8. Jean Baker Miller, 1986, *Toward a New Psychology of Women,* 2nd ed., p. 65.

9. Elsie Bliss, 1991, "Why Isn't a Nice Person Like You Married?"

10. Jean Baker Miller, 1986, *Toward a New Psychology of Women,* p. 93.

11. David Burns, 1992, *Feeling Good: The New Mood Therapy,* p. 311.

12. David Burns, 1992, *Feeling Good,* pp. 311–26.

13. David Burns, 1992, *Feeling Good,* p. 344.

14. Gail Sheehy, 1995, *New Passages: Mapping Your Life Across Time,* p. 142.

15. Cited in Caroline Bird, 1995, *Lives of Our Own: Secrets of Salty Old Women,* p. 229.

16. Colette Dowling, 1990, *The Cinderella Complex: Women's Hidden Fear of Independence.*

17. Colette Dowling, 1996, *Red Hot Mamas,* pp. 92–93.

18. Colette Dowling, 1996, *Red Hot Mamas.*

19. Christopher Hayes, Deborah Anderson, and Melinda Blau, 1993, *Our Turn: The Good News about Women and Divorce,* pp. 149–55.

20. Germaine Greer, 1991, *The Change: Women, Aging and the Menopause,* p. 325.

21. Christie Burke, 1994, "HIV and Safer Sex," in Paula Doress-Worters and Diana Laskin Siegal, eds., *The New Ourselves, Growing Older: Women Aging with Knowledge and Power,* pp. 96–97.

22. Gena Corea, 1992, *The Invisible Epidemic: The Story of Women and AIDS.*

23. The nationwide survey of ten thousand people was conducted at the University of California. Cited in Colette Dowling, 1996, *Red Hot Mamas,* p. 192.

24. Colette Dowling, 1996, *Red Hot Mamas,* pp. 191–97.

25. Carin Rubenstein, "The *Lear's* Report: How AIDS Has Changed Our Sex Lives," *Lear's,* Nov. 1992, pp. 62–67.

26. Christie Burke, 1994, "HIV and Safer Sex," p. 96.

27. National Women's Health Network, 1998, *AIDS: Women and HIV/AIDS.*

28. Germaine Greer, 1991, *The Change,* p. 110.

29. Grace Baruch, Rosalind Barnett, and Caryl Rivers, 1984, *Lifeprints: New Patterns of Love and Work for Today's Woman.*

30. Frances Leonard, 1993, *Money and the Mature Woman: How to Hold On to Your Income, Keep Your Home, Plan Your Estate,* p. 5.

31. Esther Madriz, 1997, *Nothing Bad Happens to Good Girls: Fear of Crime in Women's Lives.*

32. Christopher Hayes, Deborah Anderson, and Melinda Blau, 1993, *Our Turn,* p. 162.

33. Peter Kramer, 1997, *Should You Leave?* p. 233.

34. "Are There Dating Services for Seniors?" *Modern Maturity,* Apr.–May 1993, p. 84.

35. Otto Kroeger and Janet Thuesen, 1988, *Type Talk: The 16 Personality Types That Determine How We Live, Love, and Work,* pp. 123–24. The book analyzes people on the basis of personality type using the Myers-Briggs Type Indicator.

36. Isabel Briggs Myers, with Peter Briggs Myers, 1980, *Gifts Differing: Understanding Personality Type,* p. 126.

37. Peter Kramer, 1997, *Should You Leave?* p. 88.

38. Otto Kroeger and Janet Thuesen, 1988, *Type Talk,* p. 133.

39. Peter Kramer, 1997, *Should You Leave?* pp. 201–2.

40. Peter Kramer, 1997, *Should You Leave?* p. 55.

References

Abelson, Reed. "Our Portfolios, Ourselves." *The New York Times,* Oct. 15, 1995, sect. 3, pp. 1, 4.

Aley, James. "Where the Jobs Are." *Fortune,* Sept. 18, 1995, p. 53.

American Association of Retired Persons. "Are There Dating Services for Seniors?" *Modern Maturity,* Apr./May 1993, p. 84.

———."Facts About Financial Planners." Rev. ed. Washington, D.C.: author, 1994.

———."Fannie Mae Offers Reverse Mortgages." *AARP Bulletin* 36.11 (Dec. 1995): 3.

———."Negative Stereotypes Still Plague Older Workers on the Job." *AARP Bulletin* 36.4 (Apr. 1995): 3.

———. *Returning to the Job Market: A Woman's Guide to Employment Planning.* Washington, D.C.: author, 1992.

———. "Tapping into the Benefits of Self-Help/Mutual Aid Groups." *AARP-Online.* Washington, D.C.: author, 1994.

American Psychological Association. "How to Choose a Psychologist." Washington, D.C.: author, 1995.

Anderson, Carol, and Susan Stewart, with Sona Dimidjian. *Flying Solo: Single Women in Midlife.* New York: W. W. Norton & Company, 1994.

Antonucci, Toni. "A Life-Span View of Women's Social Relations." In *Women Growing Older: Psychological Perspectives.* Ed. Barbara Turner and Lillian Troll. Thousand Oaks, CA: Sage, 1994. 239–69.

Apter, Terri. *Secret Paths: Women in the New Midlife.* New York: W. W. Norton & Company, 1995.

Armstrong, Alexandra, and Mary Donahue. *On Your Own: A Widow's Passage to Emotional and Financial Well-Being.* Chicago: Dearborne Financial Publishing, 1993.

Ascher, Barbara Lazear. "How to Free Yourself from Anger." *Self,* Feb. 1995, pp. 142–.

"The Backlash Begins." *Notes from Emily,* Mar. 1996, pp. 1–2.

Bair, Dierdre. *Simone de Beauvoir: A Biography.* New York: Summit Books, 1990.

Banner, Lois. *In Full Flower: Aging Women, Power, and Sexuality.* New York: Vintage Books, 1993.

Baruch, Grace, Rosalind Barnett, and Caryl Rivers. *Lifeprints: New Patterns of Love and Work for Today's Women.* New York: New American Library, 1984.

Beardstown Ladies Investment Club, with Leslie Whitaker. *The Beardstown Ladies' Common Sense Investment Guide.* New York: Hyperion, 1994.

Bennett, Janet. "Many Happy Returns." *The Washington Post,* Feb. 18, 1997, p. D5.

Benson, Herbert. *The Relaxation Response.* Avenal, N.J.: Random House/Value, 1992.

Benton, Debra. *Lions Don't Need to Roar: Using the Leadership Power of Professional Presence to Stand Out, Fit In and Move Ahead.* New York: Warner Books, 1993.

Bird, Caroline. *Lives of Our Own: Secrets of Salty Old Women.* Boston: Houghton Mifflin, 1995.

Birren, James, and Linda Feldman. *Where to Go from Here: Discovering Your Own Life's Wisdom in Your Second Fifty.* New York: Simon & Schuster, 1997.

Black, Pam. "Buoying Women Investors." *BusinessWeek,* Feb. 27, 1995, pp. 126–27.

———. "A 'New-Girl' Network Starts to Take Root." Special Report. *BusinessWeek Online,* Oct. 2, 1995.

Bliss, Elsie. "Single Bliss." *The Single Parent. Journal of Parents Without Partners,* Dec. 1979, pp. 9–10, 38.

———. "Why Isn't a Nice Person Like You Married?" In *Interactions: A Thematic Reader.* Ed. Ann Mosley and Jeanette Harris. New York: Houghton Mifflin, 1991.

Bobala, Bob. "The Tempers." *The Washington Post,* Apr. 5, 1996, p. F5.

Bolles, Richard. "How to Face the Future Unafraid." Talk at the World Bank in Washington, D.C. on Apr. 1, 1996.

———. *The 1997 What Color Is Your Parachute?* Berkeley, CA: Ten Speed Press, 1996.

Bond, Marybeth, ed. *Travelers' Tales: A Woman's World.* San Francisco: Travelers' Tales, Inc., 1995.

Boughton, Barbara. "The Healing Arts." *Modern Maturity,* Sept./Oct. 1996, p. 70.

Boyd, Malcolm. "When Change Is a Must." *Modern Maturity,* Jan./Feb. 1995, p. 78.

Brand, A J. *A Common Sense Guide to Divorce.* Northfield, IL: Divorce Reform Publishing, 1996.

Brown, Fern. *Daisy and the Girl Scouts: The Story of Juliette Gordon Low.* Morton Grove, IL: Albert Whitman and Co., 1996.

Burke, Christie. "HIV and Safer Sex." In *The New Ourselves, Growing Older: Women Aging with Knowledge and Power.* Ed. Paula Doress-Worters and Diana Laskin Siegal. New York: Simon & Schuster/Touchstone, 1994. 96–97.

Burns, David. *Feeling Good: The New Mood Therapy.* New York: Avon Books, 1992.

Byrne, A., and D. G. Byrne. "The Effect of Exercise on Depression, Anxiety and Other Mood States: A Review." *Journal of Psychosomatic Research* 37.6 (Sept. 1993): 565–74.

Caine, Lynne. *Being a Widow.* New York: Viking/Penguin, 1988.

Cameron, Julia. *The Artist's Way: A Spiritual Path to Higher Creativity.* New York: J. P. Tarcher/Putnam, 1992.

Campbell, Gillie, and Caroline Chauncey. "Money Matters: The Economics of Aging for Women." In *The New Ourselves, Growing Older: Women Aging with Knowledge and Power.* Ed. Paula Doress-Worters and Diana Laskin Siegal. New York: Simon & Schuster/Touchstone, 1994. 187–203.

"Can Stress Make You Sick?" *Harvard Health Letter* 23.6 (Apr. 1998): 1–3.

Carpi, John. "Stress: It's Worse Than You Think." *Psychology Today,* Jan./Feb., 1996, pp. 34–.

Chalfie, Deborah. *The Real Golden Girls: The Prevalence and Policy Treatment of Midlife and Older People Living in Nontraditional Households.* Washington, D.C.: AARP, 1995.

Chandler, Susan. "Closing the Gender Gap—With Capital." *Business-Week,* Apr. 18, 1994, p. 110.

Chandrasekaran, Rajiv. "U.S. to Train Workers for Tech Jobs." *The Washington Post,* Jan. 12, 1998, pp. 1–.

Cole, Al. "Right on the Money." *Modern Maturity,* Jan./Feb. 1997, p. 77.

Corcoran, Mary, Greg Duncan, and Michael Ponza. "A Longitudinal Analysis of White Women's Wages." *Journal of Human Resources* 18 (Fall 1983): 497–520.

Corea, Gena. *The Invisible Epidemic: The Story of Women and Aids.* New York: HarperCollins, 1992.

Corinne, Tee. "Telling the World." *The Women's Review of Books* 13.10–11 (July 1996): 23.

de Beauvoir, Simone. *Old Age.* Middlesex, Eng.: Penguin Books, 1970.

———. *The Second Sex.* New York: Knopf, 1993.

Deets, Horace. "Job Program That Helps Now Needs Help Itself." *AARP Bulletin* 36.3 (Mar. 1995): 3.

Delbanco, Andrew, and Thomas Delbanco. "A.A. at the Crossroads." *The New Yorker,* Mar. 20, 1995, pp. 50–63.

Deutsch, Helene. *Confrontations with Myself: An Epilogue.* New York: W. W. Norton & Company, 1973.

Dowling, Colette. *The Cinderella Complex: Women's Hidden Fear of Independence.* Seattle: Peanut Butter Pub., 1990.

———. *Red Hot Mamas: Coming into Our Own at Fifty.* New York: Bantam, 1996.

Drake, Emma. *What Every Woman of Forty-five Ought to Know.* Philadelphia: Sylvanus Stall, 1902.

Elliott, Laura. "Help for Your Head." *The Washingtonian Magazine,* Apr. 1998, pp. 76–.

Ellzey, Jean. "Running Full on a Road Less Traveled." Speech at the Women's Forum, Naperville, IL, Jan. 12, 1996.

Epstein, Mark. "Opening Up to Happiness." *Psychology Today,* Jul./Aug. 1995, pp. 42–.

Epstein, Robert. "Capturing Creativity." *Psychology Today,* Jul./Aug., 1996, p. 43.

Faludi, Susan. *Backlash: The Undeclared War Against American Women.* New York: Crown, 1991.

Feldman, Linda. "Having the Time of Their Life Writing the Times of Their Lives." *Los Angeles Times,* Feb. 13, 1994.

FitzGerald, Nora. "Martha: Soup or Art?" *The Washington Post,* Mar. 17, 1996, p. C1.

Florence, Mari. *The Enterprising Woman.* New York: Warner Books, 1997.

Folliard, Patrick. "Working Out Your Network." *The Washington Post,* Nov. 1, 1995, p. D5.

Franklin, Mary Beth. "Group Learns to Play the Market, Garners 'Outstanding' Profits." *Washington Senior Beacon,* June 1994, p. 18.

Friedan, Betty. *The Fountain of Age.* New York: Simon & Schuster, 1993.

Galston, William. "One Day at a Time." *Washington Post Book World,* Apr. 3, 1994, p. 4.

Gazze, Nancy. "Wake-Up Calls and Ambulance Promises." *The Washington Post,* Jan. 12, 1996, p. D5.

Gill, Brendan. *Late Bloomers.* New York: Workman Publishing/Artisan, 1996.

Glassman, James. "Her Case of Nerves Needs Stock Treatment." *The Washington Post,* Dec. 15, 1996, p. H1.

Glazer, Helen. "I Wouldn't Want to Be Young Again." *The Washington Post,* Feb. 28, 1995, p. D5.

Goldsmith, Olivia. *First Wives Club.* New York: Poseidon Press, 1992.

Gray, Kevin. "Getting Help (The Kind People Don't Want to Mention)." *The Washington Post,* Jan. 14, 1997, p. C5.

Greenwood-Audant, L. M. "The Internalization of Powerlessness: A Case Study of the Misplaced Homemaker." In *Women: A Feminist Perspective,* Ed. J. Freeman. Palo Alto, CA: Mayfield, 1984.

Greer, Germaine. *The Change: Women, Aging and the Menopause.* New York: Fawcett Columbine, 1991.

Gregory, Vikki. *Making Ends Meet: Midlife and Older Women's Search for Economic Self-Sufficiency: Through Job Training and Employment.* Washington, D.C.: Older Women's League, 1992.

Grimsley, Kirstin Downey. "The Ax That Cuts Both Ways." *The Washington Post,* Nov. 5, 1995, p. H1.

Gross, Jane. "Divorced, Middle-Aged and Happy: Women, Especially, Adjust to the 90's." *The New York Times,* Dec. 7, 1992, p. A14.

Grumbach, Doris. *Extra Innings: A Memoir.* New York: W. W. Norton & Company, 1995.

———. *Fifty Days of Solitude.* Boston: Beacon Press, 1995.

Gutmann, David. *Reclaimed Powers: Men and Women in Later Life.* Evanston, IL: Northwestern University Press, 1994.

Hahn, Hannelore. "The Essence and History of the IWWG." Reprinted from *Network,* The IWWG Newsletter, 1993. New York: International Women's Writing Guild, 1997.

———. *On the Way to Feed the Swans: A Memoir.* New York: Tenth House Enterprises, 1982.

Hanson, Cynthia. "Want a Raise? You've Got to Ask for the Salary You Deserve." *Chicago Tribune,* Feb. 11, 1996, sect. 13, p. 7.

Hayes, Christopher, Deborah Anderson, and Melinda Blau. *Our Turn: The Good News about Women and Divorce.* New York: Pocket Books, 1993.

Heilbrun, Carolyn. *Reinventing Womanhood.* New York: W. W. Norton & Company, 1979.

———. *Writing a Woman's Life.* New York: Ballantine Books, 1988.

Heller, Ann Conover. "How to Make Money by Risking It." *Lear's,* Sept. 1991, p. 77.

Helson, Ravenna, and Laurel McCabe. "The Social Clock Project in Middle Age." In *Women Growing Older: Psychological Perspectives.* Ed. Barbara Turner and Lillian Troll. Thousand Oaks, CA: Sage, 1994. 68–93.

Henkoff, Ronald. "So You Want to Change Your Job?" *Fortune,* Jan. 15, 1996, p. 54.

Holland, Barbara. *One's Company: Reflections on Living Alone.* New York: Ballantine Books, 1992.

"How to Stop Living on the Edge." *Harvard Health Letter* 23.9 (July 1998): 1–3.

Hudson Institute. *Workforce 2000: Work and Workers for the Twenty-first Century.* Indianapolis: author, 1987.

Huizinga, Johan. *Homo Ludens: A Study of the Play Element in Culture.* Boston: Beacon Press, 1995.

Imber-Black, Evan. "Rituals of Stabilization and Change in Women's Lives." In *Women in Therapy: A Framework for Family Therapy.* Ed. Monica McGoldrick, Carol Anderson, and Froma Walsh. New York: W. W. Norton & Company, 1991.

Jacobs, Ruth Harriet. *Be an Outrageous Older Woman.* Rev. ed. New York: HarperPerennial, 1997.

———. "Expanding Social Roles for Older Women." In *Women on the Front Lines.* Ed. Jessie Allen and Alan Pifer. Washington, D.C.: The Urban Institute Press, 1993. 191–220.

Jacobson, Stanley. "Overselling Depression to the Old Folks." *The Atlantic Monthly,* Apr. 1995, pp. 46–.

Jamieson, Kathleen Hall. *Beyond the Double Bind: Women and Leadership.* New York: Oxford University Press, 1995.

Judd, Karen, and Sandy Morales Pope. "The New Job Squeeze." *Ms.,* May/June, 1994, pp. 86–90.

Kabat-Zinn, Jon. *Full Catastrophe Living: Using the Wisdom of Your Body and Mind to Face Stress, Pain, and Illness.* New York: Delacorte Press, 1990.

Kalmanoff, Jean. "Lament." In *Solo Flight.* Pleasant Hill, CA: Small Poetry Press, 1991. 13.

———. "Painting Session." In *The Continuum.* Durham, N.H.: University of New Hampshire Press, 1997.

Kaplan, Dinha. "When Less Is More." *Psychology Today,* May/June 1997, p. 14.

Katz, Stan, and Aimee Liu. *The Codependency Conspiracy.* New York: Warner Books, 1991.

Kramer, Peter. *Should You Leave?* New York: Scribner's, 1997.

Krasnow, Iris. "The Fellowship of Women." *The Washington Post,* Aug. 6, 1996, p. B5.

Kroeger, Otto, and Janet Thuesen. *Type Talk: The 16 Personality Types That Determine How We Live, Love, and Work.* New York: Dell/Tilden Press, 1989.

Labouvie-Vief, Gisela. "Women's Creativity and Images of Gender." In *Women Growing Older: Psychological Perspectives* Ed. Barbara Turner and Lillian Troll. Thousand Oaks, CA: Sage, 1994. 140–68.

Lapsley, Hillary. "Mentoring in Women's Lives." Talk given at the Center for Research on Women, Wellesley College, Feb. 27, 1992.

Lelen, Kenneth. "Four Walls, Memories—and Tough Choices: Newly Widowed Wrestle with Whether to Sell." *The Washington Post,* May 13, 1995, p. E1.

Leonard, Frances. *Divorce and Older Women.* Washington, D.C.: Older Women's League, 1987.

———. *Money and the Mature Woman: How to Hold On to Your Income, Keep Your Home, Plan Your Estate.* Reading, MA: Addison-Wesley, 1993.

Lewis, Robert. "Career Changers Find Road to Success Marked by Perils." *AARP Bulletin* 37.6 (June 1996): 1.

———. "Escaping from the Jobless Maze." *AARP Bulletin* 35.9 (Oct. 1994): 2.

———. "Up and Away: Second Careers Taking Off." *AARP Bulletin* 37.5 (May 1996): 1.

Lieberman, Annette, and Vicki Lindner. *Unbalanced Accounts: Why Women Are Still Afraid of Money.* New York: Viking Penguin, 1988.

Lindemann, Eric. *Beyond Grief: Studies in Crisis Intervention.* New York: Aronson, 1979.

———. "Symptomatology and Management of Acute Grief." *American Journal of Psychiatry* 101 (1944): 141–48.

Maddox, Rebecca. *Inc. Your Dreams.* New York: Viking, 1995.

Madriz, Esther. *Nothing Bad Happens to Good Girls: Fear of Crime in Women's Lives.* Berkeley, CA: University of California Press, 1997.

Mainiero, Lisa. "The Longest Climb." *Psychology Today,* Nov./Dec. 1994, pp. 40–.

Maisel, Eric. *Fearless Creating: A Step-by-Step Guide to Starting and Completing Your Work of Art.* New York: J. P. Tarcher/Putnam, 1995.

Manning, Doug. *Don't Take My Grief Away: What to Do When You Lose a Loved One.* San Francisco: HarperCollins West, 1984.

Mattfeld, Jacquelyn. "Close Relationships, Meaning-in-Life, and Well-Being: A Qualitative Study of Urban Women in Late Life." Master's Thesis in the Department of Psychology, Northeastern Illinois State University, May 1996.

Mayer, Donna Damico. "Segment #15: Rolling Stones Tune Helps Woman Turn Life's Corner." Aired on *All Things Considered* on National Public Radio, Jan. 18, 1996.

McCarthy, Colman. "A Perfect Match-Up." *The Washington Post,* Aug. 10, 1995, p. C5.

McCollum, Audrey. *The Trauma of Moving: Psychological Issues for Women.* Newbury Park, CA: SAGE, 1990.

McGoldrick, Monica. "Women and the Family Life Cycle." In *The Changing Family Life Cycle: A Framework for Family Therapy.* 2nd ed. Ed. Betty Carter and Monica McGoldrick. Boston: Allyn and Bacon, 1989. 29–68.

"Mental Health: Does Therapy Help?" *Consumer Reports,* Nov. 1995, pp.734–39.

Miller, James E. *What Will Help Me? 12 Things to Remember When You Have Suffered a Loss.* Fort Wayne, IN: Willowgreen, 1995.

Miller, Jean Baker. *Toward a New Psychology of Women.* 2nd ed. Boston: Beacon Press, 1986.

———. "What Do We Mean by Relationships?" Work in Progress Paper No. 22. Wellesley, MA: The Stone Center, 1986.

Mulligan, Kate. "Heilbrunian Adventures." *AARP Bulletin* 37.2 (Feb. 1996): 16.

Mullins, Terry. "How to Land a Job." *Psychology Today*, Sept./Oct. 1994, pp. 12–13.

Myers, Isabel Briggs, with Peter Briggs Meyers. *Gifts Differing: Understanding Personality Type.* Palo Alto, CA: Davies-Black Publishing, 1995.

Myerson, Allen. "Wall Street Addresses Women's Distinct Needs." *The New York Times,* July 31, 1993, p. A33.

National Center for Women and Retirement Research. *Women and Divorce: Turning Your Life Around.* Southampton, N.Y.: author, Long Island University-Southampton Campus, 1993.

National Women's Health Network. *AIDS: Women and HIV/AIDS.* Washington, D.C.: author, 1998.

Nemy, Enid. "'What? Me Marry?' Widows Say No." *The New York Times,* June 18, 1992, p. C1.

Nolen-Hoeksema, Susan. *Sex Differences in Depression.* Stanford, CA: Stanford University Press, 1990.

Oates, Joyce Carol. "American Gothic." *The New Yorker,* May 8, 1995, pp. 35–36.

Oldenburg, Don. "Women at the Top." *The Washington Post,* Aug. 1, 1995, p. E5.

Oldenburg, Ray. *The Great Good Place: Cafes, Coffee Shops, Community Centers, Beauty Parlors, General Stores, Bars, Hangouts, and How They Get You Through the Day.* 2nd ed. New York: Marlowe & Company, 1997.

Older Women's League. *The Path to Poverty: An Analysis of Women's Retirement Income.* Washington, D.C.: author, 1995.

Osterweis, Marian, Frederic Solomon, and Morris Green, eds. *Bereavement: Reactions, Consequences, and Care.* Washington, D.C.: National Academy Press, 1984.

Parkes, Colin Murray. *Bereavement: Studies of Grief in Adult Life.* Harmondsworth, U.K.: Penguin Books, 1983.

———, and Robert Weiss. *Recovery from Bereavement.* New York: Aaronson, 1995.

Pennebaker, James, and R. C. O'Heeron. "Confiding in Others and Illness Rate Among Spouses of Suicide and Accidental Death Victims." *Journal of Abnormal Psychology* 93 (1984): 473–76.

Pistotnik, Bradley. *Divorce War!: Fifty Strategies Every Woman Needs to Know to Win.* Holbrook, MA: Adams Media Corp., 1996.

Pittman, Frank III. "A Buyer's Guide to Psychotherapy." *Psychology Today,* Jan./ Feb. 1994, pp. 51–52.

Pollan, Stephen, and Mark Levine. *Starting Over: How to Change Careers or Start Your Own Business.* New York: Warner Books, 1997.

Population Reference Bureau. "Women: Still in Transition, A Policy Perspective for the 21st Century." Unpublished proposal to the Ford Foundation. Washington, D.C.: author, March 1992.

———. *What the 1990 Census Tells Us About Women: A State Factbook.* Washington, D.C.: author, Nov. 1993.

Ratey, John, and Catherine Johnson. *Shadow Syndromes.* New York: Pantheon Books, 1997.

Rayman, Paula, Kimberly Allshouse, and Jessie Allen. "Resiliency Amidst Inequity: Older Women Workers in an Aging United States." In *Women on the Front Lines: Meeting the Challenge of an Aging America.* Ed. Jessie Allen and Alan Pifer. Washington, D.C.: The Urban Institute Press, 1993. 133–66.

Roberts, Paul. "Goofing Off." *Psychology Today,* July/Aug. 1995, p. 35.

Roberts, Roxanne. "The *Other* Big 'A' Word." *The Washington Post,* July 11, 1995, p. E5.

Roseman, Janet Lynn. *The Way of the Woman Writer.* Binghamton, N.Y.: Haworth Press, 1994.

Rubenstein, Carin. "The *Lear's* Report: How AIDS Has Changed Our Sex Lives." *Lear's,* Nov. 1992, pp. 62–67.

Rubin, Lillian. *Women of a Certain Age: The Midlife Search for Self.* New York: Harper Colophon, 1979.

Schlachter, Gail. *The Back-to-School Money Book: A Financial Aid Guide for Midlife and Older Women Seeking Education and Training.* Washington, D.C.: American Association of Retired Persons, 1994.

Seligman, Martin. *Learned Optimism.* New York: Knopf, 1991.

———. *What You Can Change and What You Can't.* New York: Fawcett Columbine, 1993.

Sellers, Patricia. "Cocktails at Charlotte's with Martha and Darla." *Fortune,* Aug. 5, 1996, pp. 56–57.

Shaw, Lois, and Rachel Shaw. "From Midlife to Retirement: The Middle-Aged Woman Worker." In *Working Women: Past, Present, Future.* Ed. Karen Shalcross Koziara, Michael Moskow, and Lucretia Dewey Tanner. Washington, D.C.: Industrial Relations Research Association, 1987, pp. 299–331.

Sheehy, Gail. *New Passages: Mapping Your Life Across Time.* New York: Random House, 1995.

Shields, Laurie. *Displaced Homemakers: Organizing for a New Life.* New York: McGraw-Hill, 1981.

Singer, Stacey. "Divorce-Law Crusade Backfires." *Chicago Tribune,* Nov. 2, 1995, sect. 2 SW, p. 1.

Skrzycki, Cindy. "Stock Recipe Needs a Grain of Salt: Beardstown Ladies Miscalculated Investment Returns." *The Washington Post,* Mar. 18, 1998, pp. 1–.

Sommers, Tish. "Changing Society and Ourselves." In *The New Ourselves, Growing Older: Women Aging with Knowledge and Power.* Rev. ed. Ed. Paula Doress-Worters and Diana Laskin Siegal. New York: Simon & Schuster/Touchstone, 1994.

Sommers, Tish, drawings by Genny Guracar (Bulbul). *The Not-So-Helpless Female.* New York: David McKay Company, 1973.

Sowell, Carol. "Starting Over." *Modern Maturity* 29.3 (June/July 1986): 64–65+.

Starr, Jennifer, and Marcia Yudkin. *Women Entrepreneurs: A Review of Current Research.* Wellesley, MA: Center for Research on Women, 1996.

Stearns, Ann Kaiser. *Coming Back: Rebuilding Lives After Crisis and Loss.* New York: Ballantine, 1988.

Stoner, Kay. "Cracking the Husk." *The Sage Within* 1.1 (Winter Solstice 1995): 2.

Stradling, Richard. "The Golden Girls." *The Washington Post,* Feb. 28, 1995, p. D5.

"Strategies for Smiles." *Psychology Today,* Jan./Feb., 1994, pp. 22–.

Strazewski, Len. "Jobs on Rise for Retirees." *The Chicago Tribune,* Dec. 31, 1995, sect. 18, pp. 56–58.

"Strength Training after Sixty." *Harvard Health Letter* 18.9 (July 1993): 6–8.

Strober, Myra. "Comment." In *Women in the Labor Market.* Ed Cynthia Lloyd, Emily Andrews, and Curtis Gilroy. New York: Columbia University Press, 1979. 271–77.

Stroebe, Wolfgang, and Margaret Stroebe. *Bereavement and Health: The Psychological and Physical Consequences of Partner Loss.* Cambridge, U.K.: Cambridge University Press, 1987.

Tannen, Deborah. "For Argument's Sake: Why Do We Feel Compelled to Fight about Everything?" *The Washington Post,* Mar. 15, 1998, sect. C, pp. 1, 4.

Tannen, Deborah. *The Argument Culture.* New York: Random House, 1997.

Taylor, Eugene. "Desperately Seeking Spirituality." *Psychology Today,* Nov./ Dec. 1994, pp. 54–.

Taylor, S. E. "Adjustment to Threatening Events: A Theory of Cognitive Adaptation." *American Psychologist* 38.1 (1983): 161–73.

Thacher, Gladys. "Seize the Day: The Coming of Age and the Age of Becoming." *LifePlan Center: Comprehensive Planning for Later-Life Transitions,* Apr./May/June 1995.

Thrailkill, Diane. *Temp by Choice.* Hawthorne, N.J.: Career Press, 1994.

Triere, Lynette, and Richard Peacock. *Learning to Leave.* New York: Warner Books, 1993.

Tyson, Laura, chairman of the National Economic Council. Interview by Charleen Hunter-Gault on the PBS-TV "News Hour with Jim Lehrer," Aug. 27, 1996.

U.S. Bureau of the Census. "Marital Status and Living Arrangements: March 1992." *Current Population Reports, Series p-20, No. 468* (Dec. 1992).

Vachon, M. L. S., A. R. Sheldon, W. J. Lancee, W. A. L. Lyall, J. Rogers, and S. J. J. Freeman. "A Controlled Study of Self-Help Intervention for Widows." *American Journal of Psychiatry* 137 (1980): 1380–84.

Viorst, Judith. *Necessary Losses: The Loves, Illusions, Dependencies and Impossible Expectations That All of Us Have to Give Up in Order to Grow.* New York: Fawcett Gold Medal, 1987.

Vuko, Evelyn. "Overdoing: A No-No." *The Washington Post,* Aug. 23, 1996, p. D5.

———. "What's a Little Cancer Among Friends? Part 2: A New Circle of Friends." *The Washington Post,* Aug. 9, 1996, p. B5.

Weber, Robert. "This Is Mrs. McBride from Marketing." Cartoon. *The New Yorker,* July 8, 1996, p. 52.

Weiss, Francine. *Older Women and Job Discrimination: A Primer.* Washington, D.C.: The Older Women's League, 1984.

White, Barbara, and Edward Madras, eds. *The Self-Help Sourcebook: National Guide to Finding and Forming Mutual Aid Self-Help Groups.* 5th Ed. Denville, N.J.: American Self-Help Clearinghouse, St. Clares-Riverside Medical Center, 1995.

Widmaier, Eric. "So You Think This Is the 'Age of Stress?'" *Psychology Today,* Jan./Feb. 1996, pp. 41–.

Williams, Wendy Swallow. "50 Things to Do Before I Die." *The Washington Post,* July 4, 1996, p. C5.

Women Employed. "The Glass Ceiling: A Women Employed Fact Sheet." Chicago: author, n.d.

Women Work! The National Network for Women's Employment. *Program Directory.* Washington, D.C.: author, 1998.

———. *Women Work, Poverty Persists: A Status Report on Displaced Homemakers and Single Mothers in the United States.* Washington, D.C.: author, 1994.

Women's Legal Defense Fund. *Employment Discrimination against Midlife and Older Women: How Courts Treat Sex- and Age Discrimination Cases.* Washington, D.C.: American Association of Retired Persons, 1996.

Wuthnow, Robert. *Sharing the Journey: Support Groups and America's New Quest for Community.* New York: Free Press, 1994.

Yapko, Michael. "The Art of Avoiding Depression." *Psychology Today,* May/June 1997, pp. 37–.